CRITICAL REALISM FOR PSYCHOLOGISTS

David Pilgrim

Routledge
Taylor & Francis Group
LONDON AND NEW YORK

First published 2020
by Routledge
2 Park Square, Milton Park, Abingdon, Oxon OX14 4RN

and by Routledge
52 Vanderbilt Avenue, New York, NY 10017

Routledge is an imprint of the Taylor & Francis Group, an informa business

British Library Cataloguing-in-Publication Data
A catalogue record for this book is available from the British Library

Library of Congress Cataloging-in-Publication Data
A catalog record has been requested for this book

ISBN: 978-0-367-22356-4 (hbk)
ISBN: 978-0-367-22358-8 (pbk)
ISBN: 978-0-429-27449-7 (ebk)

Typeset in Bembo
by Taylor & Francis Books

In memory of Professor Andrew Collier; a critical realist philosopher who understood the paths and pitfalls of psychology.

CRITICAL REALISM FOR PSYCHOLOGISTS

This is the first dedicated text to explain and explore the utility of critical realism for psychologists, offering it as a helpful middle ground between positivism and postmodernism.

By introducing its basic concepts, Pilgrim explains critical realism to psychologists and shows how the interface between the natural and social worlds, and the internal and external, can be used to examine human life. This both/and aspect of human life is important in another sense: we are both determined and determining beings, making choices but within the material constraints of both our bodies and the social context of our unique existence. The book offers an exploration of academic and applied psychology with that inward and outward curiosity in mind, beginning with the premise that both inner and outer reality are the legitimate interest of psychologists. In doing so, it shows how critical realism endorses the remaining advantages of positivism and postmodernism, while discarding their philosophical errors.

A range of case studies are presented to show how psychologists can use critical realism when working with real life problems, as researchers or practitioners.

David Pilgrim is Honorary Professor of Health and Social Policy at the University of Liverpool, UK, and Visiting Professor of Clinical Psychology at the University of Southampton, UK.

CONTENTS

ACKNOWLEDGEMENTS

I would like to thank a number of colleagues, who have helped me during the writing of this book. First, a group of psychologists interested in the topic gave their time to reading draft chapters and offering me feedback: Becky Band, Ryc Aquino, Mei Yee Tang and Teresa Corbett. This informal reader group helped me to do my best to make critical realism understandable to psychologists, though any shortcomings in the text ahead are wholly my responsibility.

Second, in the past few years conversations with the editors of the *Journal of Critical Realism*, Mervyn Hartwig and Leigh Price, have proved invaluable in sharpening my arguments. This has been useful given that critical realism is a philosophy and I am not a philosopher, but have been a 'jobbing' clinician and social science researcher. The (reasonable) fear of getting critical realism wrong, when we opt to use it as a resource, rather than making any claim to producing or developing it as a philosophy, has been assuaged at times by them. This was also the case when I could check on the direction of my first book on the topic produced in 2015 (*Understanding Mental Health: A Critical Realist Exploration*) with Roy Bhaskar just before his death.

Third, during my career I have worked at the boundary of psychology and sociology, which has proved to be both challenging and creative, especially when being involved in the interdisciplinary fields of health and social policy research. There, a number of people helped me to examine the interplay of human agents in their affording and constraining social contexts. These included: Richard Bentall, Joanna Bornat, Tim Carey, Chris Dowrick, Jon Gabe, Ray Holland, Carl May, Ann McCranie, Paul O'Reilly, Catherine Pope, Anne Rogers, Cas Schneider, John Shotter, David Smail, Floris Tomasini, Andy Treacher and Fiona Williams. More recent conversations with Priscilla Alderson, Ivo Vassilev and Karin Zotzmann have helped me to understand how to apply and translate the insights of critical realism to the arena of human science.

Finally, some of the chapters are elaborations or translations of pieces published by me in the *Journal of Critical Realism*. The one examining torture is based on a collaborative piece with Nimisha Patel, whose extensive practical and research understanding of the topic proved invaluable. The chapter on protest was possible, in part at least, thanks to the help given to me from a leading psychological researcher in that field, Martijn van Zomeran.

David Pilgrim

INTRODUCTION

Psychology courses in schools and universities are popular, and for understandable reasons. From an early age, most of us are interested in ourselves and some of us are also particularly curious about others. That mixture of inward preoccupation and benign voyeurism is common in those of us pursing a professional career in psychology (including this author). This book offers an exploration of academic and applied psychology with that inward and outward curiosity in mind. It begins then with the premise that both inner and outer reality are the legitimate objective interest of psychologists.

This both/and aspect of human life is important in another sense: we are both determined and determining beings. We make choices but within the material constraints of both our bodies and the particular current and past context of our unique existence. Those bodily and environmental contexts are fluid; they are an open not closed system. Prediction in open systems is difficult and at times nigh impossible, as psychologists have found when leaving the laboratory where they had controlled (or controlled out) aspects of reality for methodological and empirical credibility. Their subsequent findings are neat but they are meaningless or precarious when and if they do not generalise successfully to real life situations in their various forms.

To get to grips with the complexities of our inner and outer lives, it is helpful to return to an older tradition that made a claim to the authoritative understanding of the mind: philosophy. During the 20th-century Western psychology developed as a separate identity from philosophy; a point I will be returning to more in Chapter 2. It found its feet and confidence during this separation from an important, and at times domineering, parent. However, I believe that it has paid a price, when losing contact with its philosophical origins and when losing competence and confidence in reflecting on its own premises of enquiry.

Whatever the original irritation posed by the constraints of philosophy, it did at least know how to reflect on basic questions (that was its *raison d'être*) even if clear answers did not always emerge. Many psychologists I have worked with in the past 40 years, as professional colleagues or as students I have taught, have been genuinely interested in those basic questions. However, often they have struggled with the confidence to address them or they have been unaware of the tools available for the task. This book offers a resource for the latter, by following the footsteps of those developing the philosophy of critical realism.

The most important leader in this recent tradition was Roy Bhaskar (1944–2015). He picked up on the advice of the empiricist philosopher John Locke (1632–1704) that it was a central task of philosophy to 'under labour' for all the other disciplines. The unique selling point of philosophy, which takes it beyond its own esoteric internal debates, is that it can go down into the foundations of a discipline and clear away the rubbish that might be getting in the way of a clear view. To extend the metaphor, there is little point in being proud of a shiny building and its pleasing features, without knowing if its foundations are built on solid ground and are doing their job well. It may (or may not) be all show and no substance. At some point the building may collapse or a legitimate case might be made for its demolition.

In the past 100 years mainstream academic psychology has been underpinned by two main philosophical currents. The first and dominant current, which was established at the turn of the 20th century, has incorporated both empiricism and positivism. In Chapter 2 I will be rehearsing the strengths and weaknesses of that orthodoxy; what critical realists call 'naïve realism'. The second current is derived from idealism. This has focused on ideas, perspectives, narratives, discourses and representations and is language focused. It gained considerable momentum during the postmodern or linguistic 'turn' during the 1980s. I will rehearse the strengths and weaknesses of this in Chapter 3.

The fact that both of these philosophical currents are appraised for their strengths, not just their weaknesses, already indicates that neither of them are implausible. Both have garnered substantial support from intelligent and enthusiastic supporters in both academic and applied psychology. However, the early chapters will offer a critique of both. Critical realism treads a middle way between them, trying to reject their errors but also retain their legitimate assumptions, when that is warranted.

Turning to the structure of the book, the first three chapters address these competing philosophical currents relevant to human science. My concern in these early chapters is to highlight the advantages of critical realism but, more importantly, to invite the reader to reflect on their own preferred assumptions about ontology, epistemology and ethics (whatever they are). The subsequent chapters, phrased as self-assigned essay questions, do not exhaust the field of the discipline of psychology. However, they are diverse enough to introduce newcomers, be they students, researchers or practitioners, to the aim of the book, implied by its title.

I first look at larger questions about personhood and neuroscience, before moving on to some specific case studies to illuminate the practical relevance and insights of critical realism, when chafing at the boundaries of naïve realism on one side and strong social constructivism on the other. My final chapter considers the possibility of a critical realist human science and the conditions required for its achievement. In particular I focus on the need for interdisciplinarity, which implies an exploration of human experience and conduct in unique contexts, with psychology, like other cognate disciplines, playing an important but not singular and unique role in that task.

Before I move to the chapters, I provide a glossary of terms commonly used in critical realism. They might be of help to the reader new to the philosophy. Apart from in the first and final chapter, these terms, when they initially appear in the text, will be placed in bold as a cue to the return to the glossary if required by the reader. Further information about these and other terms can be found in Mervyn Hartwig's *Dictionary of Critical Realism* (Hartwig, 2007).

GLOSSARY

Axiology The study of values or what is valuable in life. Axiology contains an exploration of both ethical and aesthetic aspects of human existence, though the first of these tends to predominate in discussions about values in human science.

Concrete singularity The particular and unique expression of concrete universal phenomena. Critical realism rejects abstract universals in favour of the latter. Take the example of the concept of 'woman'. Every woman will share some commonalities with other women but also be different from them in various ways. Women also come from different times and places, inflecting what it is to be a woman here and now, as well as there and then. Finally, a particular woman has unique features as a person, shared by no one else.

Covering laws The erroneous assumption from positivism that there are permanent and fixed laws discovered by science that describe the workings of the world. These laws are then deemed to be applicable in all times and places. (See **empirical invariance**.)

Emergence A fundamental premise of critical realism is that events come and go in the world as a result of underlying generative mechanisms operating alone but, more typically, in interaction with one another creating a constant dynamic mixture of homeostasis and change. The complexity and flux of open systems affords the constant possibility of new events. Also because reality is laminated, new characteristics or capacities emerge at higher levels of systemic organisation than lower ones. For example, language has arisen in humans, not other primates, because of our cerebral characteristics. In another example, a graphite pencil cannot cut glass but a diamond can, even though both are made of carbon. Diamonds emerge from graphite under geological conditions of high pressure and temperature. (See **generative mechanisms**.)

Empirical invariance Refers to the misleading claim from positivism that there are lawful patterns in reality that occur across all times and places. This assumption can only be made about closed systems but human systems in the real world are open not closed. Critical realism proposes that in open systems there is empirical variance, though some patterns may be more regular or probable than others (demi-regularities and tendencies). That variance happens in all living systems, with human agents adding to it. (See **covering laws**.)

Epistemic fallacy This is when statements about the world are reduced to statements about knowledge. When this happens we confuse the map with the territory. This, and the closely related ontic fallacy, are common errors in research and its applications. (See **ontic fallacy**.)

Epistemic humility A reminder that we need to be cautious at all times about our knowledge because it is fallible and partial. We do not understand, and may never understand, much of what is real. (See **the empirical**; **the actual**; and **the real**.)

Epistemological relativism This refers to competing and shifting forms of understanding across time and place, within and across individuals. As language users we can make statements about the world and statements about statements (meta-statements). This intriguing complexity has often been a central preoccupation of Western intellectualism. However, this narrow focus on epistemology (the study of knowledge) can divert us from the importance of ontology (the study of being). For example, before chemists understood that graphite and diamonds were constituted by the same essence (carbon atoms) people would name and discuss them as being unrelated substances in their lives. (See **epistemic fallacy**; and **ontological realism**.)

Explanatory critique This is the exploration of how a theory came into being and is sustained, even if it is flawed. For example, we could explore the roots of creationism and the interests it serves today, even though it is an untenable theory.

Four planar social being This is the assumption in critical realism that our experiences and decisions as moral agents, in particular social contexts (the constraints of social structures and their emergent processes), also take place in the natural world. This elaborated version of structure and agency then implicates four planes: 1) material transactions with nature (our bodies and the physical world around us); 2) our interactions with other people (relationality); 3) social (including economic) structures particular to our world at a place and time; and 4) the unique stratification of our particular embodied personalities (our concrete singularity). (See **structure and agency**; **laminated reality**; and **reductionism**.)

Generative mechanisms The focus of critical realism is on underlying mechanisms, which may or may not be actualised. When they are actualised, then they are the same as our common-sense notion of causes but even if their causal powers are not actualised they are still real. By contrast, naïve realism (the compound of empiricism and positivism) focuses on events primarily, not underlying mechanisms. Once events come into being, they may themselves trigger new ones so they can become part of a generative mechanism. Positivism has a narrow conception of the inference of causality, based upon the premise of 'constant conjunctions', bequeathed to the philosophy of science by the empiricist philosopher David Hume. These constant conjunctions (sequences between two empirically measurable occurrences in time and proximal space) limit our understanding of causality and obscure its depth and complexity. (See **structure and agency**; **covering laws**; **the actual**; **the empirical**; and **the real**.)

Immanent critique This involves taking a knowledge claim or theory seriously on its own terms, rather than merely rehearsing an immediate oppositional criticism of its inadequacy. This form of critique is called 'immanent' because it entails going inside a claim and then working outwards to see if it then really works in practice. Does it do what it says it should do?

Intransitive aspect of reality This refers to the world that exists independent of our thoughts and actions. This reflects ontological realism but is not conceptually identical to it. Ontological realism refers to a premise about the existence of the natural world, which is separate from our existence as individuals and a species, whereas intransitivity refers to the many ways in which we are unable to influence that world, individually or collectively. Very occasionally our actions can modify it though, when we alter our natural environment and its properties, but many features of the latter are not open to influence. For example, we cannot alter the speed of light, the force of gravity, the fact of our eventual death or our chromosome count. Note also that ipso facto historical aspects of reality are always intransitive because they cannot be changed. (See **transitive aspect of reality**; **ontological realism**; and **four planar social being**.)

Judgemental rationality The human capacity to weigh up what is likely to be true in a particular context. This can be contrasted with judgemental relativism: the proposal that truth cannot be established and that there are only perspectives about the world. The latter error is a feature of postmodern philosophy. Human judgements are fallible and open to revision and so judgemental rationality does not necessarily imply a permanent verification of some aspect of reality (an aspiration of positivism). (See **epistemic humility**.)

Laminated reality The assumption that reality is multi-layered and has depth both inside us and outside us. Lower levels of reality are required for higher ones to exist but the explanation of the character of the higher ones cannot be reduced to that of the lower ones. For example, cells in our bodies need to exist for our organs to function but, in explanatory terms, physiology cannot be reduced to cytology and histology. (See **four planar social being**; and **reductionism**.)

Omissive critique This entails examining silences and absences in knowledge production. Why is question A being pursued in research but not question B? Why was the data interpreted in this way and not that way?

Ontic fallacy A form of faulty reasoning in which we use a concept or notion to name an aspect of reality. We then deploy that named concrete aspect as *proof* of the concept or notion that we used in the naming at the outset. It is the opposite side of the same coin as the epistemic fallacy. For example, a flat earth enthusiast, might use a spirit level to show that a sea promenade is completely flat in order to demonstrate a characteristic of the world they favour (that it is not round but flat). The ontic fallacy entails knowing in advance and with certainty what X is, and then seeking evidence of specific events to confirm the truth X to anyone in doubt. Sometimes critical realists use the compound concept of the 'epistemic-ontic fallacy', as they are closely related in their (faulty) logic. (See **epistemic fallacy**.)

Ontological monovalence This is the implication of empiricism; we limit our understanding of reality only to what is positively present and observable. This creates a misleadingly superficial and thin account of reality and its fixity. Reality is largely absent not present and it changes, it does not remain the same. (See **the empirical**; **the actual**; and **the real**.)

Ontological realism The premise that the world exists independent of our understanding of it. The world is simply there; it is not a product of human thought. This is part of the 'holy trinity' of critical realist premises (along with epistemological relativism and judgemental rationality).

Reductionism Events and processes at one level are explained by those at another in a fixed, non-dynamic manner. Typically this refers to higher levels of reality being reduced to lower ones, but it can be applied in the other direction at times. The term may refer to ontology (e.g. 'we are what we eat') or epistemology (e.g. 'neurochemical theories will explain all mental processes and behavioural outcomes'). The term is also used when discussing simplistic explanations in a field of complexity (e.g. 'fog caused the car crash') and in relation to narrow disciplinary arrogance or imperialism; hence 'sociological reductionism' or 'psychological reductionism'. (See **epistemic humility**; **laminated reality**; and **four planar social being**.)

Retroduction This is a form of inference that works back from what we currently observe to how it came into being. This can be contrasted with induction (inferring the general from a particular) and deduction (inferring a particular from the general). These two forms of inference are detached from context, whereas retroduction is always a contextualised form of reasoning. It deals with a recurring and fundamental question for critical realists: what would the world have had to have been like in order for us to observe what is before us now? It works back to identify likely generative mechanisms to account for what we observe in the here and now.

Structure and agency This refers to the relationship between our variable capacity to be conscious reflective agents, who make choices, and our embedding structures, both natural and social, which enable or constrain that capacity. In social science more generally 'structure' tends to allude to economic conditions and our normative context, i.e. what is expected of us by society in terms of rule conformity and role expectations learned during our primary socialisation as children. Thus social structures are enduring aspects of our embedding social system but they can and do change over time. They both constrain human action and can be altered by it; societal stasis and change coexist. This theorisation of the relationship between structure and agency entails some sort of concession that we are both determined and determining beings, i.e. it is not one or the other. (See **four planar social being**.)

The actual That aspect of reality that actually occurs, whether or not it is observed. If we limit our understanding of reality to the actual ('actualism') then this does not exhaust our task of exploring reality. This is because underlying mechanisms exist and they may not be actualised. (See **generative mechanisms**; and **the real**.)

The empirical That aspect of reality that is observed. If we limit our scientific understanding of reality to the empirical ('empiricism') then this does not exhaust our task of exploring reality. Many actualised and non-actualised aspects of reality exist beyond what we observe. Also we are not merely passive observers of reality, we are actively involved in its affirmation or alteration. (See **structure and agency**.)

The real That aspect of reality beyond and beneath the empirical and the actual. It includes powers, tendencies and mechanisms. It contains both presence and absence. For critical realists, the total domain of the real then subsumes witnessed experiences of the world + actual events in the world + underlying generative mechanisms, bearing in mind that events may not be witnessed and mechanisms may not be actualised. (See all other entries in this glossary.)

Transduction This refers to the dubious form of inference, when we extrapolate from closed systems (such as the psychological laboratory) to everyday life, which is an open system. (See **retroduction**.)

Transitive aspect of reality This is that created by human thought and its enactment. This is reflected in epistemological relativism and it includes perspectives, narratives, theories, ideologies, theologies, as well as forms of practice that may flow from them. Occasionally the intransitive can be altered by the transitive, for example when we use genetic engineering on crop production. The more politically dramatic example is the design and mass production of the internal combustion engine and its impact on the melting of the ice cap. Thus our thoughts can become generative mechanisms (they are 'causally efficacious'). They may affect our world, when and if our motives and intentions are enacted. When this happens then it could alter the status quo or help to maintain it. (See **intransitive aspect of reality**; and **generative mechanisms**.)

1

THE UTILITY OF CRITICAL REALISM

Introduction

This first chapter introduces students, researchers and practitioners of psychology to the considerable advantages of the philosophy of critical realism. The reader can also consult the original work of its main founder, Roy Bhaskar (Bhaskar, 2016; 1997). There is a nearby literature in sociology also offering good introductions, which might help psychologists new to the philosophy (Archer, 2000; Sayer, 2000; Porpora, 2015).

Critical realism is not a dogma or a prescription for practice. However, it has implications for reflecting on good practice in two senses. First, it guides us in what is the best way to understand the natural and social worlds we enter, exist in and then depart. Second, it encourages our reflexivity about our presence in the world and our ethical obligations as professionals and human beings. My hope is that these points will become clearer as this chapter and subsequent ones are read.

The chapter proceeds with these early thoughts in mind. To make the best use of the potential of critical realism, psychologists need to familiarise themselves with its basic assumptions and broad recommendations to orientate good theory and practice. What follows below then are guidelines to aid that familiarisation. The chapter offers my version of those guidelines, with my colleagues in the discipline of psychology specifically in mind. Because it is my version, then a short reflexive statement might help to account for the style of the guidelines and the content of the chapters to come.

Short reflective statement

Having trained as a clinical psychologist and then embarked upon a PhD in psychology while practising, my interests became more and more sociological. I was working in the NHS in England and became interested in the daily politics of being a mental health practitioner working in the field. The PhD looked at the workings of NHS psychotherapy using personal accounts. At that time (during the 1980s) I became familiar with the work of Roy Bhaskar, and critical realism provided a framework to guide my stumbling efforts in research with a little more clarity.

Fortuitously, my PhD supervisor was John Shotter (who I discuss more in Chapter 3). His own approach, as a leading social psychologist and theoretician, was not aligned with critical realism but he kindly tolerated my callow efforts and the thesis was completed successfully. We agreed to differ philosophically but he understood, more than I at the time, the reasons why this was the case. What we disagreed *about* (ontology and epistemology) continued to preoccupy me. As time progressed I found myself as a psychological practitioner and researcher bouncing between the rock of implausible positivism and the hard place of implausible postmodernism.

With this discomfort I figured that maybe the answer was to escape permanently or temporarily from psychology and went on to complete a part-time Masters in sociology. Working at the boundary of psychology and sociology was useful. I found that those in the first had their feet on the ground and could think methodically about practical problems but they tended to lack confidence, or saw no point, in understanding their own historical and philosophical context (the positivists). By contrast at the time, the emerging postmodern psychologists, emboldened by French poststructuralism, were disappearing into a foggy cul-de-sac full of words, irony and cynicism.

But what I then found in sociology was no less encouraging or comforting. Less grounded and of less practical utility, sociologists too wobbled constantly between the claimed certainties of positivism (with its covering laws of social determinism for all occasions) and postmodern nihilism. They all agreed on the importance of social context (their shared point of disciplinary legitimacy) but were not of one voice about it. Without any obvious practical relevance, sociologists could either compensate for that inadequacy by shifting, often creatively, to interdisciplinary working, such as in health services research, or they could make grander claims to scarce sociological insights or become preoccupied with internal debates about postmodern social theory.

One common outcome of this 'postmodern turn' was the argument that 'everything is socially constructed'. With that came the expectation of unique methodological expertise in discourse analysis and deconstruction. During discussions of practical matters, with a feigned weak smile and flicking their fingers in the air, postmodernists would put particular words like 'reality' and 'truth' in speech marks, in a weary signal of knowing intellectual scorn. Some isolated voices in the sociological literature judged this to be a collective form of madness (Craib, 1997), which may have been fair comment (see Chapter 3).

Every time that I saw postmodern sociologists or psychologists signal speech marks, I wondered what would be there in their absence. Was *everything* just words and, if not, then what was left of reality itself? But on the other side of the same coin, within psychological orthodoxy did the experimentalists and personality theorists have any insight, for example, into the false trail of closed system reasoning or the historical relationship between scientific psychology and eugenics? Was their preferred version of realism largely just ideology dressed up as science?

What I found in critical realism was a refreshing offer: we can enjoy philosophical clarity about both social and natural science. There are underlying philosophical premises that illuminate both of these academic currents, whilst recognising the differences between their limits of theory and practice. What was obvious to me was that the tension between a natural scientific and a social scientific approach to psychology was confusing at times. However, it was also a healthy tension to tolerate and encourage curious exploration. With these initial thoughts in mind, I now offer my version of some guidelines for the reader.

Guidelines about basic critical realism

These are now listed in a particular order for clarity. They introduce the assumptions and axioms of critical realism and also explain their implications for practice. As the name suggests, the philosophy is *critical* and so those implications are largely about types of critique that can be helpful in our work, as well as an invitation to think in a critical and reflective way about our theory and practice. The ordering of the guidelines is not a hierarchal checklist (i.e. with the least important points at the end). The exception to that principle is the first one on the list, because it is so axiomatic.

1) The 'holy trinity' of critical realism

We can think of the foundations of critical realism as three core axioms or premises. Like all philosophical arguments they are fundamental assumptions. In the case of critical realism these are ontological realism; epistemological relativism; and judgemental rationalism (or sometimes in critical realist texts 'judgemental rationality'). For emphasis I re-visit here items in the glossary:

Ontological realism is the premise that the world exists independent of what we know or think about it. Our individual existence is part of the world temporarily but the world existed before we were born and will do so after we die. Reality in large part then is mind-independent. It does matter what we think about it though, while we are around. Those thoughts, descriptions, discourses or notions are themselves part of reality but their existence emerges from an external and independent material world. Mind- or language-related aspects of reality are products of real evolutionary processes that preceded, and so were independent of, them. But now language has evolved to afford us personal agency then we as well must consider the next important premise. The assumption about ontology is primary in critical realism. Without real material conditions, we would not have evolved as a species and the next two aspects of the 'holy trinity' could not have emerged.

Epistemological relativism is the premise that we construe the world we live within and reflect upon and talk about. Those construals might be fanciful and idiosyncratic tastes and assertions (e.g. the view that heavy metal exemplifies good music) or profound and serious (e.g. the passion for proving, with evidence, the reality of global warming and campaigning about its dire consequences for the survival of humanity). Heavy metal music exists but people hold different views about its merits and its definition and range of indicative bands. Global warming exists but people debate its sources, consequences and degree of threat. Some construals might be honest and persuasive (e.g. persistent inequalities in health mean the poor will be sicker and die younger than the rich on average) or dishonest and unfounded (e.g. there are no health inequalities only 'health variations' and being healthy is merely a matter of personal choice).

These examples point up that epistemological relativism is not the same as *truth relativism*. As Elder-Vass (2012) points out, knowledge is socially contingent but truth remains independent of 'historical specificities in systems of belief' (ibid.: 231). For example, 'the world is round' is a statement of truth. A flat earth claim is now a minority epistemological position but the world is, as it has always been, round. When and if our species becomes extinct, the world will still be round, unless evidence is brought forward to support the flat earth position, which at the time of writing has not occurred. (See my discussion of the ontic fallacy below.)

As we are socialised in a culture, construals will change over time and they will vary from place to place. They are mind-dependent and that mind-dependency can be reflected on within, or explored at the level of, the individual's account of their biography or collectively (in our shared cultural assumptions, ideologies, cosmologies or discourses). In the academy, some forms of knowledge are deemed to be inherently superior to those of everyday wisdom, opinion or prejudice. However, even academic construals are socially-situated and they will always reflect the context of their production to some extent and in particular ways. Their emphasis on empirical evidence, theoretical coherence or methodological transparency and rigour might *improve their claim* to superior knowledge but the latter can still be addressed sceptically; a cue for the next premise.

Judgemental rationalism is the premise that in light of the first two above we are able to weigh up truths and likelihoods. Those judgements might be made cautiously because all knowledge is fallible; but they can, and sometimes must, be made. This can be distinguished from judgemental relativism, whereby we tolerate the merits of all construals and abandon adjudicating criteria. More will be said about this in Chapter 3 when querying the tendency of judgemental relativism within the theoretical traditions of metaphysical idealism in general, and postmodern psychology in particular.

A good example of judgemental rationalism is given by Porpora (2015). If we are faced with discerning the truth when faced with closely competing knowledge claims, as critical realists we would opt for the third of these statements as the best fit:

1. Six million Jews died in the Nazi holocaust.
2. Six million Jews were killed in the Nazi holocaust.
3. Six million Jews were murdered in the Nazi holocaust.

The first is true but is incomplete because it omits the reality of mass homicide. The second is true but killings might have accrued for a range of intentional or unintentional motives and so may mislead us about the context of the deaths. Only the third captures the full picture: mass murder planned and executed by the Nazi state in its 'Final Solution' for the 'Jewish problem'. There was the deliberate industrial destruction of an ethnic group blamed by Hitler for undermining Germany and its vaunted master race.

When asked about these options, people may opt for the first or second statements, possibly in the belief that the last is emotive and others more neutral and considered. Positivism may help that slide in thinking (by claiming to remove values from facts). Postmodernism offers us only perspectives and so are all three statements of equal value? If not, then how is one account better than another, without recourse to a complex description of how the Holocaust came into being as a fact, not merely as a set of narratives? This would mean postmodernists taking reality seriously and not with a wan smile putting it in speech marks (see Chapter 3).

The above three core premises are aligned with common sense and critical realism has been described as its 'enlightened' version (Bhaskar, 2016). Professional philosophers have given common sense a mixed press. For example, Bertrand Russell called it 'the metaphysics of the savage' but Thomas Huxley called science 'common sense at its best'. What common sense does do is provide us with the cognitive capacity for judgemental rationality, which is the basis for *both* dealing with everyday life *and* pursuing intelligent forms of academic activity. For this reason, the closeted academic has grounds for envying the street-wise teenager and *vice versa*.

Academic enquiry is predicated on a shared starting point and that entails us learning the difference between words and things, as well as being aware of our inner and outer reality. From a young age we recognise the reality of the world around us and within us. We learn that a flame hurts our hand but also that what we desire is not always achieved and our dreams are not the same as our waking thoughts. We might wake up to a bird singing or a bomb bursting. Cars on the road might injure or kill us. Our parents are usually more trustworthy than strangers. Adults have power over children. Food and drink are necessary and enjoyable. Rules apply to what is wise and permissible and what is not. We feel our way into this rule-bound world. Bit by bit we learn about the world, but also how to make good (or bad) judgements about it and what others expect of us.

Our capacity to use judgemental rationality in our lives can be directed at matters which are interpersonal and subjective (the centrality of attachments and relational expectations in our developing life) and others which seem to be about the natural world more generally (the dangers of flames and cars and the importance of eating and drinking for survival). Common sense tells us that this is a both/and not an either/or real world. Relationships are important but so is everything beyond people *per se*. Our primary preoccupation, understandably, may be with our personal attachments and support from others. But if we were lost alone in a forest we would take the reality of our immediate natural environment very seriously in order to survive. An unpeopled world with no conversations is still the world. None of us require a training in philosophy or science to come to these conclusions about our shared personal and impersonal contexts.

Also, as time progresses, we become aware that we do not know everything and life is often mysterious. We are in a state of constant ignorance but know enough to cope with the messy reality of our lives much of the time. We are thrown into a world not of our making but slowly make decisions about that world and how to act upon it (or not) in a state of partial knowledge. Life is sort of predictable (the seasons guide our clothing expectations) but exceptions constantly prove rules to be wrong (the mild day in mid-winter or the surprise of the 'Indian summer'). Nothing is certain but some things seem to have stronger patterns that connect through time than others. These generalisations about the contingencies and flux of being human are the bread and butter of a critical realist approach and so it is aligned with everyday common sense and, as I have just argued, the latter provides us with judgemental rationality.

2) The transitive and intransitive dimensions to reality

Much of reality is not open to change by our thoughts and actions. A distinction can be made then for analytical purposes between that which we cannot change (the intransitive dimension of reality) and the way that we talk about and construe our world (the transitive dimension of reality). There is what exists in the world and there is what we think and say about it, with their prompts for action. To be clear, the intransitive does not necessarily mean stable and semi-permanent, though it can mean that in many instances. It refers to what we cannot change, such as everything in the past and the speed of light in the present.

Broadly, the intransitive reflects ontological realism and the transitive epistemological relativism but occasionally that linkage can be broken in human interactions because of action (praxis). Also, it is obvious that inner reality is more prone to rapid sense making and that might blur the line at times between the transitive and intransitive. For example, if I have a dream (a real inner event) I can describe its content and then revisit its meaning over and over again if I choose. The first part of this process has an intransitive character (the dream has been and gone and it had a particular content) but the second is about construal and re-construal (*post hoc* interpretations) and so has a transitive character. (For a wider discussion of the transitive and intransitive in human science, see Richards (2018).)

3) The Empirical, The Actual and The Real

We sit in a garden and comment on the beauty of a bird singing (our agreement on the Empirical). The bird flies and settles on a branch half a mile away in a deserted wood and starts singing (an Actual event) but we are unable to hear it (there is no empirical verification but note that the bird is still singing). Moreover, the physiology of the bird and its evolutionary history that afford its capacity to sing in its unique way are hidden from us, whether or not we hear the bird; they are part of the Real. The underlying mechanisms of birdsong exist even when birds are silent.

Thus whilst all three levels of the totality of reality are important, at times our understanding may be seduced by, or reduced to, the empirical alone (Empiricism) or the actual alone (Actualism). Moreover, if we concede that the Real and the unwitnessed Actual are part of a large domain of the totality of reality, then most of the latter is absent not present. Most events have been and gone, have not yet happened and are not obvious to our senses (and never will be). Critical realism then focuses on reality being absent not just present (contra positivism – see Chapter 2) and it being laminated and differentiated. This is mentioned because some realist psychologists consider the world to be ontologically undifferentiated (e.g. Mackay and Petocz, 2011).

4) Ontology and emergence; closed and open systems

Critical realism can be positioned within the tradition of Heraclitus who said that reality was in constant flux: 'A man cannot step into the same river twice, for fresh waters ever emerge around him'. By contrast, another pre-Socratic philosopher, Parmenides, endorsed a form of reality fixed and given by the gods. I return to these different versions of ontology in Chapter 2 when discussing positivism, but we can see a fundamental difference here between one premise claiming that reality is fluxing and another that it is fixed.

Within the Heraclitan tradition, critical realism emphasises the emergence of events and processes in the world based on prior forces, powers, causes or generative mechanisms. All biological systems are open systems. What makes human systems *special* forms of these is that one of the inputs to them, which might inflect stasis or change, includes personal agency (both individual and collective). The latter is not all important though, so we need to avoid the misleading *voluntarism* to be found in some variants of humanistic psychology, with its unending fetish for personal choice and responsibility. The man chose to step into the river but he and the river changed over time in ways he could not totally control or fully understand.

Moreover, in open systems probability and trends apply but the predictability of events does not. The train time table provides good intentions and expectations but an individual train may be very late (due to an episodic points' failure) or may fail to occur at all (the tree on the line or the lack of a driver). Psychologists, relying on the laboratory, control out factors that apply in the real world and so they generate dubious data. Precise data out of a real context is fairly meaningless. The world is an open system, whereas the laboratory is a closed one offering misleading forms of explanation and the false promise of prediction (an error of transduction).

5) Generative mechanisms

Whereas empiricism is concerned with the reality of witnessed events, critical realism discounts this narrow focus as being misleading. Instead the emphasis is on generative mechanisms because they are there, whether or not the events emerge into being or are actualised and whether or not the latter are verified by human senses (see above). Powers may be present but may not be active (for example in a dormant bulb). One power may cancel another out to block an event (for example antibodies preventing an infection turning into bodily signs and symptoms – see below). Also events may emerge because of the synergy of more than one force (such as fog appearing in a dip, on an otherwise clear road, crossing a boggy area on a still winter's morning). In another example, a person may have plunged into suicidal despair when their partner left them, just after they were made redundant and a close relative had suddenly died. They may have coped with one of these events alone but life defeated them contingently, when they all came together. The term 'perfect storm' has come to signal this feature of open systems.

6) Scientific inference: 'DREIC' and 'RRREIC'

Critical realism is pro-science not anti-science but it approaches science sceptically (contra positivism which makes a fetish out of the empirical method and assumes covering laws awaiting discovery). This can be contrasted with the tendency in postmodern philosophy *fundamentally* to query modern science in terms of its methods and claims. Bhaskar provides us with a sequence in optimal scientific discovery. His emphasis is on how backward reasoning *in context* is superior as a form of inference than relying upon the traditions in research of induction and deduction, which are decontextualised forms of inference. Bhaskar uses two mnemonics to capture what good researchers do in practice to produce knowledge about the world: DREIC and RRREIC, which will be outlined one after the other.

In DREIC there first is a **D**escription of an event or phenomenon. Second, the investigator makes a serious and systematic attempt at **R**etroduction (identifying a relevant underlying generative mechanism). Third, having rehearsed some imagined conditions of possibility that might account for that evidence present, some are discounted immediately, or eventually, in a process of **E**limination. Fourth, in the wake of the first three stages the **I**dentification of the most likely efficacious causal mechanism at work is made by the investigator. Fifth, that mechanism is considered in the light of past findings in a process of **C**orrection to them.

The DREIC sequencing typifies research seeking to understand causal mechanisms, for example in experimental science in the laboratory. However, when the focus shifts primarily from the mechanism of interest to an event to be accounted for in open systems (for example in applied research about human beings) then an elaborated or modified version of DREIC becomes RRREIC. They both contain a similar overall logic of backward reasoning, in order to account for a current picture with past events. However, RRREIC takes on a new shape when studying human conduct, rather than purely investigating mechanisms in the natural world. Retrodiction (working out what has happened and possibly why) and retroduction (identifying generative mechanisms implicated in the latter) intertwine in applied human science. In Chapter 8 I discuss the challenge of validly identifying victims of torture. The latter is an underlying mechanism but we have to weigh up whether that mechanism operated in a particular case to account for a person claiming that they have been tortured. I say more about the overlap of retrodiction and retroduction in human science below.

With the latter in mind, to illustrate the distinction between DREIC and RRREIC, imagine an initial encounter with a crime scene. Suspicious neighbours, upon seeing a window open over a few days when it is normally closed, try and fail to rouse the resident of a house and so they call the police. The police arrive and they force entry into the property and find a corpse slumped in a chair. They look for a range of possibilities initially to account for the dead body. The deceased may have died from natural causes and not be a victim of a crime at all and so discernment is needed at the outset; that initial description needs to be resolved to the satisfaction of the investigators. However, what looks like a bullet wound at the base of the scull is visible to the officers. Congealing blood is evident down the back of the corpse. No weapon is evident nearby in the room or anywhere else inside or outside the home. A window at the back of the house is indeed open, but expensive items were left not taken etc. A picture of the scene is built up and recorded and the pathologist is soon there to offer a view. Forensic scientists arrive to take relevant material for laboratory examination. Eventually the body is released for a post-mortem examination. Suspects are identified and sought out for apprehension.

In this scenario, the first **R** of RRREIC refers to **R**esolution of what is evident to the police. What seems to have happened to this person leaving them as a slumped corpse in their own home in the circumstances that prompted the neighbours to call the police? This leads then to the second **R** which refers to **R**edescription, which paves the way to clarifying provisionally the most likely reason, for the dead body being there in the state it is in. It looks very unlikely that the person died of natural causes and foul play at the hands of a third party seems to explain the death. At this stage the corpse and their fate is being *contextualised* more and more in the inferential deliberations of the investigators. They start to agree upon the 'best fit' explanation, at this stage, for the corpse (they have been murdered). (In philosophy the term 'abduction' is sometimes used to describe 'best fit' inferences and in some literature it is simply conflated with 'retroduction'.)

The deliberations move then more specifically to consider all of the possible ways the death occurred and motives for it, i.e. questions about who was the possible murderer, what method of killing might they have used etc. This is the third **R** which is **R**etrodiction, all of the various circumstantial possibilities leading up to the murder are postulated (see more on this below). This triggers more evidence gathering from pathologists and forensic scientists and statements from those who knew the victim. This then leads to a process of **E**limination of possible suspects of the crime (because of lack of motives, clear alibis etc.), perpetrator intentions (a bullet in the back of the head does not suggest a chaotic accidental shooting) and cause of death (this could not have been an act of suicide). By now the inferential process helps to narrow down the most likely antecedent scenario for the death. A picture is built up about who is likely to have been the murderer from the evidence and their motives for committing the crime. This then is an **I**dentification of a particular suspect's presence at the murder scene, their reasons for being there, as well as their homicidal intentions when committing the crime. If that suspect is identified the police then set out to arrest them.

The end point is then a **C**orrection of what was known at the outset (the mysterious presence of a dead person in their home). However, the conclusion may still remain suggestive not definitive because prosecutors need to be confident that the evidence gathered will be convincing in a court of law. As we know from crime stories, real and imagined, this RRREIC process can stall at any stage and the 're-set button' may need to be hit. Homicides may remain unsolved and murderers may not be validly identified; those arrested may prove to be 'false negatives' or 'false positives'. All forms of evidence gathering, and inferences from it, imply caution or the need for epistemic humility. Scientists and detectives can and do 'get things wrong'.

Both DREIC and RRREIC focus upon tracing antecedents and so they are versions of causal analysis, which are typical most of the time in any systematic investigation. The pragmatic driver of science or police enquiries leads to the use of overlapping versions of retrodiction and retroduction, *not* deduction or induction. Deduction starts with an assumption of a general rule and then infers a particular outcome and induction generalises from the particular. Both of these can fail. Sometimes general rules fail to hold because of the emergence of new events and because the underlying *assumption* of that the rule is valid may prove to be wrong. Induction may fail because the current description of a case does not generalise to other contexts. Both deduction and induction fail because they are not *contextualised* forms of inference. This is not the case with retroduction. This is not a fail-safe but it is a superior form of inference to induction and traditional deduction, idealised by positivist science (see Chapter 2).

Bhaskar (2016: 3) explains that a retroductive argument 'asks what would, if it were real, bring about, produce, cause or explain a phenomenon'. Retroduction then refers to the application of the investigator's imagination to trace a *causal mechanism*. This complements and intersects with a wider form of inference which is 'retrodiction'. This starts with *an event* (such as the imagined crime scene above) and looks to trace the range of causal powers that may have interacted to bring about that event.

Science (and detective work and good investigative journalism) proceed by combining these close-by forms of inference, which reflect contextualised 'backward reasoning'. Psillos (2007: 257) refers to their shared character as forms of inference from the known to the unknown, namely:

> Retroduction and retrodiction (inference from effects to causes or from later to earlier states of systems via retroduced explanatory structures, e.g. when a doctor infers from a symptom in a patient that one of the generative mechanisms involved is an influenza virus).

Note the phrase from Psillos, 'one of the mechanisms', in relation to retrodiction. The emphasis is on a case of flu that implicates the presence of a virus (a causal structure). However, the latter may be necessary but not sufficient. For example, some people infected may not become symptomatic because *other* mechanisms in the body are present to resist this outcome, such as natural immunity or that induced by vaccination. In open systems neat correlations between two variables rarely exist and there is empirical variance, despite similar circumstances obtaining (say here an influenza outbreak in a particular population). Standard deduction fails us and a combination of retroduction and retrodiction would be our better guide to understand underlying mechanisms and account for particular cases. For example, some vaccinated people still get influenza and some who are not vaccinated still avoid the disease.

Take another example about wrongly *deducing* the inevitable link between gastric ulcers and stress. It went like this. All stressed people have an increased flow of stomach acid (seemingly a general rule). If increased volumes of stomach acid are found in all people with stomach ulcers, then *this* case of a stomach ulcer has been caused because the patient is highly stressed, implying their need for some form of psychological therapy or anxiolytic drug treatment.

But this deduction may be plainly wrong. Even a calm Yogi might develop a gastric ulcer when and if they are affected detrimentally by the presence of the bacterium *Helicobacter pylori* (Marshall and Warren, 1984). Moreover, as with the flu example given above, many of us contain this bacterium in our stomach all of the time and yet we do *not* develop a gastric ulcer. Also, despite that bacterium being the most likely aetiological cause, a minority of patients may develop ulcers without being infected but for other reasons, such as the iatrogenic effect of anti-malarial medication (Pilgrim, 2018c). Open biological systems are complex and are best approached with epistemic humility by deploying retroduction and retrodiction in psychological research.

7) Natural and social science

As a discipline, psychology exists tantalisingly, and for some irritatingly, at the cusp of natural and social science. Bhaskar's critical realism emerged initially by focusing on the work of natural science. He objected to the false logic in the philosophy of science, derived from Hume, that the natural world contains fixed laws of causation, which apply across time and space and are incrementally discovered by science. These laws then report 'constant conjunctions', with the assumption that the world is permanent, unstructured and unchanging. (This accords with the view from Parmenides noted above.) By contrast if the world is impermanent or in flux but it is also structured or laminated then science needs to proceed in a different way than simply seeking out constant conjunctions and implausible fixed laws.

Because natural science deals in the main with the intransitive dimension of reality then it might seem to signal a quite distinct realm of enquiry to that dealing with the transitive in the main (the humanities and the social sciences). Natural scientists normally assume a *detachment* between scientists and their interest of enquiry (events and processes occurring in the natural world). By contrast social science is in a different position. Sociologists study a society that they are part of and psychologists study other human beings but they are human beings themselves (I pick this point up again in Chapter 2).

This strong embeddedness means that the rhetorical claims of natural scientists (that they are detached from what they are investigating) cannot be sustained plausibly by social scientists. However, Bhaskar made the point that there is an important overlap between natural and social science, even if we need to bear in mind their differences as well. Both are forms of social practice and their questions and methodological priorities, and favoured interpretations of evidence, are situated in time and space.

Natural scientists may be concerned with the intransitive and empirically detached world much more often than social scientists but their activity still remains *human* activity, shaped and determined by the personal choices they make as reflexive agents, within their social context of origin and sustenance. Another overlap is that both natural and social science have shared a commitment, since the Enlightenment, to positivism (see Chapters 2 and 3). Both have made claims to value-free detachment, and in turn the pursuit of the discovery of universal laws. They both then risk offering knowledge claims which are ideologically laden, while claiming the very opposite (Hume's misleading stricture about the fact-value separation and pretensions towards 'disinterestedness'). 'Scientism' is when science functions as an ideology and that ideology then includes the firm denial that it is an ideology at all. This can be the outcome of naïve realism in general and positivism in particular.

The overlap between natural and social science still leaves us with distinctions because of the greater transitive emphasis of the latter, especially in relation to normative differences across time and space. For this reason, social scientists have been prone to eschew the natural scientific aspiration of explanation (*erklären*) and they have been more comfortable with description and interpretation (*verstehen*).

8) Epistemic and ontic fallacies

If the character of the world (its ontology) is not the same as what we say about it (our preferred epistemic depictions), then to conflate the two is an error. Our common ignorance of that conflation may not matter that much as we live our daily lives. Bhaskar (2016: 23) gives this example:

> … if I ask you how far London is from New York and you tell me it is about 3,500 miles, and then I ask you whether that is a statement about your knowledge or about the world, you might understandably be taken aback.

Bhaskar calls this everyday conflation the 'natural attitude' and indeed it matters little for much of the time. However, if that lack of distinction is carried over into academic theory and practice, then errors of reasoning and false claims will inevitably ensue. A bridging example that many readers will understand is the truism that 'the map is not the territory' (Korzybski, 1933). If we are walking in a strange area and rely on a map that was accurate 50 years ago but is no longer (say because of the appearance of new buildings, paths and roadways) then we may well make several wrong turnings and be bemused, as our eyes shift from the map to what we actually see around us. Generally maps are fine, but they may not be and so they may lead to us getting lost.

Critical realism formulates these pitfalls using three closely related terms: the epistemic fallacy; the ontic fallacy; and the epistemic-ontic fallacy. The epistemic fallacy reduces the world to our knowledge of it. Statements about being are reduced to statements about knowledge. Take the example of the putative existence of 'schizophrenia'. (Uncritical) mental health practitioners, when asked what this *is*, will allude to *definitions* in psychiatric textbooks or refer you to the

Diagnostic and Statistical Manual of the American Psychiatric Association or maybe the International Classification of Diseases produced by the World Health Organization. They are adopting the 'natural attitude' of not separating the putative ontology of schizophrenia from the knowledge they are committed to unreflectively about schizophrenia.

If we subject this conflated claim about the ontology of schizophrenia to an immanent critique, then we find that we have no scientific grounds at all for claiming that it exists. What we have instead is a recurrent psychosocial challenge in many societies. It appears in concrete scenarios, where the *conduct* of some people emerges from voices they hear but others do not ('auditory hallucinations') or from their fixed *and unusual* beliefs ('delusions'), i.e. the latter are not aligned with the norms of thinking and talking in a society at a moment in time. Thus the referral by the uncritical mental health practitioner to authoritative psychiatric literature about 'schizophrenia' is not illuminating but mystifying.

A related concept to the epistemic fallacy is the ontic fallacy, which might be thought of as the opposite side of the same coin. This is when we utilise an observation in a particular part of the world as clinching evidence to demonstrate knowledge we simply assume is valid. A few years ago I presented my case about the epistemic fallacy and its implications for 'schizophrenia' to a psychiatric audience. One of the psychiatrists there dismissed my immanent critique with a trump card saying, 'of course schizophrenia exists. I can take you to my ward and show you a schizophrenic'. For her the concrete manifestation of a universal medical condition, schizophrenia, was sitting on her ward for anyone to see (even an exasperating and wrong-headed speaker like me). The exemplary patient was, as it were, living *proof* of 'schizophrenia'. But the psychiatrist was wrong and her error was an example of the ontic fallacy.

The constant interplay of epistemic and ontic fallacies means that some critical realists discuss them together as the 'epistemic-ontic fallacy'. What they share is that they are artefacts of human activity or knowledge-in-practice. Their implications may be irrelevant (as in Bhaskar's notion of getting by in life with the 'natural attitude'). However, they may lead to walkers who are using an out-of-date map getting lost. This might be a mere inconvenience but the consequences could be life threatening. And in academic life it can lead to researchers getting things hopelessly wrong with a myriad consequences, from wasted resources to wild goose chases about theory development and application.

Conclusion

Roy Bhaskar offered us his authoritative summary, of what he called the 'distinctive features of the critical realist approach to philosophy', in his final and posthumously published work *Enlightened Common Sense* (Bhaskar, 2016: 1–4). Taking his cue from John Locke, Bhaskar argued that critical realism begins with an acknowledgement that it is the job of philosophy to 'under-labour' for all other disciplines. As will be clear in the next chapter, this is a particular challenge for psychology as a discipline because it began life in the academy by attempting to actively *reject* philosophical authority. Bhaskar also insisted that when we are being philosophical, then it should be done in a spirit of seriousness. Psychologists like philosophers can, if they wish, examine trivial matters; studying optical illusions and being a consultant to silly reality TV programmes come to my mind. Instead, they could choose to use their talents to ensure human flourishing and survival (see Chapter 12). Some psychologists committed to rising to the challenge of climate change really do understand this distinction between the trivial and the serious (e.g. Riemer and Reich, 2011).

Critical realism offers psychology and other disciplines resources to do their jobs well. These include using immanent, explanatory and omissive critiques to check on the adequacy of their preferred theories. Also we could ensure that we are critically reflective at all times in our work and that we clarify our starting assumptions. Bhaskar called that 'explicating presuppositions'. Without such philosophical work, our tacit or unexamined assumptions will exist in our work but will be without critical reflection. Given that those starting assumptions are bound up often with the history of our discipline, then I would argue that a form of historical sensibility is particularly important to cultivate.

This critical and historically informed approach increases our chances of not taking anything for granted in psychology. Bhaskar followed the lead of the Egyptian sage Hermes, who encouraged this constant scepticism and a refusal to accept anything on authority. He calls this orientation of constant sceptical checking the 'principle of hermeticism'. We can develop that orientation by combining the above elements of guidance about critique and criticality at all times. During the 20th century, psychologists have been diverted from these necessities by two dominant philosophical orientations, which I will now address in the next couple of chapters: positivism and postmodernism.

2

THE LIMITS OF NAÏVE REALISM

Introduction

The academic discipline of psychology has a long history and a short past. The long view tells us that matters psychological were the concerns of very many ancient philosophers, whether in Greece, China or India. The short view tells us that psychology only became truly 'scientific' just over a hundred years ago (notably in North America, Russia and Europe). Richards (2010) makes the point that a range of ways of exploring psychological matters were still evident with the growth of modernity (the unbroken trend stretching back to antiquity). However, Psychology with a capital 'P' made its bid for legitimacy as a natural science to demarcate itself from that ancient trend.

The problem, as will become clear throughout this book, and that I summarise in Chapter 12, was that its theoretical coherence never became established in that role as a putative natural science (Smith, 1997). Moreover, to the annoyance of the professionalisers in the early 20th century, many community-based clubs focusing on practical psychology, especially variants of self-help, continued to use the term 'psychology' (Thomson, 2007; Hallam, 1925). An early example of this tension was that when the British Psychological Society was formed in 1901 using the name of the 'Psychology Society', innumerable other bodies were using the same. Accordingly 'British' was added in 1906. By the turn of this century, this split between 'lay psychology' and the discipline with its strong scientific pretension posed a problem for its public credibility and relevance (Jones and Elcock, 2001).

With regard to the 'hard sell' of psychology being simply a new version of a natural science, in the late 19th century, the science laboratory seemed to be a safe bet for the new discipline. An important factor in that trend was the morphing of physiology into psychology, such as the bridging work of Ivan Pavlov on animal conditioning, Wilhelm Wundt on psychophysiology and Charles Sherrington on neurophysiology. The expectation that physiology might prompt an understanding of *psychological* phenomena within a tradition of natural science created an ambiguity present today and pertinent to two competing possibilities of interest to critical realism: **reductionism** and **emergentism**. Might our complex thoughts, feelings and intentions ultimately be *reducible* to the physiology of our central nervous system? Alternatively, might the latter *afford new possibilities* that have to be accounted for and explored in new ways? More will be said on this in Chapter 4.

Although, more widely, physiology and medicine began to influence and define the early concerns of modern psychology, in the academy it was philosophy that was the dominant constraint on its emerging autonomy. Until the turn of the 20th century philosophy had cornered the market, with some confidence, on the nature of mind and the exploration of human existence. One of its main journals was (and still is) called *Mind*. It was established in 1876 but its intellectual pedigree could be traced back over 2000 years. Eleven years passed before the first volume of the *American Journal of Psychology* appeared. A tactical gambit open to the 'new kid on the block' was that psychology might distance itself from philosophy in all ways possible. This point is exemplified by the very first editorial issued in the *British Journal of Psychology* by James Ward and William Rivers:

> Psychology, which till recently was known amongst us chiefly as mental philosophy and was widely concerned with problems of a more or less speculative and transcendental character, has now at length achieved the position of a *positive science*; one of a special interest to the philosopher no doubt but still *independent of his control*, possessing its *own methods*, its own specific problems and a distinct standpoint altogether its own. 'Ideas' in the philosophical sense *do not fall within its scope*; its inquiries are restricted entirely to *facts*.
>
> *(Ward and Rivers (1904: 1), emphasis added)*

This endorsement of empiricism and positivism and the rejection of philosophical idealism and reflection is clear and to the point. Note Ward and Rivers make sure that it is the very first page of the very first volume of the new journal. They were setting out their stall for a new scientific discipline and letting their readership know what psychology was and was not now going to look like.

The rhetorical flourish in the editorial statement sounded persuasive enough. However, it contained within it two problems, which create problems for psychologists even today. The first was that the justification for a reliance on facts was itself based upon a philosophical legacy of a form of realism: empiricism. Psychologists in their struggle for disciplinary autonomy could not reasonably understand the *case* for empiricism without understanding the strengths and weaknesses of it as a *form of philosophy*. Kicking away the justificatory ladder of philosophical empiricism left psychologists asserting a reliance on empirical neatness, transparency and integrity (methodological rigour). What was not left was a philosophical rationale. The rhetoric of 'methodologism' began to substitute for full metaphysical insight and reflection; more on this in Chapter 12.

Related to this shift to unreflective empiricism was the claim that psychology was a new no nonsense 'positive science'. The logic of this assumption was that it would lead to our understanding of fixed universal laws (**covering laws**) about inner experience and outward behaviour. By severing their historical ties with philosophy, psychologists were making themselves further vulnerable. *Both* of the traditions of empiricism and positivism were being relied upon, at the very historical moment (the turn of the 20th century) when the traditional disciplinary authority on the mind – philosophy – was being scorned for being outmoded.

When convincing themselves that psychology now should have little or nothing to do with the older and controlling discipline, Ward and Rivers in 1904 were encouraging the beginnings of a long period of collective amnesia. The trajectory they (and other disciplinary leaders of the time) were setting of a self-confident scientific but *de-philosophised* rhetoric has had consequences for psychology students to this day. During the first of half of the 20th century, when leaders of the discipline acted as if the battle had now been won about the nature of scientific psychology, they were left with little or no philosophical confidence and competence to justify that claim.

The consequence of this collective amnesia was a series of crises about what psychology should be doing and why, as a number of commentators were to note by the mid-20th century (e.g. Bergmann, 1957; Westland, 1978). If the first part of the 20th century brimmed with the positivistic optimism of Ward and Rivers, the second part was awash with self-doubt in the discipline about the very possibility of scientific psychology (e.g. Howard, 1986; Snoeyenbos and Putney, 1980). This trope about psychology being a discipline in crisis has not gone away, with the same frustration and *angst* still being expressed now, just as it was 30 years ago (e.g. Smedslund, 2016; Hughes, 2018).

By the late 20th century, this left those defending the old positivist orthodoxy to fear for the fragmentation of the discipline. For example, Hans Eysenck lamented 'the continuing failure of the two scientific disciplines of psychology – the experimental and the correlational – to come together and mutually support each other' (Eysenck, 1997a: 1224). A strong synergy between the closed system of the laboratory and the Humean emphasis on constant conjunctions was the *only* way forward for scientific psychology: there was no alternative. Eysenck was re-stating the position of Ward and Rivers offered at its start, in defiance of the discipline's dissenters and critics but he was wrong: these doubters were offering credible alternatives, it was simply that he refused to recognise their legitimacy.

The amalgam of empiricism and positivism in orthodox psychology

If we are to remember, rather than forget, the empiricist and positivist foundations of much of modern psychology, then what is relevant to recall from the perspective of critical realism? Empiricism and positivism are bedfellows but have different philosophical emphases. The first narrowly defines trustworthy knowledge by our agreement about sense data. Sensing (typically seeing) is believing and the more that we sense the same event and repeatedly, then the more trustworthy the knowledge claim. The second presumes (*a priori*) that external reality contains lawful relationships, which science can reveal by proper investigation. In this way, science will incrementally establish how the world works. In the case of psychology, this assumes that, over time, the discipline will map out, with increasing sophistication, permanent covering laws of human (and for some also animal) experience and behaviour. At first glance, both of these orientations about reality seem to be entirely reasonable. However, if we interrogate them they are highly contestable.

Empiricism is a flawed guide to science

For critical realism, empiricism misleadingly uses **the empirical** domain of reality to describe the totality of reality. **The real** and **the actual** are collapsed into the empirical. This creates a flat and thin misconception of our inner and outer worlds (**ontological monovalence**). The latter focuses narrowly on what is present, which common sense will tell you is a sort of nonsense. Most of reality is absent to us but it is still reality. Thus, ontological monovalence, implied by empiricism, also hints at its bedfellow within naïve realism (positivism) discussed more below: reality is only considered real when it is *positively* present.

The following four points elaborate this starting point of empiricism for many psychologists and its weaknesses according to critical realism.

1. *Beyond the observable*. Reality contains more than observable events. Many events are not observed but still actually occur. Also some real powers are not converted into events at all. The amoral fantasy about killing those that we hate (thankfully) converts into practical action fairly rarely. Our murderous fantasies and our capability to kill others are both real enough but they are not in all (or indeed many) circumstances actualised. Thus we cannot limit our understanding of psychological phenomena to the domain of the empirical; we must consider the actual and real as well.
2. *Human agents and the* ***transitive aspect of reality***. Psychologists are part of the society they study and they, like their subjects, are reflexive human agents. They are far less detached empirically from their topics of interest than say an inorganic chemist. The latter looks at and muses at the reaction in their test tube. When a psychologist metaphorically does the same, then the test-tube looks and talks back (Bannister, 1966). While postmodernism has oversold the role of language in human science (see next chapter) language use is an emergent quality in *Homo sapiens*, which requires special consideration. For a start it draws us into **epistemological relativism**, which is a unique manifestation of our species. We not only use language to make statements about reality but we can go on and on making statements about statements (meta-statements).
3. *Naïve realism fails to respect human complexity*. If we limit our psychological knowledge to what is known empirically then it tempts us to scorn other legitimate ways of investigating our inner and outer reality. For example, sometimes our insights into the complexities of human functioning might be

more elaborate and nuanced if we read novels and poetry, rather than relied upon empirical psychology. We know so little and so we can explore cautiously what it is to be human in so many legitimate ways beyond the confines of the discipline (see **epistemic humility**). Creative artists or political visionaries explore imagined possibilities, which have not yet occurred in the future, or have already happened but are beyond formal empirical verification. Critiquing empiricism does not deny that the empirical is a very important *aspect* of reality, not at all. It simply does not exhaust our task of appreciating reality in its totality.

Take the example of empiricism's earnest philosophical commitment to the transparent inter-subjective confirmation of reality (via co-present observers or replicated experiments). An exemplar of a disruptive critical realist objection for psychologists is the imagination of the solo creative artist. A painter with strong visual imagery could paint a tortoiseshell cat sitting on a purple leather chair, with the sun shining from a window to the left, all from her mind's eye. No one else can see this image just the painter. The internal image is real to her but it cannot be validated by others. Her capacity to imagine and then put that capacity into goal-directed practical action demonstrates this point, when an admiring audience eventually sees the painting of the cat in a gallery. However, that complex form of reality would also be *true* even if the artist, in an act of dissatisfied self-denial, destroyed her painting with no witnesses present a day later.

Similarly, a song writer can play around with options in their mind about developing a tune and elaborating helpful supporting chords. During their internal experiment, unknown to anyone other than themselves, real though transitory possibilities emerge and are discarded as options. Nobody else has access to that aspect of their reality but it could be the basis for producing a pristine song for others to eventually appreciate when performed (or not at all). What is not in doubt though is that a true enough, albeit transient, inner reality was … real. It was unobservable by others but it was undoubtedly real.

4. *Empiricist psychology has been inconsistent about inner reality.* When contemporary psychology relies on its empiricist past, embedded in a type of oft forgotten philosophy, it is not merely being prey to historical ignorance. It is also still dealing with one of empiricism's own enduring and inherent contradictions. Empiricism during the 19th century did not create a form of behaviourism (that was to come later) but instead was keen to return, again and again, to unobservable inner events.

Empiricism has conceded the legitimacy of our interiority in two senses. First, it has pursued objectivity while relying on *inter-subjectivity* as a method (i.e. consensus building about sense data). Second, empiricist philosophers took a scientific interest in our inner world, not just our outer one, for the obvious reason that *its reality simply cannot be denied.* We think and feel. We have dreams. We have fantasies. Our passions at times prompt irrational action but are the source of creativity, romantic love and industriousness in our lives. Subjective experience is

> not invalidated by empiricism, quite the contrary. It is actually *required*, both in terms of its faith in inter-subjective decision making and the very personal inner events and processes (such as accurate perception and judgement) that make any of us capable of contributing to the latter.

Those who were working at the cusp of empiricist philosophy and the upcoming de-philosophised version of 'scientific psychology', announced with a flourish by those like Ward and Rivers, had no qualms at all about their curiosity in inner events. They were the early explorers of what we might now think of as cognitive psychology. These 'associationists' and early experimentalists were interested in memory and reasoning. They took inner reality very seriously. It was even positioned as the core business of psychology, as an emerging discipline, when understanding the 'workings of the mind' in a scientific manner.

The morphing of British empiricism into a psychological examination of inner events was evident in seminal texts in modern psychology being offered by prestigious empiricist philosophers in the mid-19th century. During the 1850s, Alexander Bain's *The Senses and the Intellect* and *The Emotions and the Will* built upon Thomas Brown's *Lectures on the Philosophy of Mind* and James Mill's *Analysis of the Phenomena of the Human Mind* from the 1820s (Hearnshaw, 1964). During the same period in the USA, the work of William James also exemplified this contentment with, and interest in, inner events from the very tradition of empiricism that was to shape modern psychology.

Naïve realism: not only empiricism but also positivism

Turning to positivism in particular and the disciplinary orthodoxy it spawned in the 20th century, it relies heavily on empiricism and so subsumes its strengths and weaknesses, as just noted. However, it goes further by also appealing to rationalism and logic, when making knowledge or truth claims. When combining empirical methods and logic it then determines what is legitimately scientific by the facts ascertained at the end of a scientific investigation.

What the empirical evidence has told us morphs immediately into what is scientific truth and, by implication, sets limits on what and what is not scientific psychology (see quote from Ward and Rivers above). However, this simple and clear *a posteriori* criterion of scientific worthiness in positivism is joined by one which is *a priori*. The latter has more profound implications because of the assumption of universal lawfulness; empiricism does not logically require such an assumption, as its focus is on sense-data as the source of knowledge. Paradoxically, although positivism is for many our supreme philosophical guide to ontology, in truth it is largely concerned with knowledge. Its mission to demonstrate epistemological supremacy is not different in principle from its arch enemy rooted in idealism (radical social constructivism), which I address in the next chapter.

Positivism is positive in two senses. First, it is positive about truth derived from empirical evidence about what is present (and negative about anything else as a form of scientific claim). Second, it is positive that the world functions in a lawful manner and the job of science is to verify or confirm those permanent and universal processes, reflected in their alleged empirical invariance.

To be clear here, for critical realism ontology can be usefully separated from epistemology. Ontology contains within it tendencies set by nature, which are independent of our conception of nature (the force of gravity, the speed of light, the phases of matter (gas, liquid, solid), biological types etc.). However, positivism then overlays these legitimate assumptions about reality with another but misleading epistemological one: reality is considered to be fixed and predictable, independent of fluxing contexts. Critical realism rejects positivism's misplaced confidence in an invariant world governed by permanent laws.

Thus whilst critical realism endorses the existence of the mind-independent world and its natural tendencies, it rejects positivist assumptions about it and as importantly it recognises the need for critical reflexivity about our epistemological assumptions. By contrast positivism lacks that critical stance, relying instead on its own epistemological confidence in empirical verification, its reduction of everything that is real to the empirical and its assumption that reality is laid out in a fixed manner to be eventually discovered by science. Thereby, science becomes a positive project of confident incrementalism, taking small steps, or leaps and bounds, over time. For positivism it is a linear process of increasing certainty and sophistication about a world (including our world of experience and behaviour) that functions universally in a lawful manner. Positivism has misled psychologists for reasons just noted. This has created three mutually reinforcing and misleading assumptions, within their discipline, under its influence:

1. In addition to *methodological empiricism* (the empirical method) operational definitions set out the nature of reality in advance for the researcher to deliver a form of *meaning empiricism*: empirical findings will be judged to be meaningful to the researcher and his or her audience, once they are broadcast or disseminated. An example of this would be that a high psychometric score on 'extraversion' of an outgoing and stimulation-seeking individual confirms the meaningful reality of that concept both to scientific psychology and the world receiving its findings.
2. Once findings are established in accordance with the rules of methodological and meaning empiricism they will add to a confident stock of knowledge, which is characterised by empirical invariance. That is, unless proved otherwise by subsequent empirical work, lawful relationships between variables, it is assumed, will always apply across time and space. This reflects the contestable *a priori* assumption I noted above about universal aspects of reality.
3. This combination of assumptions about our reliance on empiricism and empirical invariance will encourage or warrant versions of *explanatory reduction*. For example, radical behaviourism argued that the systematic empirical investigation of the contingent relationship between stimulus and response will account for *all* behavioural tendencies in humans and other animals. We are nothing but the product of our reinforcement history. No other considerations are required to produce a scientific version of psychology. Or, in another example, expanding

on above, a map of our scores on psychometric instruments, measuring the 'Big Five' personality characteristics, will explain why we act as we do as individuals across settings. The blend of these scores defines who we are and explains, and might even predict, how we act in the way we do.

Responding to the points above one by one, for critical realism, empiricism does not exhaust our account of reality and so should not constrain our understanding of the complex challenge of understanding psychological aspects of reality. Moreover, whilst *some* aspects of the latter over time and place are largely invariant (the 'structural aspects' of a system) and slow to change, in open systems they are often not invariant at all but are instead unstable and poorly predictable.

Some things stay more or less the same over time and place, but many do not. Thus empirical invariance cannot be assumed at all in open systems and universal laws are very risky to assert. This is true of biological systems in general not just human systems in particular. Hence I am not special pleading here for our species but making a wider point about emergent features of open biological systems. For example, why is there not an absolute one-to-one relationship between heavy smoking and lung cancer and why do some non-smokers get the disease?

As for explanatory reductions, any explanation of human conduct requires us to consider a wide range of processes jostling together because we are *both* determined beings (under biological, psychological and social influences from the past and the present) *and* determining beings with an eye to the immediate or long-term future. Cognition and elaborate language use has afforded us the capacity for agency and reflectiveness. This emergent quality in *Homo sapiens* means that we can make choices, even if we cannot choose to do or be anything we want unendingly.

If we recall from Chapter 1 that the ancient Greek tradition of positivism can be traced to the work of Parmenides. He assumed the world was fixed and given (by the gods, but now non-religious positivists may consider it simply as being given by nature). This assumption, even more than the limits set on reality by empiricism, is queried by critical realists. They argue instead that the world is not fixed but in flux (following Heraclitus). Moreover, with flux comes a dynamic mixture of old tendencies and freshly emergent events and processes.

Human systems are open systems: inference about fluxing complexity

Critical realism rejects falsifiability as the guide to good science (cf. Popper, 1959). The well-rehearsed abstract methodological convention of the null hypothesis does not inspire confidence about how we should proceed in our research in all circumstances. For example, the law of gravity cannot be falsified, similarly with evolutionary theory. However, falsifiability as a guide to good scientific practice did not come from positivism.

Popper was *not* a positivist, in the sense that that term had been used by the sociologist August Comte or the Logical Positivists of the Vienna Circle. His approach was one of critical rationalism and he noted that the positivists had limited their considerations of truth to strict empirical confirmation or to tautology (hence the *positive* assertion typified in the Ward and Rivers citation above). We see the fruition of these principles in Skinner's philosophical behaviourism, which focused on empirical studies of S-R links and in operational definitions. Thus operationalism was a logical outcome of a positive assertion about the world (Bridgman, 1938).

The positivists had focused on positive presence and its proof (i.e. empirical verification) and argued that without this then there is no truth only superstition and meaningless claims about ourselves and the world. Popper disagreed, conceding that many aspects of life may be true but cannot currently be justified scientifically. Thus the verification focus of positivism was displaced by the falsifiability focus of critical rationalism. Popper also emphasised that science was a social activity and its merit could not be appraised by methodological matters alone (see my discussion of the shortcomings of methodologism in Chapter 12).

Thus Popper's work is a bridge in some ways to critical realism because it rejects the naïve focus on verification and concedes the social context of science; he began a trend of post-positivist philosophy of science, to which critical realism now belongs. His naivety remained though about his confidence in empiricism and covering laws, as well his assumption that open debate and peer criticism were the necessary *and sufficient* condition for confidence in science. This ignores the range of conscious and unconscious processes that shape science (in terms of the questions being posed and the ways in which data generated are interpreted). I return to this point below.

Also Popper remained an empiricist, methodologically. Bhaskar et al. (2018) cite the example of puppies:

> [Popper] ... said that we can only ever describe individual puppies and that it is not the business of science to ask the question 'What is a puppy?' For Popper then there is no real category of 'puppy', it is just something we impose on the world. However, for critical realists there is a real category of puppy, although empirically every puppy that we meet will be an entirely unique individual example of the category 'puppy'.
>
> *(ibid.: 57)*

Returning to Popper's preference for falsification over verification, we might reasonably have *confidence* in some theories, rather than others. Take, as an example, that we see around us diverse flora and fauna. In the case of fauna, we see members routinely competing for food and mates with others and defending their territory against intruders. Seeing this picture, Darwin developed his well-known historical theory that might account for these observations. His theory suggested that extinct species might well be found in fossils and that current forms of anatomy would have residual traces of past structural elements and their functional role. If Darwin was correct in his epistemic musings then his theory was a transitive aspect of reality. However, evolution as a complex set of historical ('been and gone') antecedents to account for bio-diversity was an **intransitive aspect of reality**. Evolution did not need Darwin or anyone else to describe it; it simply existed.

Creationism is a different attempt at **retroduction**, so we can exercise **judgemental rationality** about which theory is more persuasive. Were Darwin's observations about the present state of the world consistent with the rapid and recent creation of bio-diversity by God or with a very long geological period of biological adaptation between species reproducing and surviving in varied and shifting ecological contexts? (God-given fixity of the world was part of the view of reality offered by Parmenides contrasted by critical realism with that suggested by Heraclitus.)

Returning to the central point in this section, critical realism disputes the guidance of *both* verification *and* falsifiability for good scientific practice, replacing them with a different form of inference (retroduction and retrodiction), which I discussed in Chapter 1. Moreover, if open systems are complex and in flux then a *definitive* claim that something is not true is highly problematic, to say the least. In critical realism the problematic desire to infer laws of nature (an open system) from a closed system is flawed. One casualty of this process of **transduction** is our false confidence in the transferability of experimental findings, when moving from closed systems like the laboratory to the whirring complex and fluxing everyday world around us.

Thus null hypothesis logic about falsification is seductive but limited in practice in open systems. As the critical realist sociologist Porpora (2015: 85) puts it well, 'when results are contrary to null expectations, we cannot be sure that it is the null hypothesis specifically that has been falsified'. Even in a seemingly tightly controlled experiment, human error and equipment failures can undermine confidence in null hypothesis logic. If that is true of the closed system of the laboratory, then our certainties undoubtedly fall apart in open systems. The dubious utility (or futility) of null hypothesis logic has also been rehearsed by psychologists, even though its totemic status remains on the undergraduate curriculum (Cohen, 1994; Schmidt, 1996). Null hypothesis reasoning focuses on the failed association between two measured variables, say A and B, being the basis for disproving causation, reflecting the search for Humean constant conjunctions. However, A may have a genuine causative power in relation to B, but it might be blocked by the presence of one or more other variables (C/D etc.). Moreover, we only can confirm or disconfirm the certainty of events after, not before, their occurrence.

For example man A, who died in 1986, could not have murdered man B in 1987. However, the notion that in open systems we can declare something not true *in advance* is untenable. We could not have said definitively in 1985 that man A will *not* murder man B in 1987. As the saying goes, it is easy to be wise after the event (or '20/20 hindsight') but prediction is a different matter completely. The very notion that some things will *always be true or untrue* in all contexts would only be logically possible if systems are fixed and immutable (i.e. on tramlines of determination), which they are not. With or without human interference, biological systems are open and not predictable (though tendencies or demi-regularities exist often).

Barring maths and (Newtonian) physics, other forms of science have struggled to assert covering laws and appealed increasingly (from necessity) to probabilities and the need to take into account each new circumstance (the importance of context). For example, panels of horticulturalists, who are experts on plants and their physiology will advise gardeners about why this particular plant is not thriving, despite conventional forms of nurturance. They will make various suggestions to increase the chances of future prospects for thriving and offer a range of possibilities to account for failure to date. Sometimes they agree on diagnosis and cure and sometimes they do not. This is the inevitable outcome of dealing with open biological systems. Thus, whereas Newtonian physics helps a civil engineer to predict, fairly accurately, when a load on a bridge will make it collapse, biological science cannot even offer a similar certainty to a gardener about how to revive a sickly plant. And even well-built bridges may sometimes fall down when *new events* emerge, such an earth tremor from a fracking scheme, newly introduced, that shakes its foundations.

Turning from plants and bridges to people, as biological beings we do not even react predictably to a given pharmacological agent. So called 'personalised medicine' is an eventual admission from biomedicine that drugs tend to create a wide range of beneficial and injurious effects across groups of human patients. Whether it is analgesics, anxiolytics or antibiotics, we react to drugs in a range of ways. The same is true of self-administered alcohol. For psychology, this question about uncertainty in biological systems is made more complicated though by language use and our moral agency.

The focus in human science so much of the time on the transitive aspect of reality further implies the lack of wisdom of claiming psychological predictability. Natural scientists and their high level of empirical detachment from their research focus are dealing largely with the intransitive dimension of reality, whereas human scientists are dealing overwhelmingly with the transitive dimension (human thought and praxis).

Above I noted the problem that open biological systems pose for retrodictive theorists. Broad trends can be identified but predictions are dubious at the individual level. This is conceded by developmental psychologists, such as Jerome Kagan. He argues that our personal attachment style in infancy has a weak predictive validity about our later psychological development, compared to the socioeconomic status of our family of origin (Kagan, 2016). Moreover, thereafter a whole cascade of contingent events and opportunities affect where we end up in life and our state of well-being. The outcome of the cascade is inflected continuously by the meanings we attach and the choices we make. I return to Kagan's work in Chapter 4.

We are determined and determining beings. We are the product of our socialisation (in this sense socialisation theory is retrodictive in its form of inference). However, we also reflect on our experiences; people with very similar forms of parenting may be diverse in their eventual personal styles, interests etc. Some Catholic children remain devout until their death, others quickly reject the Church with scorn. Very similar adverse childhood conditions only lead to broad trends of becoming adults. Differences in the mental health of survivors confirm this point (see Chapter 10).

Following from this point, the powers exercised *via human action* (praxis) are what links social psychology to sociology: the matter of normativity. For example, the norm of men consciously and unconsciously pursuing the control over women and children reveals a repeated power of patriarchy. However, patriarchy only exists as long as it goes unchallenged. It could be eroded and abolished by political struggle, pitching some human agents against others, until this is achieved. Today we can see that struggle operating unevenly across societies. We do not know for certain where it will lead in the future. Norms (say patriarchal ones) exist and these may be sustained or changed by collective human action. Human agency does not singularly account for the character of open systems (they occur in biological systems generally) but it does *amplify* unpredictability within them.

These doubts from critical realism about a reliance on the empirical method and a closed system scientific rationale undermine any confidence in experimentalism. Bhaskar incorporated a key assumption from scientists, who had started life in the laboratory with its optimistic norms of experimentalism but were critical of its potential to generalise to everyday life (von Bertalanffy, 1968; Weiss, 1969). Their assumption, instead, was that real living systems (not just human systems) are open not closed and they are stratified (see **laminated reality**). Science should be about understanding processes not events *per se*. For these systems theorists, experimentalism decontextualises those processes and controls *out* the complexity associated with real life. This leaves us with methodological neatness but dubious findings, which are not likely to generalise to a multiplicity of other settings in a consistent manner. I return to systems thinking in conclusion in Chapter 12.

In open systems we can make broad probability statements, but we cannot make plausible specific predictions. Even in a relatively closed, rule-bound system, such as a game of soccer, where the detailed past form of the teams is highly documented and an independent referee is present to ensure fair rule compliance for all the players, then unexpected results can (and do) still occur. In a semi-final of the 2018 World Cup, the professional pundits predicted that England would beat Croatia by one goal. The reverse of this outcome actually occurred.

Psychology as a self-confident predictive science is doomed to failure in relation to individual events (barring the fact we will all die, and even some futurologists are querying this inevitability). If this is in doubt, then why do we seek comfort in religion, sneakily look at our horoscopes and contribute irrationally to the enlarging profits of the gambling industry? Predicting future human events constantly fascinates and outwits us. The psephologists who claim expertise at predicting election outcomes often have to eat their words, when the voting has stopped. Even genetic counselling for inherited diseases will only offer probability statements to anxious relatives, who are currently asymptomatic. The human genome project may enable insurers to alter their actuarial calculations but definitive predictions about the morbidity and mortality of an *individual* are necessarily tentative.

To summarise, because human systems are open systems, their predictability is precarious. Experts, even prestigious ones, taking the risk of prediction about human societies have been embarrassingly wrong. For example, the inventor of the machine gun (Richard Gatling), dynamite (Alfred Nobel) and the radio (Guglielmo Marconi) all claimed that their technological changes would reduce casualties and even eliminate war but actually the reverse happened. The economists Irving Fisher and Larry Kudlow just prior to the financial crashes of 1929 and 2008, respectively, claimed that the capitalist system was safe and secure. These and many other examples are given to us by Tom Phillips in his amusing and depressing book *Humans: A Brief History of How We F***ed It All Up* (Phillips, 2018). In so many ways it was an easy book to write.

Epistemic humility and the ubiquity of values in science

Does this leave us in a state of nihilism then in social science? The answer is 'no' but it means we should proceed cautiously with epistemic humility about what is achievable. For example, beyond the specific we can affirm general tendencies. Middle-aged women tend to be better drivers than young men; look at the motor insurance premiums. But some individual young male drivers are impeccably safe and some individual middle-aged female drivers are reckless. Poverty and social isolation predict depressive systems at the population level but some poor individuals report being happy and some loners enjoy their lives. Not all heavy smokers die young but most do and, as a consequence, pension estimates can be more advantageous to those using tobacco.

Moreover, linking this aggregate tendency point to falsification, over time a *theory* (rather than a particular hypothesis) might be genuinely falsified. For example, the theory that the earth is flat has been falsified by camera shots from space. The theory that the earth was made in seven days with all of its flora and fauna is untenable (see above discussion of Darwinism). The theory that mortality was a random act of God (anytime to anyone about any accident or affliction) was disproved as we collected actuarial data to show its clear link to social group membership (age, social class, occupation, age, sex and race). Our current life insurance industry relies on such data and it aggregates predictions or probability statements, based on data from the past.

Thus we must be humble and cautious about predicting *specific outcomes* but can be quietly confident sometimes about aggregate patterns and trends. That is why Newton and Darwin can broadly still be relied upon as sound scientific theorists. The reason why standard Popperian falsification is a wild goose chase in any science is that it focuses not on that cycle of learning as a *continuous process* but on whether at a particular *point* within it we can *definitively* test a null hypothesis. Sometimes we can test it and sometimes not; even when we can, our specific inference at the time may be erroneous.

Moving to science and values, positivism makes a specious claim that facts can be separated from values; the assumption of 'disinterested knowledge'. The fact–value distinction was made by David Hume and is honoured still today by many philosophers of science (Hume, 1854). Critical realism argues that such a separation is not possible, in either principle or practice. Facts are value-laden for a range of reasons. We make a knowledge claim to displace a previous false assumption (e.g. the world is round and so it is not flat). Thus knowledge brings with it an assumption at some level of truth seeking, which is a moral imperative. Even when knowledge is abused (say to justify oppression in some way or to mislead) that is still a value-driven process, simply one that offends its critics. An example here would be the controversy over Tony Blair's alleged evidence base for agreeing to the invasion of Iraq in 2002. A problem with the notion of the 'abuse' of knowledge is that it implies that its *use* is a value-free affair, when it is not.

An example of 'normal' psychological knowledge being value-saturated has been the widespread pragmatic success claimed for 'nudge technologies', arising from behavioural economics (Thaler and Sunstein, 2008). It has been used as a successful public health measure but also to encourage dubious consumer choices. This moral ambiguity has required nudge proponents to concede the ethical context of its application and assumptions, which are cheap and minimalist but also arguably manipulative (Sunstein, 2016). Thus our appraisal of nudge technology, or any form of applied psychological intervention, requires some form of judgemental rationalism and critical reflexivity from both their proponents and critics.

Knowledge generation emerges as a result of the commercial and epistemic interests of human beings living within particular political and moral orders. An example in the first would be the production of magic bullets to target specific diseases by Big Pharma, in order for it to make profits for its shareholders. An example of the second would be why academics maintain their careers by pursuing particular theories. (In Chapter 7 I discuss why moral panic theory is held on to irrationally by some when understanding child sexual abuse and in Chapter 10 I discuss why mental health professionals retain irrational diagnostic concepts.) If knowledge production emerges in part because of the driver of particular interests, then from the outset it is value-laden and our retroductions, within in an explanatory critique, entail working out how those interests contributed to the emergence and then maintenance of any form of knowledge.

Positivism is simply wrong to assert that we can separate facts from values. It confuses the real enough prospects of some degree of *empirical detachment* in natural science (a methodological matter) with *value-neutrality* (an ethical matter – see **axiology**). This conflation provides us with a narrow and misleading definition of objectivity. Critical realists accept objectivity but conceive it not in terms of value-neutrality or 'disinterestedness' but instead in terms of alignment to the object of its enquiry. That is, are we respecting properly the particular aspect of ontology we are observing or exploring? Objectivity then is a version of truth-seeking guided by judgemental rationality and good faith.

That attempt at psychological objectivity requires substantial epistemic humility and reflexivity about the social norms we are embedded within. Psychology cannot enjoy the degree of empirical detachment of the chemist because the test tube 'talks back'. Human agency operates in normative contexts shared by psychologists and those they try to understand as 'subjects' or 'participants' (or in the applied realm 'clients' or 'patients'). We cannot absent ourselves from our societal context in order to gain a neutral bird's-eye view of human experience and conduct. The prospect of psychologists claiming authentic and comprehensive empirical detachment from their research is not just weak and precarious, it is comical.

Points of agreement between realists

Most of the above has been about finding fault with the assumptions of empiricism, positivism and critical rationalism, which, if fair comment, should profoundly undermine our confidence in much being claimed within orthodox and respectable psychology. However, there is an important baby not to be thrown out with the bathwater. Although positivism implausibly separates facts from values and offers us universal covering laws, empiricism offers us a superficial account of reality narrowly and critical rationalism relies too naïvely on the corrective power of peer review, they are all committed reasonably to a view of an independent reality. Common sense can give confidence to any form of realism because of our primary socialisation, when making sense of our inner and outer worlds (see Chapter 1).

Thus the common-sense assumption of (most) human beings that reality exists both gives confidence to empiricists and positivists (who are human themselves) and to 'lay people' who have an understandable tendency to trust scientific experts. When the latter point out that they operate with methodological rigour in order to deliver disinterested truth claims about reality, then there seems to be a 'win–win' for both parties. Trust in fair judgements is both a rational and democratic position: why would any of us *not* trust those skilled in delivering scientific knowledge?

A more sceptical look at that trust is warranted though. It is not only about the limits of empiricism and positivism noted above but it is also about the interest work in developing knowledge claims. In psychology that interest work has been there throughout its short formal disciplinary existence. For example, there could be no 'psychology of individual differences' without the emergence of eugenic thought in the late 19th century. Intelligence testing was developed from the beginning to sort the sheep from the goats in educational policy and to warrant the warehousing of those now called 'intellectually disabled'. The concern about the 'moral fibre' of military recruits during the inter-war period of the 1920s and 1930s stimulated a psychometric interest in neuroticism. The political concern in more recent times to individualise social problems by locating them inside individual brains has been an important driver of modern neuroscience (see Chapter 4).

Given all the potential topics that invite our curiosity about human life, why do we study some things and not others? Why do some research questions secure more financial backing than others? Which interest groups offer that funding? (See the glossary entry on **omissive critique**.) Neither empiricism nor positivism are inclined to pose and answer these questions, because values have allegedly been bracketed out of science. Methodological rule following and faith in null hypothesis reasoning, not critical reflexivity about pre- and non-empirical questions, is the name of the game for naïve realism (see Chapter 12).

Naïve realism in psychology: concluding discussion

Critical realism contests features of scientific orthodoxy in modern psychology for reasons which I will return to, repeatedly, in the case studies of subsequent chapters. The empirical does not exhaust our understanding of reality and so it is both misleading and restrictive for empiricism singularly to define the norms of psychological enquiry. Moreover, the world is not fixed but in flux, with open systems containing a mixture of stable and unstable, or even very ephemeral, processes and events. For this reason, it is a futile task to seek predictability in the search for 'psychological laws' and, in particular, we cannot transfer conclusions drawn in the closed system of the psychological laboratory to everyday life. Also, reductionism is risked as a result of these errors of reasoning. Explanatory reductionism has been celebrated in psychology (e.g. we are nothing but a product of our reinforcement history), when really it should be a source of grave concern because of its lack of plausibility and wisdom.

Beyond these basic differences between critical and naïve realism we need to consider three more linked and implied matters, which throw confidence in the latter into serious doubt. First, psychology cannot be a pure natural science, no matter how much that prospect would have appealed to the its early leaders at the start of the 20th century. Whilst our experience and behaviour are always underpinned and afforded by our bodily states and features, we are much more than this. In addition, we are inevitably part of what we are a studying. Thus psychology is, in large part, a social not a natural science.

Take the metaphor offered by Don Bannister, noted earlier, of the test tube 'talking back' in the psychological laboratory. In the famous Milgram experiment about compliance with authority, about a third of the subjects refused to continue with the contrived cruelty expected of them. Psychological subjects participate in research as reflective human agents, they are not merely impassive and insensible objects of enquiry for the researcher. Reflecting this aspect of reality, increasingly psychological studies began to talk of 'participants' rather than 'subjects', bowing to this undeniable feature of the ontology of being human.

Second, an emergent quality of human beings is that they are reflexive agents, who make choices that might either reproduce or transform the world they inhabit. Reflexivity and praxis (intentional action, not merely mechanistic behaviour) are part of being human and to a limited extent, because of weaker mechanisms of internal symbolic representations in other species, they are also part of mammalian life more generally. Whereas the natural scientist can claim, as his or her subject matter, a largely intransitive domain of reality, the social scientist in addition and much more extensively is dealing with the transitive domain.

Third, positivism suggests that we can separate facts from values and thereby generate 'disinterested knowledge'. This is not the case because both natural and social scientific activity is a social form of practice and will thereby always reflect, to some extent, the norms and values of its geo-historical situation. In the social sciences, the heavy focus on the transitive dimension of reality particularly compromises the capability of psychology to generate disinterested knowledge.

By keeping *both* ontological *and* epistemological considerations in mind, we can come to our best and fair judgement about what is and is not a legitimate truth claim. This is not the same as seeking the permanent truths of covering laws aspired to by positivism; neither is it pre-emptively rejecting any notion of truth (the tendency of postmodernism). However, it does recognise contingent truths, reasonably appraised. Did this man commit the crime he was accused of? Were six million Jews murdered in the Nazi death camps? Can we trace this woman's distress to her neglect and abuse in childhood? Does human activity contribute to global warming? Can we reduce our actions and consciousness to our brain activity? These sorts of questions can be answered legitimately because they are about the contingencies of emergence in complex systems. They do not require an assumption of positivist covering laws but they do not give up (postmodern style) on truth-seeking.

This chapter has focused on the shortcomings of the naïve realist orthodoxy in modern psychology. That critique has offered critical realism as a more comprehensive and valid framework for us to explore psychological aspects of inner and outer reality. The chapter began by noting the price paid, when the politics of disciplinary knowledge at the turn of the 20th century prompted the intellectual leadership of psychology to distance itself from the traditional authority on the mind, philosophy.

This strategic position created the conditions for a form of collective amnesia, disabling empiricist and positivist psychologists from fully understanding their own philosophical roots. One implication of this was that other forms of philosophy that were influencing psychological understanding outside of the conservative academy were also not being considered. For example, empiricism was not the only relevant and lively philosophical current during the 19th century. Two others were to have a continuing relevance and would come back to haunt naïve realism: existentialism and phenomenology. This point about philosophical diversity will be considered in Chapter 6 when discussing inner and outer reality but also in Chapter 3 which considers postmodernism.

3

THE LIMITS OF POSTMODERNISM

The shortcomings of naïve realism explored in the previous chapter were to be challenged during the 1980s, and after, by some disaffected psychologists. The so-called postmodern, narrative or linguistic 'turn' in the arts and humanities reminded all concerned that the discipline of psychology still rested precariously at the cusp of natural and social science (or even for some 'art and science'). The rejection of 'grand narratives' of any sort became modish within a reaction against all certainties in the academy, but especially scientific certainties. And if science could not be trusted in general, then a science such as psychology, which was relatively new and still lacking in confidence, was a tempting and ready target for postmodernists.

Postmodernism is a confusing term even today, especially as its core rejects certainties and defined starting points of discussion. Here I will separate three broad meanings but note that those writing about postmodernism sometimes consider the entanglement of the three. First, it has been used to describe an artistic movement of eclecticism, exemplified in the architectural styles favoured in the 1980s. That pluralism and pastiche in design and the arts was certainly evident then and can still be seen today.

Second, it has been used as a description of the socio-political jumble characterising 'advanced capitalism' or 'late modernity'. The latter form of societal organisation is said to reflect a 'postmodern condition' in which production has given way largely to a culture of consumerism and national concerns have been absorbed in a process of globalisation but also coexisted. New forms of technology have encouraged this complex emergence (Lyotard, 1979). This then is 'postmodernity', with the notion of postmodernism being a way of examining its character.

Third, and the connotation I will explore more here, is postmodernist philosophy. The latter has been associated with poststructuralism. As its name suggests, poststructuralism argues that we must go *beyond* the assumptions of any form of stable causal reality (ontology) and the forms of incremental knowledge development assumed about the latter (epistemology).

For the reader recalling the main points in the previous chapter, it is clear that naïve realism was a sitting target for this type of philosophical challenge. Across the arts and humanities researchers set about rejecting positivism with its obsession with universal **covering laws** and claims of empirical invariance. Now postmodernists emphasised contextualised or situated realities, with deconstruction and discourse analysis as their favoured methods of enquiry. The core assumption of this trend, often heard as a mantra, was that 'everything is socially constructed'.

This chapter will argue that the emergence of such an intellectual movement was an understandable reaction to scientific certainties but it then threw the baby out with the bathwater by rejecting or scorning **ontological realism** and querying the very point of tracing causation in the world (**generative mechanisms**). I will first place postmodernism and its strong social constructivism within the idealist tradition of philosophy; some of its current problems exist as an inevitable legacy of the past. After that I will turn to the specific impact of these shortcomings on postmodern psychology and return at the end to the similarities and differences between postmodernism and critical realism.

Postmodernism as a version of idealism

At its most basic in philosophy, a distinction can be made between ideas as sources and ideas as outcomes. In the first pure form, ideas drive, shape and constitute society and who we are within it. This is philosophical idealism (to be distinguished from the everyday use of the word to mean 'utopian' or 'extreme optimism'). An extension of this logic about the primacy of ideas is that a mind-independent reality actually does not exist or it is unknowable or it can only be known via the process of mental representations held by us *in advance* of our apprehending our inner and outer worlds. Taking these variations on a theme from the idealist tradition:

- It can offer versions of *anti-realism* as in the work of Bishop Berkeley (Dicker, 2011).
- It can offer versions of scepticism about reality as in Immanuel Kant's *transcendental idealism*. Kant's work is an important starting point for Bhaskar's development of critical realism because of its focus on free critical thought; Kant championed the Enlightenment and the rejection of religious dogma (Seung, 2007).
- It can offer versions of *perspectivism* as in the work of Friedrich Nietzsche, which I say more about below.
- In a weak trace, it can be found in the *cautious empiricism* of John Locke, who argued that we may distort reality by our failures in apprehension and perception. His notion of a *tabula rasa*, which was then filled in during our sentient existence, via our senses, is well known but he also cautioned that this does not lead automatically to accurate perception or understanding. Thus, although Locke's work is in most ways a break from idealism, his version of empiricism converges towards it to some degree in logic. Later British empiricists, such as Bertrand Russell, were to turn against idealism more fully:

> The shared concern of these metaphysical idealists is to put the mind, not external reality, at the centre of inquiry. This encourages a preoccupation with epistemology at the expense of ontology. External reality might be denied or its existence considered a secondary matter.

Starting with Nietzsche

The postmodern philosophical current of today is traceable largely to the work of Nietzsche (Robinson, 1999). His interest was broader than science and included morality. He argued that notions of truth or of good or bad were always predicated upon the perspective adopted by individuals. He dismissed the existence of facts in preference to one of how we understand the world. Thus he emphasised a form of *interpretivism*, which *in part* would be endorsed by critical realism, as we do indeed *construe*, even if we do not *construct* reality. We do this in particular ways and those ways can alter over time and place. This version of interpretivism is that of existentialism, as it stays with the unique or idiosyncratic viewpoints of lay people in their biographically contingent contexts (see Chapter 6). It is close to the notion of everyday 'psychologies' noted by Berger and Luckmann (1967) discussed below.

Nietzsche's philosophical rhetoric is the very inverse of that offered by Ward and Rivers, cited at the start of the previous chapter and is worth reading and re-reading them together:

> Against those who say 'There are only facts', I say, 'No, facts are precisely what there is not, only interpretations'. We cannot establish any fact in itself. Perhaps it is folly to want to do such a thing. Insofar as the word 'knowledge' has any meaning, the world is knowable; but it is interpretable otherwise. It has no meaning behind it, but countless meanings.
>
> *(Nietzsche cited in Pojman, 1998: 1015)*

Those telling phrases, 'only interpretations' and 'countless meanings', are at the core of postmodern thought. Accordingly, today social constructivist psychologists compare and contrast a wide range of meanings about the word 'meaning' (Medlock, 2017).

The limits of idealism

The question for critical realism about forms of idealism is less that their case cannot be defended in part, when attacking positivism, but whether that *exhausts* our understanding of the relationship between epistemology and ontology. The risk at all times is that a lopsided preoccupation develops about the former at the expense of the latter. In the extreme it culminates in the absurdity of anti-realism. This argues for the futility of a search for truth in reality and it erases the role of causal powers that are external to mental processes. Put simply, by over-selling a mind-dependent position the credibility of idealism is always made precarious; judged by common sense it is preposterous.

Turning instead to the focus on ideas as outcome, rather than source, this has been associated broadly with the philosophical tradition of *materialism*. (This technical term can distinguished from the everyday use connoting grasping self-centred greed.) Materialism prioritises the emergence of ideas from real biological and social relations in practice. Bhaskar (1997) was emphatic that ideas were an emergent part of the natural world. Idealists by contrast put ideas as separate from, or even at times in opposition to, the ontology of the natural world.

If ideas are part of the natural world then they cannot stand outside of it. Put differently, although we can distinguish for *analytical purposes* what exists (ontology) from our fallible knowledge of it (epistemology), the latter is also subsumed by the former. That is, if knowledge is part of the world then *ipso facto* it is *also* ontological. For this reason, postmodernists, who claim there are only words, and only situated social constructions built around them, are being illogical. To have faith in the words or texts requires us to have confidence in their very existence, thereby confirming ontological realism. And once that is conceded, why only isolate words as being real and nothing else? Why special plead for language, rather than other palpable and hidden forces in our lives? This singular preoccupation with language diverts us from taking reality in its complexity and totality seriously. Critical realists reject the position for being:

> … morally irresponsible and outrageous. This is because there are serious problems that affect humanity and these problems need to be understood in an interdisciplinary way. It is vital to be able to describe them, to theorize them and to critique them. Yet strong social constructionism disallows this critique.
> *(Bhaskar et al., 2018: 81)*

A focus on ideas that attempt (and critical realists would say fail) to scorn or highly problematise ontology is only one problem for idealism of the postmodern variety. In a similar vein to Bhaskar et al. 2018, another critical realist reflecting on personhood (see Chapter 4), Christian Smith concludes that:

> Postmodernism in the end is the abandonment of social science, actually, in favour of antirealist storytelling and identity posturing. That is a dead end.
> *(Smith, 2011: 489)*

Thus narratives are an important part of reality, as is our shifting sense of identity but they do not, by any means at all, exhaust the task of trying to understand people as real individual moral agents, in relation to others and in particular social contexts. What Smith calls 'identity posturing' has now become a part of the cultural landscape created by identity politics, underpinned in part by the confidence of its intellectual leaders in postmodern philosophy.

There is also the question of the relationship between ideas and action. I noted in the previous chapter the important difference between subjective life and praxis. Ideas in themselves exist but they are largely meaningful for critical realism, when they are enacted to affirm or challenge the *status quo*. The focus on this relationship and the role of action in human relationships is definitely not an endorsement of behaviourism (see Chapter 6). It is about how ideas become manifest in the world in human activity. That embeddedness of the meaning of praxis in social relationships overlaps with points being made in postmodern psychology (such as the work of Ken Gergen, see below). Likewise Michel Foucault talked of 'discursive practices' (Hook, 2001).

I noted in the previous chapter and will discuss more in Chapter 6 that empiricist philosophers discussed ideas as part of our interiority (now resonating in today's 'cognitive science'). Thus even naïve realism in the past did not reject ideas. As an overture to behaviourism, professionalisers in psychology such as Ward and Rivers cited at the turn of the 20th century opted to reject ideas 'in the philosophical sense' and concern themselves only with 'the facts'. This naïve distinction was implausible because ideas are typically manifest in 'the facts' and so the relationship between them deserves serious psychological reflection rather than dogmatic severance. Facts are both theory-laden and value-laden, not freestanding; a point of agreement between postmodernists and critical realists.

Thus both idealists and materialists certainly respect ideas and the need to attend to their content and emergence (concepts, ideologies, models, theories, cosmologies etc.) but they have contrasting views about their understanding and prioritisation. By privileging ideas as an *a priori* concern, idealists, knowingly or unconsciously, tend to slip into a focus on epistemology, as a dominant or even singular preoccupation, within any academic enquiry.

What became clear in postmodern philosophy was that our purview of human complexity was now being skewed towards, or reduced to, ideas, representations, words, narratives and discourses (Norris, 1990). If behaviourism as a version of positivism was to develop a *mindless* version of psychology and the reduction of our humanity to S-R patterns, then postmodern psychology was to adopt the opposite error: versions of radical *mind-dependency*. Now there were no valid or reliable claims to be made about inner or outer reality, only shifting and inconsistent perspectives and representations. Everything was just a situated story created by social actors. However, we find in practice that these social constructivists, of necessity, had to call upon reality in order to reject it (see below).

Is postmodernism inherently politically radical?

The lopsided interest of postmodern thought upon epistemology includes a healthy distrust of ideas, not just a preoccupation with them. The problem is that such an ultra-scepticism can become a form of nihilism. As Rosenau (1993) pointed out, postmodernism 'rejects epistemological assumptions, refutes methodological conventions, resists knowledge claims, obscures all versions of truth and dismisses policy recommendations'. This depiction suggests that postmodernism tends to be both anarchistic and nihilistic in its reasoning; mischievous features which appeal to its followers and drive its critics to despair.

With the term 'anarchistic' in mind, postmodernism has been attributed with a radical political role in intellectual life since the 1980s. The suspicion of traditional academic, especially scientific, authority seems to position it as a left-wing phenomenon. Indeed it seemed to attract the sympathies of leftist intellectuals disillusioned with Marxist structuralism in social science. After the 1970s, they were taking a turn away from materialism and towards idealism (e.g. Laclau and Mouffe, 1985). One of these, Scott Lash, considered that postmodernism was far more threatening to the *status quo* than modernist critiques (such as Marxism) because it pervades *all* of society, whereas modernist ideas were retained only in the realm of the political elites (Lash, 1990).

However, nothing is straightforward in relation to postmodernism. Two key intellectuals providing a springboard for postmodernism, Martin Heidegger and Paul de Man were unrepentant Nazis. The role of de Man was particularly important because he was instrumental in legitimising Derrida's emphasis on deconstruction, as an overarching methodology for postmodernists within Western social science. Indeed, postmodernism has supporters across the political spectrum and so, ideologically, it has become a zero-sum game. For example, at the time of writing the notion of a 'post-truth' society has emerged from the political right in the US; compare that ideological trend to the socialist aspirations of Laclau and Mouffe, noted earlier. Nietzsche and Heidegger are now being claimed by some as the philosophical leaders of the 'Alt Right' movement in the USA (Beiner, 2018). However, we must be careful not to claim that postmodernism *led* to the post-truth society. Many of the anti-liberal and 'fake news' obsessives following Donald Trump are not likely to have heard of it or be acquainted with its metaphysical assumptions. However, its judgemental, not just epistemological, relativism does offer *post hoc* comfort to those familiar with the philosophy.

Recently Noam Chomsky has condemned postmodernism, not just for its obscurantism and lack of intelligibility (he calls it 'plain gibberish') but, more importantly, for its role in giving comfort to the forces of reaction in Western democracies: it has become 'an instrument of power' for those forces. Moreover, Chomsky laments that in third world countries that their intelligentsia has been captivated by postmodernism and has lost its connection with the everyday struggles of poor and disposed fellow citizens (https://blog.p2pfoundation.net/noam-chomsky-postmodernism-is-an-instrument-of-power/2017/07/23).

An implication of this section then is that today postmodernism can give comfort or irritation to anyone on the political spectrum, though during the 1980s it seemed to be a genuinely radical and liberating break from positivist orthodoxy in psychology; a cue for the next section.

Postmodernism and psychology

The emergence of constructivism in psychology pre-dates the postmodern turn. It can be found in George Kelly's personal construct theory (Kelly, 1955) but also in social psychology where some focused on social representations (e.g. Moscovici, 1963; Wagner, 1996). The latter trend in social psychology overlapped with a 'pre-postmodern' version of social constructivism, associated with symbolic interactionism and the one wing of the Chicago School of sociology around the Second World War. That version of social constructivism (or as appears often in psychology texts 'social constructionism') was certainly idealist in its philosophy. However, it was more concerned with revealing the shifting fine grain of everyday reality than attacking positivism *per se*. The work of Erving Goffman on *The Presentation of Self in Everyday Life* is an example of this North American version of early social constructivism, influential in psychology but absorbed from sociology, at the interface with social psychology (Goffman, 1959).

In their US–German collaborative text, *The Social Construction of Reality*, Berger and Luckmann (1967) drew liberally on Marx, Durkheim and Weber, when exploring the relationship between 'society as objective reality' and 'society as subjective reality'. Their concern was not to deny the mind-independent aspect of social reality (at all) but instead to examine how society is internalised as a set of cognitive operations inside individuals, during primary and secondary socialisation and how it is then, in response, maintained normatively in everyday social relationships.

The relationship, for example, between everyday cultural assumptions at a moment in time and space and their loyal and unquestioning acceptance by individuals was important to grasp in social science for these symbolic interactionists. This depiction of how social reality is reproduced is not the same as the stronger assertion of postmodernism that replaces ideology with discourse and readily discounts the role of selfhood in its enquiries. The symbolic interactionists were mainly concerned with researching the subjective and intersubjective aspects of our embodied existence.

Also, although the symbolic interactionists were not committed to the postmodern tendency to eliminate the human subject (see below), they did query the validity of talking about 'personality' and instead emphasised *identities*. Notably Berger and Luckmann also called these 'psychologies', thereby reframing the word 'psychology'. It shifted the meaning from the activity of an on-looking scientific discipline to the variegated everyday world of ordinary people 'doing life' and understanding themselves and others.

Moreover, the symbolic interactionists were unequivocally humanists but the postmodernists have been associated with anti-humanism or 'post-humanism'. Derrida's work in particular aims to dissolve our unique personhood into language and Foucault talks of the 'de-centred subject' and the need to completely reject humanism. As a consequence, as individuals we are like sad whales beached by the outgoing tide of words and words about words (Derrida, 1982; Foucault, 1984). Lemert (1979) summarised the latter outcome of postmodernism as 'the twilight of man'. In a similar vein, Anderson (1983) noted that postmodernism generates 'subjectivism without a subject'. This is a highly impoverished view of subjectivity and inter-subjectivity that reduces our humanity to discourse (Archer, 2000). As Elder-Vass (2012) notes, there is a contradiction at the centre of Foucault's work, which is that he problematised human agents, whilst also arguing for the promotion of new forms of nuanced subjectivity. That contradiction has been mirrored in postmodern psychology; see discussion below of the work of John Shotter and Ken Gergen. Despite their best efforts, it would seem that our individuality is a hardy perennial, not killed off by postmodern writers.

If the radical anti-individualism and anti-agentic implications of postmodernism are validly inferred, then when and if they are taken seriously, one core project of academic psychology (the study of experience and behaviour in named or nameable individual subjects) would be fatally wounded. After all, *inter alia*, psychology is an exercise in scientific humanism and postmodernism would basically deem that to be a futile ambition (given that it problematises *both* science *and* humanism).

Thus, in contrast to the earlier version of social constructivism, inherited from the 1960s, postmodernism prosecuted a bolder case against the orthodox traditions of social science. For example, the 'grand narratives' of Marx, Durkheim and Weber respected by Berger and Luckmann were now being fundamentally questioned by postmodernism. This had an impact on academic psychology during and after the 1980s as part of a wider philosophical shift in the arts and humanities away from structuralism, materialism and positivism. We can identify some key postmodernist themes in this impact on the discipline:

- the rejection of forms of truth claim derived from positivist psychology;
- the presumption of the ubiquitous social construction of all psychological topics and the methodological requirement of deconstruction or discourse analysis;
- the problematisation of the notion of 'the self' and the erasure of individuals as unique human agents;
- the rejection of humanism.

By the time we meet the 1980s, these themes were emerging in Western academic psychology, even if they were not to deal a fatal blow to the positivist orthodoxy; each reader can make their own judgement about whether this summary remains accurate still today in their experience.

A good illustrative example of postmodern psychology, from the period is the edited collection *Texts of Identity* from John Shotter and Ken Gergen (Shotter and Gergen, 1989). In the introduction to their text, they lay out their stall for a postmodern version of psychology to displace the inadequacies linked to positivism, which they describe as a wrongheaded 'optimistic romance'. In the new tradition set out by Derrida's poststructuralism, they suggest that the contributors to their edited collection hold a joint and overriding loyalty to the deconstruction of texts:

> The major metaphor underlying these explorations is the text, both the finally produced text and the textually aware activities involved in its production. For, it is reasoned, the primary medium within which identities are created and have their currency is not just linguistic but textual: persons are ascribed identities according to the manner of their embedding within a discourse – in their own or the discourse of others. In this way cultural texts furnish their 'inhabitants' with the resources for the formation of selves; they lay out an array of enabling potentials, while simultaneously establishing a set of constraining boundaries beyond which selves cannot be easily made.
>
> *(Shotter and Gergen, 1989: viii)*

This is replete with contradictions and absurdities for the following reasons. First, texts themselves are deemed to be metaphors. That is, if texts are not real but metaphorical we might then wonder what, if anything, *is* real at the outset. The very meaning of the word 'metaphor' suggests an empirical contrast with a non-metaphor (i.e. something of real substance). The word has no meaning unless it implies a contrasting *reality*. Second, the text is a medium and identities have currencies. Here we do then move on to ontological assumptions and away from metaphors. Third, the phrase 'according to the manner' suggests a way or style of acting. However, Shotter and Gergen offer us no actors as human agents. Such individuals seem to be abandoned, or conveniently ignored, in favour of impersonal or supra-personal discourses. Nonetheless, human agents are then implied, though not fully fleshed out, by the existence of an array of 'enabling potentials', operating within 'constraining boundaries'.

So for Shotter and Gergen, *who* is being enabled or constrained? Postmodernists may proudly write books that display their names or collect their salaries with named payslips from their employing universities. Is all this just a textual matter? The question about whether postmodernists do or do not accept the existence of individual human agents has dogged their credibility. For example, in his early work Foucault discarded the individual in favour of discourse but in his later work he began to consider again the ontology of individuality, in line with the very humanism he previously had scorned (Dews, 1989). Below I point out that some postmodernists have had to return to the embodied self for the case to work and by doing so have had to return to ontology: epistemology is not enough (and never will be because mind-independent reality cannot be ignored or cleverly argued out of existence).

To summarise, in this short passage we find all of the contradictions inherent to postmodern logic. The preoccupation is with texts as the sole source of social reality (and even that is deemed to be a mere metaphor). The prospect of affording texts the privilege of ontological status but it being denied to other aspects of our shared material world. There is also the erasure of individual actors in favour of discourses, whilst hinting that we do actually exist as people as well. However, we only exist as a by-product of texts and discourses: our sense of self is but a precarious and limited artefact or epiphenomena of words. A few sentences later though Shotter and Gergen suggest that this new post-positivist and post-humanist form of psychology is liberating because 'new forms of personhood are revealed' (1989: viii). The word 'personhood' brings us back as real people with unique characteristics. So do we exist beyond words after all or is this just more word play? What exactly is 'revealed', a story about reality or reality itself?

There is a consistency though in the wider work of Shotter and Gergen with their philosophical advice from Derrida. When he said there is 'no outside text' (usually mistranslated as 'there is nothing outside the text') he actually wanted to discount the intentions of the author and install instead a wider supra-personal set of considerations about the social and historical context of any discourse, which embedded both the author and the reader. In this way, all of these postmodernists despite their rhetoric still have to constantly refer to aspects of *the describable reality* of the contexts they want us to attend to.

For example, both Shotter and Gergen drew attention to the constitution of social constructed reality via praxis-in-context; a notion not too far away from a critical realist emphasis (see below) (Shotter, 1984; Gergen, 2009). This constant contradiction is replayed by postmodernists: reality (agreed grand and small events and interpersonal and societal happenings) is inevitably required in order to defend the importance of contextualised discourses and 'subjectivity without a subject' *but* the process of deconstruction then is used in order to reject the intransitive dimension of reality. Reality is like a step ladder required by postmodernists, which is then kicked away contemptuously or ironically. Also discourses are deemed to displace and negate traditional causal arguments but the central notion of power in postmodern thinking still constantly implies *causal* power (Sayer, 2012).

The implausible anti-realism of the programmatic postmodern summary from Shotter and Gergen is revealed by the use of a modicum of common sense. For example, whatever the role of texts and discourses in furnishing us with our sense of self, a poor person has that sense for many years less than a rich person, on average, because they tend to die younger. In another example, for developmental and neurological reasons the sensibility of a one-year-old about who they are is different from a ten-year-old, even though they are both children. In another example, a bright imaginative person can be reduced to a miserable cognitively disabled one by a severe head injury in a car collision. Their brain, the car crash and their lost functioning are simply there: they are not textually generated. We can all think of the ways in which the direct impact of material reality, beyond the textual world we inhabit, shapes and constrains who we are or who we are allowed to be.

Likewise the judgemental (or moral) relativism celebrated by postmodernism never survives in practice in any society because common sense, at any moment in time and place, asserts *precisely* what is to be expected (and not) of its successfully socialised citizens in a particular culture. The content of those normative assumptions certainly *vary* across time and space. However, normative assumptions of *some sort* always operate: they are not generically disposable in practice, merely because postmodernism declares such a case by fiat. An irony here, but also confirming this point, is that identity politics predicated on postmodern premises tend to be *highly* morally prescriptive and judgemental, not at all liberally permissive, as expected from judgemental relativism. As an example of this, look at the competing forms of indignation from trans-activists on one side and gender-critical feminists on the other (Pilgrim, 2018b). What Christian Smith above called 'identity posturing' comes with a top-dog approach to morality; what we now call 'virtue signalling'. The latter would be impossible unless we were sensitive to what ought to be (norms and mores), and how people ought to act accordingly moment to moment in our culture (see **axiology**).

Thus although there are limits to normative differences, they are not unending and so we cannot dispose of the reality of normativity. There are several stable general commonalities in any society, such as the existence of mores, laws, a respect for one another, the pursuit of peaceable relationships, the moral, and often legal, regulation of sexual relationships and conventional last respects for the dead. Societies (the clue is in the name) are *ipso facto* social because for evolutionary reasons, we are a socially interdependent species. As a consequence, *all* societies contain norms and mores in relation to the dramas of being born, becoming sexual and then dying; see T.S. Eliot's basic facts of life about 'birth and copulation and death' (Eliot, 1932). Sometimes norms are merely conventions, sometimes they reflect axiomatic morality, but in *some form or other* they are ubiquitous (Sayer, 2011). (A fuller exploration of normativity and critical realism is provided in the whole special edition on the that topic in the *Journal of Critical Realism* (2019, 18, 3)).

And then there is the matter of emotions. Postmodernists are preoccupied with words, maybe reflecting their role as accomplished intellectuals; emotions are less their *forte*. Feelings come and go in our lives and are tied to our experience of self, independent of words. Pre-verbal infants experience feelings and so do animals. They cannot clothe those experiences with words. Environmental stability or trauma in childhood can have profound effects on our sense of self as we mature. They are not texts *per se* and much of the time do not involve a linguistic aspect, even if they might be woven *later* into the life story of the person involved. It is insulting to the adult survivor of child abuse to say that their distressed sense of being a person is because of a 'text' or 'narrative'. Certainly life scripts and the narratives we develop about ourselves exist and are part of our sense of self (a transitive consideration) but they are built around real events in our lives that have been and gone (an intransitive consideration).

The core problem then is that epistemological relativism in relation to our experience is oversold by postmodernism, which recurrently culminates in absurd forms of linguistic reductionism and 'ontological vandalism' (Sayer, 2000). Apart from the outcome of ontological vandalism, postmodernism contains another fundamental pitfall: if there are no certainties, there are only words and texts, and everything is socially constructed, then why are *those* emphatic generalisations still permitted as certainties? The answer to this might lie in the starting point for postmodern objections: positivism. Indeed, the dialectical provocation of the latter suggests that postmodernism is tied to it in a simple oppositional logic.

This is confirmed if we look at the summary defence of postmodern psychology offered by Gergen (1992a). He sets out four key aspects of modern psychology which postmodernism challenges and seeks to rectify. First, modernism is committed to a knowable world, with the basic subject matter of psychology defined for its enquiries in advance. Second, that *a priori* assumption of modern psychology also includes the notion that its basic subject matter has universal properties. Third, that truths emerge from adherence to the empirical method. Fourth, empirical enquiries about a pre-existing world with universal features will lead to the progressive rejection of false knowledge and the positive establishment of value-neutral knowledge. Note at this juncture that similar objections to positivism and empiricism are also taken up by critical realism but they are taken to different conclusions to those of postmodernism (see Chapter 2).

Finally in this section I can note that ontological realism is a hardy perennial that postmodernists could not counter for long. Apart from their tendency to selectively alluding to some exemplary part of reality before querying the latter in principle, for psychologists there is the challenge of embodiment. We can only understand the way we construe the world by listening to the accounts of people in their embodied totality.

After his textual focus with Gergen, Shotter moved back quite quickly to this point (Shotter, 1993a, b). This was inevitable because discourses are produced from *real individuals* via their particular speech acts and written documents. Despite their evasion of this fact, it was a necessary affirmation, from postmodern psychologists, of the existence of our unique embodied **concrete singularity**. The texts and discourses that are the preoccupation of postmodernists emerge in practice from named individuals, who cease that form of production when they become cognitively incompetent or die, whichever comes first. If we attend to our **four planar social being** it is obvious to both common sense and critical realist researchers that our bodies are part of the natural world. The experience of toothache or the certainty of our death reminds us of this simple point. We can cleverly *deny* that embodiment but that does not make it go away as part of reality. A student of Shotter, John Cromby, continued with this exploration of embodiment in a weakened version of social constructivism, within psychology, which attends very respectfully to material reality (Cromby and Nightingale, 1999; Cromby, 2015).

The anti-humanism of the poststructuralists, despite all of the contradictions noted above, provided increasing confidence in forms of post-humanism and trans-humanism (Wolfe, 2010; Porpora, 2017). Each reader can take stock of their reaction to these recent developments; I find them profoundly depressing.

Responses to postmodern psychology

At the time of Gergen's defence of postmodern psychology Chaiklin challenged his premises and arguments. Chaiklin (1992) notes that postmodern psychology replaces one form of methodological rigidity (the empirical method and, stereotypically, experimentalism) with another (the deconstruction of texts and narratives). Chaiklin calls the latter form of rigidity 'regressive' and rejects its claims to displace the mirror-image and pseudo-progressive claims of empiricism. There is an irony then that, methodologically speaking, postmodern psychology does not encourage creativity and plurality, but quite narrow prescriptions are offered instead.

A second query offered by Chaiklin is that postmodern psychology is a strong form of negativism (in response to positivism). He suggests that for postmodern psychology to be persuasive it should put forward a clear alternative, rather than dwell on the negation of the shortcomings of positivism. This reminds us of the theme of nihilism in postmodern thought, which is traceable to its origins in the work of Nietzsche.

Chaiklin then proceeds to a third concern: if postmodernism emphasises local or situated knowledge then this principle should apply to itself. For example, rather than esoteric French poststructuralism in the middle of the 20th century determining good theory and practice, then what of other forms of parochial knowledge were created across time and place? How are these to be recorded and their merits compared and contrasted (if at all)?

This leads to a fourth query: is it realistic and wise to wipe the slate clean about the merits of modernist theories and findings in psychology? Are they not forms of inherited knowledge that make sense to people and have relatively enduring characteristics at times, with genuine practical utility? For example, just as a bridge is more likely to remain standing if designed by engineers who understand the mechanisms of strength and stability of materials and their construction, might the study of attention and fatigue in air control operatives increase the safety of passengers? These questions imply that the *refinement or reform* of the modernist project might actually be a wiser option than its destruction.

This prompts a final doubt from Chaiklin about postmodern psychology, which is that it is not at all simple to draw a definitive historical marker around modernism. Historians of psychology highlight much ambiguity about how the modern discipline is now constituted, with its multiple legacies and emergent forms of emphasis in the present. Put simply psychology was never the modernist monolith depicted by those like Gergen, which is fair comment. Nonetheless, Gergen was right to point to a strong *positivist orthodoxy* in the academy.

By the time the 1990s arrived, the focus on discourse had become the default position for psychologists critical of their discipline. For example, the core position of the edited collection *Critical Psychology: An Introduction* (Fox and Prilleltensky, 1997) was a form of radical anti-positivism built overwhelmingly upon postmodern philosophy. The latter pervades its pages from their 26 authors. There was some concession in some of the chapters though to the remaining relevance of the Frankfurt School (Sloan, 1997) and a single (undeveloped but favourable) allusion to critical realism on only one of its 362 pages (Parker, 1997: 296). (Parker subsequently recanted his interest in critical realism and returned to his poststructuralist intellectual allegiance.) Roy Bhaskar does not appear in the index, but it is teeming with allusions to the work of Michel Foucault.

However, the new orthodoxy of postmodernism for critical psychologists was precarious and it created a critical response of its own from realists. Henderikus Stam edited a special edition of the journal *Theory and Psychology* about 'social constructionism and its critics' (Stam, 2001). The critiques begin with Hibberd (2001) who makes that point that Gergen offers a form of philosophical conventionalism: theoretical terms are determined in whole or part by other terms within that framework or they reflect the cultural norms of researchers. She notes that this is no different from the internal reference reasoning of the alleged enemy of social constructionism: logical positivism.

Maze (2001) offers another realist response to Gergen's work and takes it to task for its internal contradictions. As I noted earlier, how can social constructionism say *anything* realistically about reality if it denies ontology? Maze pursues this line of attack and traces the vulnerability of anti-realism in postmodern psychology to the work of Derrida. A more sympathetic critique is then offered by Liebrucks (2001). He argues that in practice constructionist arguments *must* be compatible with realism in order to make their academic and political claims. It is not really a challenge to realism in principle (as it relies upon it in the pursuit of deconstruction or discourse analysis – see above). Its only persuasive special claim is methodological not metaphysical. Liebrucks seems to be saying 'problem, what problem?' in relation to the tension between realism and constructivism.

Jenkins (2001) goes on to note that social constructionism fails to distinguish content from process. Take the example of the concept of 'the self'. Whereas, versions of the latter vary across time and space, *some* version is found in all societies. Jenkins is responding then to postmodernism's implausible anti-humanism (see my points above about the subject being dissolved into texts).

Edley (2001) continues with an examination of the contradictions of social constructionism and the weakness of being concerned only with epistemic matters. This brings us back to the absence of the balance demanded by critical realism between ontological realism and epistemological relativism. Social constructionism is preoccupied with the latter unevenly, which is misleading for researchers. It culminates at some point in 'ontological vandalism'.

Stam (2001) makes the fair point that it is not easy to discuss social constructionism in its entirety (as a sort of 'job lot'). The relativism and (ironically) individualism of its contributors in psychology means that constructivists are defined or define themselves in a variety of ways. Whilst they all share a psychological interest in personal accounts, narratives and discourses, Stam was not confident that they would identify themselves as a common group with common premises, listing the work of, amongst others, Ken Gergen, John Shotter, Kurt Danziger, Rom Harré, Jill Morawski, Jonathan Potter, Edward Sampson and Margaret Wetherell.

As Stam (2001: 293) puts it forlornly 'what counts as constructionism is often dependent on the author's or critic's aims'. However, I would argue that family resemblances *do* exist within the weaker form of social constructionism derived from symbolic interactionism on the one hand, compared with the stronger form preoccupied with texts and discourses, derived from Derrida and Foucault on the other. The first version conceded social and material ontology from the outset, whereas the latter had to use it in practice, while being philosophically anti-realist in principle or rhetoric.

Gaps and commonalities

In the previous chapter I rehearsed the features of realism shared in its critical and naïve forms. Likewise this one can note some points of convergence between postmodernism and critical realism. Most of this chapter has been a dire warning from a critical realist perspective that postmodernism can descend into anti-realism and culminate in the 'post-truth society'. Indeed some critical realists such as Alex Callinicos in his book *Against Postmodernism* demolish the postmodernist case unflinchingly (Callinicos, 1991). In my view, it remains one of the best rebuttals.

However, others have cautioned against this wholesale rejection and noted some common concerns of postmodernists and critical realists. For example, we can note the critical realist focus on the 'conditions of possibility' for particular sorts of **emergence**, which was shared with Foucault (see below). Another French poststructuralist, Gilles Deleuze, was keen to explore how, despite repeated patterns in the world (what critical realists might call 'demi-regularities'), within repetition there are always new occurrences of difference or 'non-exchangeable and non-substitutable singularities' (Deleuze, 1994: 1). This chimes with a critical realist concern for understanding unique emergent features of open systems: concrete singularities. Other discussions of the degree of compatibility between poststructuralism and critical realism can be found in Hardy (2019) and Wheatley (2019). Given that critical realism seeks a metaphysical middle way between positivism and postmodernism, it is little surprising that points of contact on each side sometimes entail rejection and irritability and sometimes reveals common purposes or assumptions.

Reviewing commonalities and differences between postmodernism and critical realism, Roberts (2003) cautiously suggests four points of convergence:

1. Both critical realism and postmodernism reject positivist certainties about fixed universal laws.
2. Postmodernist thinkers, such as Derrida and Foucault, implicitly accept the intransitive dimension at times, when noting our internalisation of external features of reality, though they are unforthcoming about spelling this out in any detail.
3. The emphasis on emergentism in critical realism can account for the appearance in late modernity of postmodernism, as an alternative to the forms of modernist thought linked to the ideology of capitalism.
4. Critical realists have under-utilised a 'discourse perspective' as a legitimate and useful methodology in social science. Just because discourse analysis can become a form of methodological reductionism (when you only have a hammer everything becomes a nail), this does not mean that it cannot be a useful method, when combined judiciously with others.

My view of Roberts' points is this:

1. It is true that critical realism and postmodernism are both hostile to positivist certainties.
2. It is not surprising that postmodernists are unforthcoming about the intransitive dimension of reality because, by a slight of hand or intellectual gymnastics, it is scorned but also utilised by them, when and if it is required (Sayer, 2012). This creates an embarrassing dilemma for postmodernists. It is a bind of their own making because of their rejection of ontological realism in favour of Nietzschean perspectivism. Postmodernists try to have their cake and eat it about reality. Accordingly, critical realists have adopted a phrase that summarises emergent aspects of reality from Foucault (1965), which refers to 'conditions of possibility'. Whereas postmodernists then became singularly preoccupied with the discourses created by those conditions, they then discarded the material conditions underpinning them. By contrast, an understanding of the relationship between the transitive and intransitive dimensions of reality is part of the bread and butter work of critical realists. The latter have largely endorsed formulations of the Frankfurt School (which I deal with more in Chapter 9). That materialist

tradition encouraged the idea that, as individuals, we are a product of our time and place and we play our part in reproducing or changing the world. However, we can consciously reflect on only some of this outcome of social processes of emergence; it is largely unconscious. This is a different account of how supra-personal processes shape us as persons than one that insists that we emerge merely from texts or discourses. The first version prioritises real causal mechanisms, whereas the second offers a tangled web of words instead. Though deconstruction seeks to illuminate these tangles, that may not be the outcome for the reader, with any 'so what?' response being understandable; hence Chomsky's dismissal of postmodernism as 'plain gibberish'.

3. It is true that postmodern critiques have emerged in part because of changes in capitalism (amplified more recently with the appearance of social media), as well as the shift towards the moral regime of consumerism and neo-liberalism in the past 30 years. However, not *all* postmodern critiques challenge oppressive relationships under capitalism; some shore them up. See my earlier point about the zero-sum game of postmodernism on the ideological spectrum. Thus there is a difference between offering a critical realist account of the emergence of postmodern thought and endorsing any conclusions of the latter.
4. Critical discourse analysis is part of the methodological repertoire of critical realism, which can endorse a wide range of methods, depending on the research question being posed (Flatschart, 2016; Sims-Schouten and Riley, 2018). By contrast, deconstruction and discourse analysis put postmodern social science on methodological tramlines. Repeating the point for emphasis, it is true that critical discourse analysis has now become an important and useful part of applied critical realism, *but it is only a part.*

In addition to these four points of discussion within critical realism, about the merits or otherwise of postmodernism, I would add another one of importance. Whilst both postmodernists and critical realists refuse to separate facts from values (contra positivism), this prompts judgemental relativism in the former and judgemental rationality in the latter. These are different philosophical outcomes. Judgemental relativism relies on the Nietzschean logic that meanings and values are projected onto the world in such diverse ways, that we cannot adjudicate on what is true or untrue, or good or bad.

Judgemental rationality implies instead that human beings exercise forms of common sense in order to weigh up competing truth claims or moral expectations, in light of a range of considerations. These can include our empirical knowledge (lay or expert) about causality in the world, our practised rationality, our sense of probability and fairness, our commitment to versions of mutual obligation, our capacity to empathise with but also identify deceit in others, our insights about the motives of ourselves and others, as well as a general eye towards individual rights and collective human freedom.

This multi-layered weighing up process reflects our everyday wisdom (*phronesis*). It leads to our best shot at discerning what is true or fair about matter X or Y in our lives. Scientists acting with good faith and intelligence in their inferences and interpretations, or juries deliberating on the guilt and culpability of the accused in the dock, or the honest investigative journalist getting to the bottom of a story are common examples of judgemental rationality in practice. Taken to its logical conclusion the judgemental relativism prompted by postmodernism would simply paralyse these social actors or tempt them to abandon their task.

Above, Roberts gives credit where it is due to postmodernism, and he is right to point up overlaps with critical realism. In a similar vein, Norris (1990) attacked much of postmodernism from a critical realist perspective but saw some intellectual virtues in the work of Derrida and de Man. However, in my view, ultimately the obsession of postmodernists with epistemology, at the expense of ontology, will always make their work problematic, when and if psychologists want to engage with the reality of our inner and outer contexts. It is fundamentally incompatible with the primacy given by critical realists to ontological realism. For that reason, it culminates in the 'ontological vandalism' noted by Andrew Sayer.

For Sayer (2000) the epistemological relativism that is considered to be very important to critical realism permits us to view the philosophy as endorsing a 'weak' form of social constructivism. We find that weaker trend in a range of psychologists from George Kelly in the 1950s to those today, such as John Cromby, who I noted above with his work on embodiment. What has prompted so much objection from critical realists is the 'strong' version offered by many social scientists and its cynicism about truth claims; see the outrage signalled by Bhaskar, Danermark and Price above. Most of this offence has been created by postmodernists, but the perils of social constructivism can also be found at times in work derived from symbolic interactionism. I give an example of this in Chapter 7 when I discuss the failure of moral panic theory to account for the scale and harm of child sexual abuse.

The differing positions adopted by Callinicos, Norris and Roberts, as critical realists, highlight the challenge of steering some sort of path between positivism on one side and postmodernism on the other. The case studies in the rest of the book offer my version of dealing with that challenge. The first of these considers a matter that is both obvious and complex: on being a person.

4

DO WE EXIST AS INDIVIDUALS?

Introduction

Today, for most of us, common sense dictates that being a unique person is *both* ontologically obvious *and* it is a test bed for human rights. Without an ontological agreement on named persons, how can I claim that this computer I am typing on belongs to me and not to someone else, be tried for a crime, be buried with (or maybe without) dignity or have my name allocated on the particular birth certificate that I have used occasionally to prove my age and identity? If I am tortured (see Chapter 8) or detained unfairly in the psychiatric system (see Chapter 10) then how can I seek reparation for an injustice against me as a particular person if my uniqueness and particular lived impermanence are not respected? As I noted in Chapter 3, why do postmodernists insist on putting their unique name on the books they write and expect to be paid as named academics for their talents? The existence of individuals and their assumed rights can be a point of impassioned protest (see Chapter 9). For example, the positions adopted by the 'pro-life' and 'pro-choice' lobbies about abortion both adhere to a notion of the (competing) rights of *individuals*, which necessitates statements about their *existence*.

It is true though that some cultures do not adhere neatly to the modern Western view of child development, which is that by the time we are around three years of age we develop a unique sense of who we are. It is what Schweder (1984) describes as the problematic of a 'bounded, unique, integrated and dynamic center of judgment and action' (ibid.: 12). We are obliged then to recognise that the principle of **epistemological relativism** undoubtedly applies to the matter of being human. But it is also true that in most times and places *some* notion of individuality is noted as well, even if elites are remembered by name in recorded history more carefully than the poor and the powerless.

Traditional positivistic psychology takes the latter notion of a person as the touchstone for permanent and universal features of the skin-encapsulated individual. It can be the basis then for tracing laws of genetic inheritance and child development and the postulation of forms of personality theory, with both subjective and objective aspects of the latter being open to investigation. The psychology of individual differences (differential psychology) then flows from these forms of investigation.

In reaction to this view, during the postmodern turn, the individual was lost to discourse. One leading anthropologist following that trend was the champion of symbolic anthropology, Clifford Geertz, who questioned the legitimacy of viewing selves as being coherent and continuous. He wanted to reverse those traditional psychological assumptions, especially from humanistic psychologists related to the 'true self' and expressions of its sincerity or authenticity. Geertz (1984: 15) protests that such assumptions are unfounded and fly in the face of 'the fact that we are all wearing masks all the time through all the changes of social morphology'. The use of the word 'fact' here by Geertz is an example of strong social constructivists problematising reality but also utilising it emphatically when required for practical and rhetorical purposes.

This chapter, by steering its way between trait reductionism and social constructivism picks up some implications of the above tension between a naïve realist and a purely discursive position about exploring being a person. The comments above also alert the reader to something that cuts across our philosophical assumptions: the actual and potential distortions of uni-disciplinary authority. Psychology, anthropology and sociology (to name the three dominant players in the academy) have all created some preferred way of understanding what it is to be human. As a consequence, their methodological orientations may well, each in their own way, have narrowed or stylistically inflected a fuller understanding of being human, when considering the domains of **the empirical, the actual** and **the real**. At least some of the tension, between say the view of Geertz and developmental psychologists or personality theorists, is not because he was an anthropologist, who was concerned by the 1980s with strong social constructivist accounts and the displacement of the individual by discourse, but simply because he was *not* a psychologist. I return to the important matter about interdisciplinarity in Chapter 12.

The relationship between our individuality and our cultural context then is the recurring theme in the disputes hinted at between the idealists and materialists I discussed in Chapter 3. Is our culture maintained by shared cognitions, symbols and discourses (with these aspects of our inter-subjectivity as our primary interest, as in the work of Geertz noted), or do we examine the material conditions of emergence of culture as the primary task? What if our biology does indeed determine in whole or part who we are? That question was answered in the affirmative by many personality theorists under the influence of eugenics about inherited temperament.

On the other hand, what if our contingently learned thoughts, feelings and actions simply shape who we are, with the rules set by the social norms we are thrown into in our particular society (the narrow empirical implication of behaviourism)? In the latter regard, is it legitimate to generalise about 'the psychology' of the 'baby boomers' or 'millennials' or 'snowflakes'? However, if contingent social norms are simply maintained or reproduced mechanistically by comprehensive conformity during our primary socialisation, then how does social change ever occur? Surely beyond the real enough social conditioning of selves, the latter express degrees of individual agency as well. This does not have to be an either/or matter; it is more likely to be a both/and phenomenon.

Our individuality, when and if conceded, might emerge from material forces but in doing so it might provide us with powers to change ourselves and the world around us. For critical realists, as will become clear below, we are both determined and determining beings. To demonstrate this point it is necessary to trace the intricacies of multiple interactions in the flow of our lives. It returns us to the point made by Heraclitus that 'a man cannot step into the same river twice for fresh waters ever emerge around him'. The river changes and the man changes. He might go with the flow, swim against the current or he might be drowned by undercurrents he cannot see, or even submit to them in suicidal intent. All are possible.

Moreover, to add to the complexity, the man did not ask to be born and the river would be there before and after his death. Eventually conditions in the man and the river between them guarantee his individual demise but the river keeps flowing. As the cultural theorist Raymond Williams noted, when capturing the concurrent reality of *both* our choices, which might be for some of us of heroic proportions, *and* our inevitable fate or 'the way of all flesh':

> We become ill, we become old, we die ... To die for a cause, and be honoured for it, is one thing. To attempt to override the physical realities, which persist in and through and beyond all historical causes is quite another.
>
> *(Williams, 1980: 114)*

My critical realist take on the title of this chapter will explore the emergence of personality theory and its implications for normal and abnormal personalities, before turning to the work of Jerome Kagan, a holistic developmental psychologist and Margaret Archer and Christian Smith, leading critical realist sociologists, who have written extensively on human agency in its lived context.

Differential psychology

What were the conditions necessary for our current orthodoxy of the 'Big Five' personality traits to emerge within the modern discipline of psychology or our confidence in intelligence testing? Historically we cannot consider differential psychology separately from the political context that drove the social administrative requirement to separate people according to their psychological attributes. That process emerged with industrial capitalism and with it colonialism. The workings of the leading European and North American economies of the 19th century, the historical moment when psychology was taking shape as a new academic discipline, entailed the production of organised structures that regulated human activity, such as in schools, asylums, hospitals and armies. It also entailed the emergence of a guiding ideology to manage the masses: eugenics. Personality theory and differential psychology did not spring from thin air but emerged from the political ideology of eugenics.

In Britain, in 1904, Ward and Rivers set out the stall for positivist psychology, which I cited at the start of Chapter 2. Three years later, a young psychologist who was to dominate the leadership of differential psychology and its implications for educational policy in Britain in the first part of the 20th century, was asked to conduct research on the standardisation of the psychological tests being used for the 'anthropometric' survey sponsored by the British Association for the Advancement of Science. His name was Cyril Burt and he was already under the ideological influence of Karl Pearson, a mathematician.

Pearson, who readers may now associate with modern behavioural statistics, was a self-declared eugenicist and racist (Pearson, 1905). He had taken up the first Chair in Eugenics at University College London in 1911, bequeathed by Pearson's intellectual mentor, Francis Galton, a cousin of Darwin. The latter, when developing his theory of evolution, in passing expressed ambivalent views about its implication for human conduct and society. The task of developing Darwin's fleeting ideas was left first to Herbert Spencer and then Galton. The completed task later became known as 'Social Darwinism'.

The concerns of Galton and other eugenicists, who followed his leadership, tapped into an anxious middle-class consensus emerging across the political spectrum in Europe and North America. Although many today associate eugenics with its link to racism (via Nazi 'race science'), its very early concern in Britain, for Galton and his followers, was not with race but with social class. In particular there was a fear that the fecundity of those in poverty was outstripping that of those above them in the class hierarchy (Burt, 1946). Poverty was associated with a range of behavioural dysfunctions and disabilities: epilepsy, insanity, idiocy, prostitution, inebriation and criminality. Collectively these behavioural deviations were seen by eugenicists as a product of a tainted gene in the lower orders ('poor stock') (Galton, 1869; Pearson, 1904). Eugenic logic then inspired ways and means to reduce childbearing in the poor as a public health measure and to improve socio-economic efficiency and the vitality of the nation's population. For this reason, the early birth control movement contained eugenicists who were also feminists and social democratic reformers. Eugenics was of the left, not just the right, as a political philosophy; for example Pearson saw himself as a socialist.

A problem faced by the eugenicists was that behavioural deviations, then as now, did not seem to follow simple Mendelian rules. Accordingly the biometrician Pearson made an argument that continuously distributed variation typified such inheritance and subsequently this was accounted for by him conceding that behaviour was affected by multiple genetic influences (Burt, 1912; Fisher, 1918). The latter paved the way for 'quantitative genetics': the calculation of combined elements of genetic and environmental variance (Fisher, 1930).

Thus we find the measurement of psychological differences is rooted in eugenics. Apart from Burt and Pearson, Spearman (1904) announced that general intelligence was a naturally occurring psychological capacity that was inherited variably across a population. This extended the study of genius by Galton (1869). However, the more pressing concern, for social administrative purposes, was the measurement of the less able and this was expressed in the work of Burt and his view that 'innate general cognitive ability' dominated our functioning and that it could be 'objectively determined and measured' (Spearman, 1904; Burt, 1909).

The role of eugenics in social administrative decisions was to spread to the USA, Germany, Canada, France, Estonia, Australia and Scandinavia. Its impact in Britain was limited mainly to influencing educational policy and that governing 'mental deficiency' (Thomson, 1998). Several states in the USA embarked upon sterilisation programmes in line with eugenic advice. In Nazi Germany it became the basis for a series of measures, initiated, not just endorsed, by the German Medical Association (Proctor, 1988). This involved sterilising and murdering people with mental or physical disabilities. Medical killing centres in Germany were to become the technical rehearsal for work in the death camps of occupied Poland (Meyer, 1988). This was not merely a Germanic aberration. In 1942, an editorial in the *American Journal of Psychiatry* rehearsed the option of 'involuntary euthanasia' for patients (Joseph, 2005).

Prior to the First World War, James McKeen Cattell, who had been Galton's research assistant, set up a laboratory to study psychological differences at the University of Columbia (Roback, 1961). Robert Yerkes at Harvard conducted surveys of the intelligence of military recruits into the First World War and in 1922 sat on the Surgeon General's Committee on immigration. He was joined at Harvard by William McDougal, Burt's early mentor. McDougal queried whether the correct balance of North European to other migrants was being achieved by the US immigration policy. The USA was the most self-confident emerging expression of the capitalist system. Consequently, its socio-economic efficiency was to be a matter of constant and concerned self-surveillance. The social threats posed by a post-slavery legacy and new immigration fuelled eugenic interest in the emerging new elites, constituted by those of North European origin.

But if intellectual differences were to concern these early psychologists in civilian life, then another individual difference, neuroticism, was to be studied in the wake of the challenges of warfare. The 'shellshock' problem of the First World War prompted its anticipation when the Second World War was emerging 20 years later (Stone, 1985). At this point both Hans Eysenck in Britain and Raymond Cattell in the USA developed tests to differentiate those likely to remain stable in the face of external stress and those who might be vulnerable to psychological collapse. At this point what had been about cowardice and 'lack of moral fibre' in the military became psychologised as a personality matter by its professional advisors. Neuroticism thereby was foregrounded in personality theory as a trait.

Both Eysenck and Cattell picked up on the original work of Galton and his lexical hypothesis: that the human character is described in ordinary language (Eysenck, 1947; Cattell, 1943). Galton simply went to the dictionary. He found around a thousand character-related words. Others came up with different numbers: 700 for Partridge (1910) and 3,000 for Perkins (1926) in the English-speaking world and 4,000 for Klages (1929) in German. Subsequently, using the principle of the lexical method from Galton (1869), Allport and Odbert (1936) found nearly 18,000 character-related words in English. By the 1950s these estimates had been reduced to a few factors by Eysenck and Cattell and the 'Big Five' were installed as a psychological orthodoxy. Thus a range of Eurocentric linguistic elements, from 700 to 18,000, are boiled down to five personality features that define all of humanity in all contexts: openness to experience; conscientiousness; extraversion; agreeableness; and neuroticism.

My concern here is not to adjudicate on types of personality testing but to note some features of the brief history of ideas I have supplied. First, because it is a history of ideas it is dealing with the **transitive aspect of reality** and so the risk of the **epistemic fallacy** is ever present if we take personality test scores as a read-out of how we exist as human beings in a range of contexts from birth to death. Second, the epistemic fallacy is evident in the convention of English- and German-speaking psychologists during the 20th century asserting that descriptions of human character were a permanent scientific fact. This positivistic assumption was present but not reflected on; positivists are inside their own assumptions about universal **covering laws** and **empirical invariance** and so this lack of insight is to be expected. Personality tests contain elements that simply operationalise those five features and then measure them in order to offer us confident forms of meaning empiricism and methodological empiricism (see Chapter 1).

Third, whilst neuroticism was proposed as a core trait or dimension of personality by Eysenck and Cattell, others were emerging in their work which were a poor theoretical fit. For example, later Eysenck was to suggest another core trait, psychoticism (Eysenck and Eysenck, 1976). What the Galton-inspired lexical method had spawned was a method that tracked ordinary language descriptions of character within the social norms of the time and place, creating an epistemic fallacy. This was a form of cultural imperialism. It assumed that all people in all times and places could, and should, be described using the language of 20th-century white Europeans.

Fourth, and following from the previous point, there was a silence about norm transgressions; the focus of an indexical approach simply reflected norms *themselves*. This is why the nearby profession of psychiatry ('medical psychology') developed a form of knowledge about personality development that diverged from that of psychologists. Norm transgressions, not norms *per se*, shaped psychiatric thinking. Psychiatrists, knowingly or otherwise, rubber-stamped concerns about deviance in the lay arena, contained that deviance in institutions and, when and where it could, re-established rule compliance with therapeutic interventions; a cue for the next section.

Ordered and disordered personalities

During the 19th century, psychiatrists admitting patients to asylums at times came across those who were seemingly sane but chronically very irritating or offensive, according to those around them. Two diagnoses stood out in this trend. The first was of what, for now, is called 'obsessive-compulsive personality disorder' (Berrios, 1985). The second was of 'moral insanity', which morphed conceptually into what is now called 'anti-social personality disorder' or 'dissocial personality disorder' by diagnostic psychiatry. Quite soon the interest of Charcot and Freud in hysteria added to the mix (today and for now called 'histrionic personality disorder').

Spin forward decades and Henderson (1939) and Cleckley (1941) then suggested a hybrid diagnosis of 'psychopathic disorder', to be framed even later by the clinical psychologist Robert Hare as an admixture of anti-social, histrionic and narcissistic personality features (Hare and Neumann, 2008). Note that, mirroring his disciplinary background, Hare has viewed psychopathy as a *continuum not a category*; for him we are all more or less psychopathic. He also notes that psychopaths (i.e. those of us scoring highly on his psychopathy checklist) staying on the right side of the law are often very successful in business and politics (Babiak and Hare, 2007). Accordingly, one person's personality disorder could be another's successful and lucrative career (Board and Fritzon, 2005; Boddy et al., 2010).

Moreover, as I noted when discussing schizophrenia in Chapter 2, we are faced with empty explanations or tautologies:

Q. How do you know this man is a psychopath?
A. Because he rapes children and shows no sign of remorse or guilt.
Q. Why does he do such terrible things?
A. Because he is a psychopath.

Given this lack of etiological or *explanatory* value of functional psychiatric diagnoses, the utility of their *descriptive* coherence is particularly important. After all, descriptions minus causes *might* still be useful. They are based on behavioural checklists, which should increase the probability of reliable descriptions, but as all trained psychologists know, reliability is a necessary but not sufficient condition for validity. We may consistently describe a very poor concept and it may have poor predictive value.

Transitive and intransitive questions about personality disorder

The behavioural checklists in diagnostic systems to identify a type of personality disorder simply reflect ordinary language descriptions of people, who are under- or over-socialised in relation to current shared social norms. An example of an under-socialised person would be one who is regularly anti-social without evidence of guilt, shame or remorse. The affective response in others is typically one of fear and disgust and the evaluative one disapproval and contempt. An example of an over-socialised person is one who rigidly follows rules, obsessively checks their environment for risks and is overwhelmed with anxiety when the contingencies of life interrupt this direct personal control. The response in others is typically one of pity and frustration about the inflexibility they are faced with. These scenarios exist prior to, or are independent of, the medical codification of 'anti-social personality disorder' or 'obsessive compulsive personality disorder'.

At a moment in time then there would be a strong empirical agreement that the *conduct* subsumed by the incipient diagnosis is real enough; actually or potentially it could be empirically recorded for new independent observers to consider and confirm. I mention this because some critics of psychiatry at times lapse into the idea that its practitioners operate whimsical value judgements about conduct. Overwhelmingly they do not; what they do instead is rubber-stamp lay judgements, within a culturally shared normative context. We can discuss the conduct itself then as an intransitive matter but the way that we then discuss and label the conduct is a transitive matter.

In the examples just given, an ordinary moralisation might call the first 'evil' and the second 'pitiably or exasperatingly inflexible'. When called upon, medicine uses its own terminology, which has shifted over time. Psychiatrists disagree on the categories they prefer and are not even of one voice about whether personality disorder is clearly different from, or a version of, mental illness. For example, Cleckley called psychopathic disorder 'the mask of sanity', a view reflected later by some other psychiatrists (Kendell, 2002). Note also that the term 'psychopath', which for now has entered into the vernacular of Anglophone cultures, is not even present in either DSM (Diagnostic and Statistical Manual of the American Psychiatric Association) or ICD (International Classification of Diseases of the World Health Organization). In Britain for a while it was used as a legal category but is no longer.

A problem with all *categorical* descriptions of abnormal personalities is that they are incoherent in a range of ways. They have poor test-retest reliability, their aetiology cannot be specified and there is no specific effective treatment for them. Conceptually they cannot be distinguished often from normality on one side and other categories of psychopathology on the other. (In this regard, they are no different to all functional psychiatric diagnoses, a point I pick up on in Chapter 10.) Elsewhere I offer a longer immanent critique of personality disorder in Pilgrim (2017b), here though I want to focus on two main matters. First, the way that personality is discussed in abnormal psychology and psychiatry diverges markedly from the 'Big Five' trait assumptions noted above. Second, rather than personality disorder being formulated via the lexical method, *norm transgressions* are used to generate a different form of epistemic fallacy.

On the first count about divergent framings of personality, with the exception of a very low measured extraversion score, i.e. shyness, which taken to extreme can culminate in a description of 'avoidant personality disorder', the concerns of psychiatric diagnosticians are different from those of personality theorists (Lane, 2008). This disjuncture is because psychiatrists simply re-codify a range of chronic conduct that is distressing to the identified patient and/or those around them. It is not about their character or temperament (the concern of the Galtonian tradition in psychology) but the categorisation of mental pathology by the medical profession on behalf of those in society who are sane by common consent (the Kraepelinian tradition in psychiatry). What they shared though was a background eugenic rationale (see above and Chapter 10).

This leads to the second matter of norm transgression. If a person is *chronically distressed* then it disables them from rule/role compliance set by the norms of the society they inhabit. For example, obsessive checking of light switches and hand washing means that a person takes hours rather than minutes to leave their house to start work or catch a bus. If a person acts in an *unintelligible* manner this transgresses our expectation of mutual accountability and rational rule following. If a person is *chronically distressing* to others, then again rule transgression or role failure are implicated. Anti-social, manipulative people are to be distrusted for good reason and role compliance relies on mutual trust in our lives, because we are a social and inter-dependent species. In some cases, a personality disorder diagnosis may subsume both types of conduct, e. g. 'borderline personality disorder' (Kernberg, 2008).

A developmental frame of socialisation then is a social rather than medical way of addressing 'personality disorder'. For example, the early cases of what we now call 'obsessive-compulsive personality disorder' described an exaggeration of the normal conformist rule-bound middle-class Victorian in Britain (Berrios, 1985). In another example, the notion of 'narcissistic personality disorder' has been used within the Diagnostic and Statistical Manual of the American Psychiatric Association but *not* in the International Classification of Diseases from the World Health Organization, which points to cross-national differences in norms.

We could think of a 'narcissist' as simply an exaggeration of the norm of being a proud American individualist. For example, Donald Trump's televised performances have been replete with statements about why he is brilliant at everything he does, why people like him so much and how much property he owns. He has reduced international diplomacy and its contents to whether or not he likes people and they like him. Observers in other nations and his opponents in the USA have reacted with embarrassment to this empirical evidence of self-preoccupied arrogance, immaturity and boastful conspicuous wealth. However, those voting for him may well have adored and idealised the very same. Some of his political opponents, who are also diagnosticians, have offered an alternative view of Trump, saying that his mental disorder should debar him from office, triggering an ethical debate about the legitimacy of diagnosis at a distance (Caruso, 2017).

Cultural norms are obvious to common sense: the personal style of the average Italian is not the same as someone from Finland, which anyone visiting the public spaces of each country today can confirm. A misleading stereotype would be that *all* Mediterranean people are emotionally expressive and *all* Scandinavians are quiet, but the normative trends noted are also still true. In any culture, eight-year-olds tend to be energetic and excitable, whereas eighty-year-olds tend to be sedate and reflective. These examples highlight some intransitive aspects of social norms and the extent of behavioural conformance at the individual level, while recognising that social norms themselves vary over time and space.

As well as recognising these norms being the backdrop to any attempt to offer a fixed view of personality from positivist diagnostic psychiatry, we could drill deeper with attempts to link psychology to sociology. For example, we could discuss the (irritating) aspects of Donald Trump's arrogance and self-regard by looking at the discussion of amplified individualism in late capitalism, in the *Culture of Narcissism* (Lasch, 1978), *The Heart of Man* (Fromm, 1964) and *The Fall of Public Man* (Sennett, 1977).

The latter author in particular links the ways in which in pre-capitalist times *character* was emphasised as a consistent link between public and private life. With increasing secularisation, industrialisation and urbanisation, with the development of the capitalist mode of production, an emphasis on private life increased and character was replaced as a focus with *personality*: a set of personal idiosyncratic features, known via particular intimate relationships and forms of absorbed self-concern. 'My Way' was written by Paul Anka and popularised by Frank Sinatra in 1969. By 2012 it was the most popular song requested at British funerals; narcissism seemingly had become a new norm at the turn of this century in Western society.

Psychiatric positivism and personality disorder: a summary

The ontology of personality disorder is no more than a set of behavioural descriptions featuring distress to self or others, associated with rule transgressions or role failures in particular normative contexts. It is agreed by diagnostic psychiatrists that these sorts of conduct are a) recurring or chronic in form and b) not accounted for by a notion of mental illness but, as I noted above, even this second criterion is queried by some psychiatrists. Rule transgressions and role failures can occur acutely (such as in states of inebriation or in a stress reaction), so it is the *chronicity* of a form of distressed or distressing conduct that seems to warrant a diagnosis of personality disorder. When that diagnosis is made, and it is not accounted for by the person being mentally ill, then the patient tends to be held accountable for their actions ('they know what they are doing'), which prompts contempt or frustration in others.

Thus distressed or distressing *conduct* in a particular normative context is the ontological feature of what is called 'personality disorder'. By contrast, the *diagnosis* is an epistemological matter that continues to be controversial. The controversy is fuelled by a number of concerns. What is the point of a medical label if it does not trigger effective treatment? This is the recurrent query about the 'treatability' of personality disorder (Salekin, 2002). Also, because the judgements are normative prior to diagnosis (the incipient patient is chronically distressed or distressing to others), then applying a diagnosis simply codifies ordinary moral judgements (Blackburn, 1988). The diagnostic label then reinforces demoralisation and stigmatisation for the identified patient.

Also, the diagnosis is allegedly about a chronic stable state (it describes personality, which is purportedly about stable features of an individual) and yet it is often changed in favour of another as time progresses (Cacciola et al., 1998). Thus treatment interventions are of dubious effectiveness and yet the diagnosis does not hold over time in individual cases. Given all of this confusion, understandably critics of the diagnosis question what, if anything, is being added by medicalising forms of incorrigible conduct in society. Is medicalisation in this case just a mystified form of moralisation about those who others find offensive or burdensome?

When psychiatrists talk of patients 'having' a personality disorder this is an epistemic fallacy. Personality disorder is a *codification* of some forms of socially-situated *conduct* that has become a chronic concern to the diagnosed patient and/or those around them (more often the latter). It is not a 'thing' inside distressed and distressing people, like having a heart or kidneys. It is a relational not simply a skin-encapsulated matter summarised in a medical label. Such a dubious psychiatric description would be plausible and legitimate if it engendered some clear benefit to the person labelled, guided kindly and efficient amelioration of the problems experienced and created by them and offered retrodictive and predictive clarification for all concerned. However, that does not seem to be the case. It is true that childhood adversity predicts a diagnosis of personality disorder but that is also the case for all forms of psychiatric diagnosis (Read and Bentall, 2012). I return to this important point in Chapter 10.

The important work of Jerome Kagan, Margaret Archer and Christian Smith

Given that psychological and psychiatric positivism fail fully to persuade, in light of the shortcomings just noted, we could resort to postmodern accounts, which celebrate the death of 'personality' (Gergen, 1992b). The problem then is that persons are erased in favour of texts (see Chapter 3). That is fine if you are content with having no sense of a stable self and are casually indifferent about respecting people as unique individuals in your particular life. However, as I noted at the outset, it is difficult to identify any society to date that does not consider named individuals to really be separate human agents with rights and responsibilities.

It is not merely a modern Eurocentric claim that individuals are considered universally to be important. The importance of individualism may certainly be stronger in Western cultures now than in Eastern cultures, both now and in the past. However, named individuals in elites loom large in *any* recorded social or historical account of any society. The meek who, according to Christianity will inherit the earth, have their own implied personal role to celebrate, admittedly less often but they are on record, from the Tomb of the Unknown Soldier to the history of the six named Tolpuddle Martyrs (see Chapter 8).

I will suggest a way forward in this impasse about postmodern dismissals of personality and its reductive descriptions from the eugenic-positivist tradition, by considering the work of Jerome Kagan, Margaret Archer and Christian Smith. I have chosen them because of their similar titles: *On Being Human: Why Mind Matters* (Kagan, 2016); *Being Human: The Problem of Agency* (Archer, 2000); and *What Is A Person?* (Smith, 2011). First, I look at Kagan's work because of his standing in modern American psychology and the sophistication of his reasoning about the interaction of temperamental (genetic) and contextual factors in becoming who we are as individuals. For Kagan, context of our species brings with it the emergent quality of us being choosing agents and so this connects with Archer's sub-title. Kagan is not a self-declared critical realist; indeed he has researched and written without any knowledge of the philosophy (Kagan, 2018, personal communication).

Kagan's book consists of a series of essays connected by some key themes. The first is that he is concerned that his discipline has surrendered too readily and unreflectively to neuro-reductionism. I come back to his views and those of others on this matter in Chapter 5. Second, his defence of anti-reductionism in psychology is more than this point about the neural substrate. In particular he is concerned that animal models favoured by positivists in psychology, who wish to adhere too closely to the rhetoric of natural science, miss the point about the emergent qualities that arise from cognition (see also Bannister (1968) on this point). Our use of elaborated language means that whatever we have in common with other species (which is quite a lot of course), our tendency to allocate unique situated meanings (personal construals) to events and relationships in our lives makes us humans, not other animals. Third, he emphasises that in a range of ways different contextual factors shape and inflect that meaning allocation.

Taking these together, Kagan is opposed to sociological not just biological reductionism. For example he argues that high rates of incarceration, teenage pregnancies and academic failure in African Americans cannot be reduced *only* to poverty, parental child-rearing practices or poor urban schools. In addition he says we must add the *collective* attribution of failure made about black people in the US and an abiding sense of grievance about being the target of white hostility. This confirms a critical realist assumption that we will find complexity in open human systems.

He gives another example of complexity but now introducing (unwittingly) other critical realist strictures about unpredictability, retrodiction and **retroduction**. He uses the metaphor of a pinball machine, which means that predicting outcomes of children by their psychological profile at say two years of age is futile. Extending the metaphor, Kagan says that the obstacles of life are like the obstacles in the machine as the ball progresses on its course. The weight of the ball symbolises the child's temperamental biases and the position of the ball at the top of the machine before its unique kinetic energy starts to ricochet through the obstacles, and this is a metaphor for the child's class and cultural starting point in life. He concludes: 'an understanding of a person's profile at a particular moment requires a narrative that begins with the present and proceeds backwards in time' (Kagan, 2016: 197). Kagan describes retroduction here without using the term.

Turning to Margaret Archer, her work is not only informed by critical realism (cf. that of Kagan), but is one of its most important expressions, spelling out the implications of the philosophy for social theory. The themes of anti-reductionism and **emergentism** evident in Kagan's work are expressed here as well, but this time they are explicitly philosophised.

Archer focuses on our emergent powers as human agents to be reflexive beings and to reinforce or change the world we are thrown into. Because we are reflexive language users, this means that we are engaged in our own biographically-situated version of an 'inner conversation'. According to Archer, people (individually and in groups) can reflect on their position in relation to their social context and vice versa. Reflexivity then is a mental capacity, which is common but can vary in its efficiency or sophistication – some of us are better at it than others. As she puts it, 'the "inner conversation" is how our personal emergent powers are exercised on and in the world – natural, practical and social – which is our triune environment' (Archer, 2000: 318). The relationship between our inner and outer worlds is in constant interplay until we die. (Remember from Heraclitus that the man and the river change over time.) For Archer our particular version of the 'inner conversation' constitutes who we are as unique individuals or, in the language of critical realism, it provides us with a **concrete singularity**. Because we have this reflexive mental capacity *and* we often share contexts for it, this affords us other emergent capacities such as empathy and compassion.

Deep subjectivism could rest on the laurels of this interiority, but Archer makes an important complementary point. Our inner conversations are not just about our view of the world (the way we construe it) but are also *about reality*. This is a reminder of the transitive and intransitive aspects of reality and the co-existence of ontological realism and epistemological relativism.

Echoing Sartre, Archer adopts an existential frame of reference by arguing that our inner conversation shapes our 'being in the world'. Echoing Marx, she emphasises though that the determination of our being in the world is not of a time of our choosing. This point is important because it brings us back to the dual consideration of us being both determined and determining as unique individuals. It can be contrasted with the lopsided voluntarism we find in some forms of humanistic psychology that we are nothing but a product of our choices in life. It can be contrasted with behaviourist assumptions that we are nothing but our conditioning histories.

If we are fallible unique human agents then, according to Archer, this leaves us with three recurring 'problems' or 'concerns': our physical wellbeing; our competence as social actors in practice; and our sense of self-worth. This is aligned with the summary I cited earlier from Raymond Williams about unique selves that will eventually get sick and die (or be killed off prematurely by outer events and agents). We cannot choose to defy physical reality and its implications for our wellbeing, social competence and sense of self-worth. However, we can adopt a range of positions about the existential challenges they pose for us all in unique ways. We can play the hand we are dealt with, this way or that way.

Moreover, as we are social agents those challenges occur within variable relational settings (family, friends, fellow pupils, neighbours, workmates etc.). For this reason, our praxis is embedded in social relationships; we are not freestanding agents operating in isolation. Thought experiments defying that norm, but also validating its truth, include *Desert Island Discs*, the longstanding BBC Radio 4 programme, and Bob Dylan's song, 'Talking World War Three Blues'. The first is an imagined future alone on a desert island, the second refers to the unenviable position of being the only survivor of a nuclear war. Both are unbearable scenarios because we are relational beings. Even the isolated monk in his silent cell prioritises an imagined relationship of some sort (with God).

Also our actions impact on the world we are thrown into and we can exercise some control some of the time of that world through our choices put into practice, though nothing is certain. Archer is not a narrow rationalist, in the sense of limiting human agency to our rational choices. Thoughts for her are important but so are our feelings. The non-rational aspects of our agency bring into play forms of psychology (from existentialism to psychoanalysis). We are not only determined and determining we are *both* rational *and* non-rational in variable ways in our unique lives. Our beliefs that are a meld of logic and leaps of faith can also become causes when we act upon the world. We can choose to reproduce the world we live in (Archer calls this 'morphostasis') or we can seek to transform it. I return to this tension in Chapter 9 when discussing why we protest or fail to protest.

These themes from Archer are also picked up in the work of Smith. He focuses on *both* our biological substrate *and* our biographically-situated social context to account for personhood. That field of possibilities contains what Smith calls 'causal capacities'. Our brains afford us the capability to function as moral agents (see Chapter 5 where I discuss this more). The sum of these causal capacities does not then simplistically equal being a person, but creates the conditions of possibility for personhood to emerge. This focus on **emergence** is central to critical realist philosophy, so Smith's work, like that of Kagan and Archer is worth reading to understand people as people in their unique social contexts.

With this focus on emergence Smith argues that our unique capacities as humans come from our bodies interacting with their natural and social environments. Within that fluxing process, much of which is mysterious and so requires **epistemic humility**, we find that human beings have a range of capacities that make them who they are. It is useful to compare this position to the insulting reductionism of trait theory and the 'Big Five'.

Smith lists a number of these capacities, which include: consciousness; an unconscious life; our ability to understand quantity, quality and time and space; the use and communication of mental representations; volition; practical consciousness (moment-to-moment steering our way through life); the formation and pursuit of interests (alone or with others collectively); feelings (experienced, expressed and codified); efficient monitoring of the effectiveness of our actions (both as intent and as *post hoc* reflection); self-transcendence (an appreciation of non-me, especially the existence and needs of others); symbolisation and language use; an understanding of virtue; aesthetic appreciation; and interpersonal communion and love. This list gives us a strong sense from a critical realist perspective of what it is to be human. It is assertively humanistic (cf. postmodernism) and emphasises causality (but without the errors in this regard of naïve realism). Along with others like Gregory Bateson, who I come back to in Chapter 12, Smith offers a respectful holistic sense of being human.

A final relevant note about Smith is that prior to his commitment to critical realism as a philosophy, he was an established sociologist concerned with interpreting narratives. He began to recognise that *limiting* social science to understanding stories risked social constructionism 'driving us over a cliff'. Whilst he realised that understanding meanings was very important (interpretivism or hermeneutics), there was no point in tracing those social meanings unless they point us to some underlying causes operating in our lives and society. Critical realism offered Smith an escape from these shortcomings of the idealism, which I discussed in Chapter 3.

Thus Kagan, Archer and Smith converge on much when they consider what it is to be human (anti-reductionism, agential powers, the importance of social context and the mixture of cognitive and affective aspects of our interiority and our actions). The fact that Archer and Smith are knowing critical realists but Kagan developed his work in ignorance of the philosophy is interesting. It reminds me of the point I made in Chapter 2 about a de-philosophised disciplinary norm in psychology. Despite this, the simple honesty derived from our shared common sense (epitomised in the intelligent reflections of Kagan) means that many psychologists may operate as *de facto* critical realists but without any inkling of the philosophy.

Even without a knowledge of critical realism, many psychologists know that reductionism is implausible and in practice creates absurdity. Applied psychologists in particular know that we must understand human experience and conduct in its *particular situated context* and that each case brings its unique considerations for a psychological formulation. They know that we are human agents but cannot simply choose to be anything we want to be.

Conclusion

The three main sections of this chapter have highlighted the limitations of any positivist discussion of us being unique individuals in our particular biographical contexts. The latter include the particular world we pass through, defined by time and places from birth to death, having been thrown into it without any choice. As we develop, our competence as choosing agents increases but none of us ever become freestanding decision makers as our lives are embedded in relationships with others and our natural world, as well as living in social structures we did not make and much of the time we are unaware of. Our 'inner conversation' shapes who we are within the constraints of particular external events and processes. It also is a commentary about a reality that will eventually determine our death.

By considering our personhood in this way, as suggested by Kagan, Archer and Smith, we can avoid the positivistic errors and unreflective simplifications of Galtonian personality theory and Kraepelinian psychiatry. If the reader prefers a postmodern account then it is still there to be embraced, but in my view it throws the baby out with the bathwater by locating us in texts and erasing us as individuals who are reflexive moral agents. I now turn to some thoughts already introduced by Kagan and Smith about the pitfalls of neuro-reductionism. If postmodernism renders our unique humanity invisible in textual reasoning and unending deconstruction, then it is erased by reductive neuroscience using a different logic.

5

DOES THE BRAIN CAUSE BEHAVIOUR?

Introduction

An exciting prospect for those psychologists in the naïve realist tradition has been that the brain is the primary source of explanation for all experience and behaviour. If this fundamental premise were to be true then psychologists could sit alongside other more established disciplines in the natural sciences, such as neurology and biochemistry. The older aspiration for psychology to be a behavioural science, defended by behaviourism as a philosophy, not merely a scientific method (Skinner, 1971), could now be superseded by a grander possibility: it could be a key player within the interdisciplinary field of neuroscience.

This chapter has as its focus the errors of **reductionism** and **transduction**. Neuroscience today is an interdisciplinary field of enquiry, with psychologists being enthusiastic members of a community of scholars with a faith in the central causal role of the brain in human functioning. When I provided a short account of reductionism in the glossary I noted as an example, 'neurochemical theories will explain all mental processes and behavioural outcomes' and noted the importance of interdisciplinary research. The field of neuroscience is certainly interdisciplinary but its willing collaborators constantly run the risk of 'neuro-reductionism'. The latter risk is not always actualised, with many psychologists being aware of the distinction between the brain explaining experience and behaviour and the brain affording or constraining them – a general point I get to by the end of this chapter.

To be clear at the outset then, I am not claiming that neuro-reductionism inevitably flows from neuroscience but only that it is a perennial risk unless those working in the field exercise constant critical reflexivity (see Chapter 1) and **epistemic humility**.

The current legitimacy of neuroscience

Neuroscience now has a particular global legitimacy. An academic compact between neuroscientists from a range of disciplines emerged during the 1960s with the establishment of the International Brain Research Organisation (1960); the International Society for Neurochemistry (1963); the European Brain and Behaviour Society (1968); and the Society for Neuroscience (1969). The legitimacy of neuroscience in the academy is confirmed now by the presence of over 50 high status journals.

The role of the brain in our lives then has taken on a particular salience in recent decades, especially for politicians. They probably support research in the field because skin-encapsulated explanations for say anti-social conduct, or mental disorder or wellbeing in society, function to deflect attention from more complex explanations and their profound political implications for social change. If there are clear social, rather than psychological and neurobiological **generative mechanisms** relevant to our lives, then these are at risk of exclusion by neuroscience, creating a convenience for conservative policy makers.

The logic of neuroscience, which is to close off supra-individual complexity (see below), supports the *status quo* by this limited focus. This point is manifest in for example the extensive government funding allocated to George Bush Senior's 'Decade of the Brain' in the 1990s (Jones and Mendell, 1999) and Barak Obama's more recent 'Brain Research through Advancing Innovative Neurotechnologies (BRAIN)' initiative. Given that the US is prone to fiscal restraint, individualism and a cultural evasion of public rather than philanthropic funding, an ideological reflection is invited about neuroscience and its advantages to policy makers.

Such a trend has not been unique to the USA. For example we find in Europe the *Human Brain Project (HBP)* (HBP-PS Consortium, 2012). This provides a very clear methodological imperative for the neuroscience programme, which explicitly decouples the brain from its social context:

> The evolutionary function of a brain is to control *the organism's behaviour* in their environment. In principle, therefore, *the only way* to test or characterise the high-level behavioural or cognitive capabilities of a brain model is to create *a closed loop* between the model and a body acting in an environment and to interrogate the model through well-designed experiments ... Once a set-up has successfully replicated we can then identify causal mechanisms by lesioning or manipulating specific brain regions, transmitter systems, types of neuron etc.
>
> *(ibid.: 49, emphasis added)*

I have italicised part of this stricture from the EU-funded consortium to highlight three key points from a critical realist perspective. First, there is a methodological reduction (this is the *only way* of doing the science). Second, the deliberate creation of a closed loop celebrates closed-system reasoning and creates the error of transduction. A fundamental flaw of naïve science is to privilege and idealise, rather than avoid and doubt, closed-system reasoning (see Bhaskar, 2008: 115–116). Thus in neuroscience the risk of reductionism is ever present, in both its methodological and epistemological ambitions. Third, according to the position cited, human science is not human at all. It is about 'the organism's (sic) behaviour'. This entails a double reduction: allegedly we are like all other organisms *and* we merely behave (i.e. we do not conduct ourselves as human agents). As I will explore now, this convention of neuroscience runs the risk of reducing our humanity, with our common, albeit variable, capacities as moral agents, embedded in fluxing social contexts, to fixed considerations about the brain alone.

Note as well the reference to the organism's 'environment'. That word is also well rehearsed more generally in the behavioural science tradition and its underpinning methodological or philosophical behaviourism. 'Environment' is a legitimate broad description compatible with our critical realist assumptions about both **ontological realism** and the **intransitive aspect of reality**. However, its rhetorical function in disciplines that operate 'below' political science, anthropology, economics or sociology, such as psychology, physiology and neurology, converts *context* into a diffuse and undifferentiated common background, or 'constant' part of the 'variance', rather than a highly complex fluxing sphere requiring its own detailed exploration. Once the simple word 'environment' is deployed, with its creeping positivist implication of **empirical invariance**, then this pre-empts the richness and contingent flow and uncertainty of 'context'. It deprives us of the necessary scrutiny of both **epistemological relativism** and the **transitive aspect of reality**. Having complained then of the pervasive risk in neuroscience of reductionism, what it the alternative?

A non-reductionist account from critical realism

The above caution, about the aggregating risks of both transduction and reductionism in neuroscience, should not be confused with a rejection of the role of biology (in this case neurobiology) in any understanding of human beings. For critical realists our natural world (which includes our bodies) is an aspect of reality, in accordance with our **four planar social being**. For that reason, of course our brains are important to understand and warrant with causal significance, but they cannot *exhaust* any psychological account for the very reason that the other three plains (our relations with others, the social structures surrounding us past and present and our unique personalities) also are important. Without my brain and its sufficient level of efficiency I cannot type this book. It affords my ability to see what I am typing and to use my fingers accurately and speedily on the keyboard. The neural efficiency of my cortex, and indeed its very existence, has stored the information I need to both type and to furnish the content of this sentence. If I have a massive stroke during the writing of the book it probably will not be completed.

An obvious analogy, though not homology, here is the working of a computer. We will never understand the content of its installed software by an unending exploration of its hardware. Of course the latter needs to be turned on and functioning properly for the software to run, but the software is ontologically separate. This is an analogy not a homology because, in addition, in human functioning agency is a relevant species-specific product of evolutionary **emergence** (Broad, 1925; Clayton and Davies, 2006). To reinforce this point, the existence of both the hardware and software of computers, as well as their utilisation by us, is only present because of human praxis. The likely degree of future autonomy and intentionality of computers is a matter of conjecture but their current existence is clearly a product of human decision making and action.

To continue with the point about the *partial* role of neurobiology in human science, my brain cannot explain a number of matters relevant to my typing of this book. These refer to my personal history and its social context. An exploration of this psychosocial complexity would unpack a wide range of decisions and experiences in my life, especially since I began to be confident as both an applied psychologist and social science researcher, but also from my younger days when my common sense had not been sullied by too much theorising about life. These have culminated in a unique emergent event: I decided to write a book called *Critical Realism for Psychologists*. This points up the question of human agency and the role that neurobiology plays. In simple terms then our brains are the *necessary but not sufficient* condition to explain our experience and conduct.

Below I want to emphasise some key features of our existence and our actions, which put the role of neurobiology into a necessary and wider context, if we are to provide a non-reductionist account. To do this we can return to the flaws in the statement I cited above from the rhetorical flourish from the *Human Brain Project* which I can highlight with three key points:

1. *We are people not just organisms.* We use language (an emergent characteristic of our species) and this means we can make statements and meta-statements about ourselves and our world. This creates the capacity for both personal agency and **judgemental rationality** (Archer, 2000). This should caution us about reducing our experience and behaviour to neural antecedents alone.
2. *Neuroscientific research is a way of studying human life but it is not the only way.* Any claim that it is the superior and single method is a form of unwarranted epistemological imperialism from neurobiology. This confidence would soon dissolve, if we were to consult those outside of neuroscience such as moral philosophers, artists, sociologists, novelists, poets, anthropologists, historians, economists, cosmologists, lawyers, geographers, literary theorists, political scientists, archaeologists, musicians, cultural theorists and faith leaders, to name but a few. Whilst neuroscience is indeed already an interdisciplinary field of enquiry, those collaborating do not extend to this long and legitimate list of researchers and commentators on what it means to be human.
3. *We are part of an open system.* The 'closed loop' and 'brain lesioning' approach to psychological investigation will create errors of transduction, if relied upon as our sovereign guide to psychological science. Evidence replicated in the laboratory, which sets out deliberately to isolate human beings from their wider open system of daily life, will lead to results that are at best partial and at worst actively misleading. The false promises associated with the project of

positivism in both natural and social science, such as **covering laws** and empirical invariance, are what neuroscience seems to be offering us as researchers, practitioners and citizens. This naivety invites our critical reflection but the gravitas of conservative policy makers and the high rankings of neuroscience journals in the academy deflects us from the task. Just because positivists have a complacent confidence in the contents of neuroscience journals or politicians enjoy the instrumental advantages of neuro-reductionism does not mean that we are obliged to accept these preferences. For reasons just listed that confidence in neuroscience is substantially misplaced.

Sceptical commentators

The triumphalism of neuroscientists has not gone unchallenged. For example, the physician and poet Raymond Tallis has attacked the arrogant naivety of his colleagues when accusing them of 'neuromania' (Tallis, 2011). Similarly, Rose and Rose (2012) point up the 'Promethean promises of the new biology' (the sub-title of their book attacking neuro-reductionism and its suppression of considerations of social context). Amongst other things their sceptical analysis discusses the eugenic roots of biological determinism and its modified expression eventually in forms of socio-biology that simply justify the existing social order (Wilson, 1975). Rose and Rose point out that evolutionary psychology has been slightly less reactionary in its assumptions. For example, it says that our psychological nature was basically fixed in the Pleistocene period and *Homo sapiens* have not had the time yet to adapt to its consequence but the racial differences claimed by eugenicists are excluded from this trend. (I discuss eugenics and bio-determinism more in Chapter 10.)

This focus then is on how neuroscience implicitly promotes a form of genetic, not just biological, determinism (or fatalism) that puts us all on tramlines and creates a version of TINA ('there is no alternative') in society. This tramline logic of course excludes the fact that evolution also has accounted for language production and the emergence of human agency. Thus whether we endorse positivist neuroscience or are sceptical about it, we might want to check if we do indeed conflate biology and genetics, which occurs at times in discussions within human science.

This is a false conflation for the very reason that our biological characteristics are being constantly shaped by post-conception events and processes, which implicate our own actions at times. The most profound of these are the epigenetic effects congenitally and in infancy, though our environment affects our neurochemistry throughout our life span in a range of ways. These include toxic reactions (e.g. hangovers) and loss reactions (e.g. acquired disabilities). Those of us getting gloomy in the deep midwinter know even how day length can alter our mood. Some diabetics report a range of environmental contingencies, such as weather conditions, that might affect their physical and psychological state. Acts of nurturance, such as stroking a pet or a mother feeding her baby will lead to neurochemical changes in the brain etc.

Put simply, biology is more than genetics as common sense will tell the reader. Epigenetic effects are particularly important and necessitate open-systems reasoning. For example, observations that pregnant women traumatised in the Twin Towers attacks of 9/11 had markedly lower cortisol levels, shows that this could impact the neural development of their infants (Yehuda et al., 2009). Similar research on stress in animals affecting germ cells post-conception are important to note (Bohacek and Mansuy, 2015). Thus from a critical realist perspective provided that neurodevelopmental effects are studied and interpreted within an open not closed system, this is scientifically legitimate. The problem is to insist on closed-system methodologies (see above).

Neuroscience has also emerged in a commercial context. The psychiatrist and psycho-pharmacologist David Healy has offered an elaborate critique of the interest work of the drug companies. They promote neuroscience research in order to sell their 'magic bullets' for putative mental disorders (Healy, 2004). A common version of neuroscience both creates profits for the pharmaceutical industry and reifies scientifically implausible and socially decontextualised diagnostic categories (Lakoff, 2005). Neuroscience then is not a 'disinterested' enterprise at all. It feeds industrial profits and it allows politicians to evade policy challenges at the aggregate or supra-individual level of causation (see above).

The positivist logic of much of neuroscience leads to what Wolman (1981) called 'hoped-for-reductionism', which is common more generally in human science and has been around for the past century. Such an epistemological tendency runs the risk of negating or subverting the legitimacy of psychosocial generative mechanisms pertinent to understanding the relationship between experience and behaviour. The three layers of our four planar social being, other than the natural world that includes our embodied biological features, all contain their own admixture of causes and consequences for human thought and action. Moreover, once neuroscientists over-value hope-for-reductionism, then that can elide into a false assumption of a scientific 'mission completed'. It is as if the long-standing arguments about understanding human thought are over with the forward march of neuroscience, when in open systems that explanatory closure is not tenable.

Take the example of the hoped-for-reductionism about mental activity, which Freud as a neurologist believed would eventually be explained at the neural level (see Chapter 11). By the turn of this century although this outcome had not been achieved in practice, some neuroscientists were claiming a version of that 'mission completed', a view even endorsed by some psychoanalysts (Solms and Turnbull, 2002). This *took for granted* that Freud's early hope as a neurologist has now been fulfilled in practice. Two examples can be given to illustrate this claim.

First, the report of the HBP-PS cited above goes on firmly to describe *functional* psychiatric disorders as being *brain* disorders (ibid.: 98). Second, epidemiologists studying mental disorders continue with the same explicit but fundamentally faulty assumption (e.g. Wittchen et al., 2011) as do psychiatrists studying the biological substrate of 'schizophrenia' and 'depression' (e.g. Kandel, 2018). This is a glaring error from both neuroscience and any form of epidemiology that follows its lead.

These proponents of neuroscientific logic and success fail to acknowledge that functional disorders, such as 'schizophrenia' or 'depression', *ipso facto* do not *have* a clear aetiology. After all, that is the very reason why they are designated as 'functional' rather than 'organic' disorders. By a discursive sleight of hand, that important distinction is erased in favour of all dis-valued psychological differences in society being reducible to faulty brain functioning, even though there is no evidence to warrant the erasure. We see at this point then how neuroscientific claims are ideologically driven but not scientifically plausible for all their methodological trappings of experimentalism and brain lesioning.

In the case of neuroscientific ideology, critical realists do not go down the road of either hoped-for or taken-for-granted neuro-reductionism. This is done though while respecting the role of biology in our lives. Not to do so would be anti-realist and offer its own version of reductionism of a psychological or social variety. Some system theorists, such as Humberto Maturana who, note, is a biologist and neuroscientist, have elaborated a defence of holism. With his student Francisco Varela, another neuroscientist, he developed the notion of 'autopoiesis', which is a feature of open biological systems. It refers to the capacity of biological systems to sustain and reproduce themselves in unique ecological settings (Maturana and Varela, 1980).

Maturana and Varela were preceded by those developing general systems theory before the Second World War, Ludwig von Bertalanffy and Paul Weis, both of whom were biologists and began life as laboratory scientists (Mingers, 2011). By focusing on open systems (a core emphasis of critical realism) these systems theorists provided an early warning of the problems of transduction, now evident in the rhetorical position of neuroscience, exemplified by the mission statement of the European *Human Brain Project*.

The work of these systems theorists is a constant reminder of both the risk of neuro-reductionism and how to combat that risk. Picking up on the points above from the systems theorists trying to avoid the pitfall of transductionism (and by implication any form of reductionism, including neuro-reductionism), a critical realist summary of how we might proceed in a non-reductionist fashion has been offered recently by (Tortorello, 2017).

Tortorello, like other critical realists, is not at all hostile to biology or neuroscience in principle. Problems arise though with decontextualisation and errors of transduction. He cites Francis Crick from the naïve realist tradition of science to illustrate this problem as follows:

> You, your joys and your sorrows, your memories and ambitions, your sense of personal identity and free will, *are in fact no more than* the behaviour of a vast assembly of nerve cells and associated molecules. You are largely the behaviour of a vast population of neurons.
>
> *(Crick, cited in Tortorello 2017: 236, my emphasis added)*

The italicised phrase points to a celebration of neuro-reductionism (not a shameful confession). The emergence of human cognition and language shapes and is shaped by the types of societies we inhabit by affirming their traditional priorities, power structures and forms of organisations (stasis and reproduction) or altering them (reform or revolution). We can codify rules to follow and roles to adhere to and we can teach these to our children, in order to enable them to be successfully socialised adults. We can also reflect on the moral order, which then ensues, and we can choose to endorse and reproduce it or to critique and change it. Maturana and Varela noted that complexity then has both an external connotation (in this case our context embedding our experience and conduct) and an internal one (in this case our unique experience and conduct).

Where then does all of this identification of complexity and unique emergent features leave our brains? The answer for Tortorello, speaking on behalf of critical realism, is that *brains afford, but they do not determine*, human experience and action. This is aligned with common sense but it is problematised by positivists, with their proneness to both reductionism and a misplaced faith in transduction from the artificially controlled laboratory to everyday life. In reaction to positivism a different error can emerge: some strong social constructivists might render our biological reality irrelevant, because the totality of understanding purportedly resides in discourses and texts (see Chapter 3) (Benton, 1991; cf. Rose, 2013).

In this strong constructivist scheme, the brain itself could be rendered as a mere social construct, with no material ontological substance, independent of its discussion or description. However, note that some neuroscientists now use the term 'socially constructed' to mean 'socially influenced' or 'socially mediated', permitting both causes and meanings, and allowing meanings themselves to become causes (e.g. Eisenberg, 2006). This then becomes a real and dynamic interactive process from epigenetics onwards, implicating contingent conditions impacting our lives for good or ill (e.g. Landecker and Panofsky, 2013; Lederbogen et al., 2011). As I describe in Chapter 3, these forms of research are completely consistent with a weaker notion of social constructivism, which is one way of conceiving critical realism (e.g. Sayer, 2000).

These types of study highlight that any reduction of psychological phenomena to brain mechanisms will unreasonably exclude the disruptive impact of, for example, child sexual abuse, warfare, poverty, domestic violence, insecure employment, racism or bullying in schools and workplaces. We can invert these influences as positive processes that would increase the probability of our wellbeing as adults and of our developing ontological security as children. This fluxing and variable complexity is obscured from our analysis if we become overly preoccupied with studying the brain, in the manner suggested by the neuroscientists promoting their wares from the *Human Brain Project*.

The risk of neuro-reductionism has stimulated a critical commentary in relation to neuroscience. One strand of this is the growth of neuro-ethics (Conrad and De Vries, 2011). Another can be found in discussions about the role of neuroscience in contemporary society, especially in relation to mass media depictions and popular books on science. The latter are written by authoritative experts, such as Antonio Damisio, Joseph LeDoux and Steven Pinker, so this is not commentary about journalistic misunderstandings or inaccurate summaries of information from a position of ignorance. Johnson and Littlefield (2011) following on from the critique of Fahnestock (1998) note a number of features of this popular science offered to us by neuroscientists.

First, doubts and contradictions tend to be smoothed over, when evidence is summarised for the lay reader. The writer may cut quickly to certainty and even hyperbole (e.g. Iacoboni, 2008). Second, the tendency to simplify and offer certainty, when it is not warranted, appeals to policy makers who want simple messages about simple solutions; see my point above about the challenging complexity of our four planar social being. Third, in journals scientists, mindful of their peers reviewing and reading their work, will be cautious and limit themselves strictly to the implications of their findings, i.e. they follow the convention of not 'going beyond the data' and often offer epistemic humility in their conclusions. By contrast, writers of popular science books are 'cut loose' from this inhibition and might leap to wider speculations about covering laws about human nature, as was noted by Varghese and Abraham (2004).

Fourth, some of these wider generalisations have popularised simplistic claims about our educational potential as human beings and about our gender identity being built into our inherited or epigenetically shaped neurological hardware. This points up the controversy of the 'male and female brain' (Brizendine, 2006; Baron-Cohen, 2003). Bio-determinism can feed in readily then to the contested domain of gender politics, with claims and counter-claims being made by feminists and transgender activists (e.g. Fine, 2008; cf. Smith et al., 2015). As Johnson and Littlefield (2011) note, broad and simplified findings from neuroscience can soon become invoked in arguments about other forms of identity politics (see for example Nadesan (2005) in relation to autism and 'neuronormals'). Given that neuroscience is now embedded in the worlds of both identity politics and policy formation, this invites us to exercise particular critical reflexivity about its role in society, both now and in the future.

The tendency towards simplification in popular science books (written, note, again by neuroscience experts, not journalists) is not only about authorial self-promotion and the shift from caution to rhetoric, it also belies their background in positivism. These writers within that philosophical tradition really believe that covering laws *will* emerge from neuroscience; they, as it were, are simply offering an early announcement about those certainties.

Another implication for critical realists, from the above summary from sceptical commentators, is how scientists reason in the background (i.e. their more cautious journal article presentations and private accounts of how science actually proceeds behind the data that is tidied up). Scientists rely on trial and error **retroduction**, with its false trails and ambiguities in their daily practice, even if neat claims of deduction are then made in scientific journals, which might then go on to be speculatively extrapolated to covering laws in their writing of popular books. What actually happens in science, as in problem solving and detective work of any kind, with their doubts, uncertainties, hunches and loose ends, is hidden from the general public and policy makers by simplified popular science books celebrating the tradition of positivism. The reader is left with neat simplifications about context-free human functioning, which they may welcome or fear.

Summarising the case for a non-reductionist neuroscience

Our conduct cannot be reduced to one or more brain mechanisms. When our brain is impaired then this certainly impacts our agency. Brain-injured and dementia patients are living examples of this point. However that does not mean that we can simply work back confidently, in a process of retroduction, to explain a currently observed action by a readily identifiable brain mechanism *alone* that reflects covering laws for all contexts.

Varela, cited in Tortorello (2017), gives the example of a man trembling at his daughter's wedding. The shaking might be a symptom of Parkinsonism. On the other hand, supposing he normally does not tremble but instead in *this particular context* he is simply overcome with pride and nostalgia about someone he loves. Any retroductive exercise about human conduct cannot limit itself to neural pathways alone but must include a range of psychological and social factors as well, depending who is being studied and which aspect of their conduct is being interpreted.

If behaviour cannot be traced to neural pathways in simple terms, even in relation to just one action, such as trembling, then we would be unwise to argue that complex social-existential states (for example, what are called 'mental disorders') are readily reducible to brain states. And yet, that is precisely what neuro-reductionism from the *Human Brain Project* encourages (see above but also further discussion in Chapter 10). Moreover, for now we cannot even glean a clear and unambiguous account of how the brain creates consciousness in principle, let alone look to it to trace specific causal pathways of behaviour (Searle, 2007).

As critical realism emphasises repeatedly, human experience and conduct are part of an open system and so their unique complexity needs cautious interpretation and must always be set in a situating context of time and place. Covering laws about brain mechanisms allegedly causing conduct out of context are untenable as complete psychological accounts. The external and internal complexity described by Maturana and Varela (1980) not only reflect the character of open systems, but they provide the conditions of concrete singularity, which human scientists need to attend to, from person to person, each with their own unique biographical features.

All of the above evidence and arguments leads us to a non-reductionist version of neuroscience that would give due and appropriate weight to neurobiology but within unique social and biographical contexts. This means that we do not need to 'throw the baby out with the bath water'. Biology is important but it is not all important. Here are some examples of proceeding more wisely within the strictures of critical realism.

1. We can utilise the useful findings that environmental impacts in the womb and in infancy shape gene expression (e.g. Galea et al., 2011).
2. Both chronic stress and acute trauma affect neurotransmitter activity. For example, urban living makes us psychologically vulnerable to symptoms of both anxiety and depression (e.g. Lederbogen et al., 2011). Some research also

suggests that urbanicity inflects the probability of psychotic symptoms, despite the strong eugenic tradition insisting that the latter reflect inherited brain disorders (see Chapter 10).

3. Some biological states, such as diabetes, can affect emotional wellbeing and mood states (e.g. De Groot et al., 2016). This may also be true of the relationship between bacterial activity in the gut and mood states (Cryan and Dinan, 2012). These examples confirm that biology does not mean necessarily *genetics* (the eugenic trope just noted and still around at times today in relation to mental health). The health of the gut and the pancreas are affected postnatally by our eating preferences and habits. These emerge from the norms of food consumption surrounding us in childhood and our embedding economic system that contains a profit-driven food industry. In turn this inflects the probability of both obesity and malnutrition in the general population. These biological links with behaviour confirm looping biopsychosocial interactions, which require a whole system form of understanding (Pilgrim, 2015b). (See my return to the importance of our four planar social being in Chapter 12.)
4. Planned action, from jogging and swimming to meditation and yoga, can alter our brain chemistry (e.g. Erickson et al., 2015). This point applies too in the altered conduct that emerges from the insights of psychological therapy. Thus our choices as human agents are implicated in our conduct (for example, those fit to do so may still opt not to exercise), which in turn can affect our biological functioning.
5. Childhood adversity is a strong predictor of mental health problems, independent of diagnostic labels attached to its victims (see Chapter 10) (Cutajar et al., 2010; Pilgrim et al., 2009). Thus child protection policies and norms of child-rearing affect neurochemical activity in its various expressed forms of concrete singularity.
6. The complex and intersecting material contingencies of social group membership and adverse conditions of life (especially poverty and warfare) affect *both* our physical and mental health (Rosenfield, 2012). This means that holism, not reductionism, is implied. Disciplinary imperialism and reductionism (from psychology and sociology not just biology) undermines that holistic imperative (see Chapter 12).

These summary six points confirm that critical realism does not reject neuroscience, only its reductionist tendencies and so alerts us to its risks. Critical realism, as it were, puts neuroscience in its place, giving it due weight but not overvaluing or sacralising its explanatory power.

Conclusion

The answer to the question in this chapter's title is that the brain does not *cause* our behaviour but it does *afford* our experience and conduct. With no brain we are dead and with an impaired brain our efficiency in the world is less than optimal. The implication of this is that critical realism does not reject neuroscience but it does proceed cautiously. Covering laws claiming neurological or neurochemical causation of behaviour separated from its particular context are untenable but tendencies can be conceded. Moreover, the brain is part of a wider open biological system for all animals, with the causal interplay between genes and the environment from epigenetics onwards being important to study. With increasing agency our choices then enter that complex mix of multiple generative mechanisms, which together then might account for our experience and conduct.

In the case of humans, the emergent cognitive capabilities of language-use provide a unique dimension to our complexity (see Chapter 4). The latter has both an external dimension (our particular embedding environments fluxing over time and place) and an inner one (we all have unique thoughts and feelings about the world as we develop and age, which are open to change). The concrete singularity of each person can be explored psychologically. At this point we can recall the Heraclitan roots of critical realism in relation to the man stepping into the flowing river: both the man and the river change with time.

Finally, the above exploration raises two important matters. First, neuroscience is prone to errors of transduction, when naïve realists celebrate the narrow research confines of closed systems and the certainties of findings allegedly flowing from them. Accordingly, this is not a cause for celebration at all, but grounds for serious critical reflection for neuroscientists. Second, it is an encouraging start that neuroscience has been associated with interdisciplinary collaboration. However, this has been far too limited. To develop a fully human science we need a much larger community of scholars than those in the biological and cognitive sciences alone. I return to the matter of interdisciplinarity in Chapter 12.

6

DOES LIFE FLOW ON WITHIN YOU AND WITHOUT YOU?

Introduction

When George Harrison penned the song 'Within You Without You', for The Beatles' concept album, *Sgt. Pepper's Lonely Hearts Club Band*, he was in the thrall of Eastern mysticism. The lyrics reflect the influence of the Vedanta sub-tradition of Hinduism and its notion of non-dualism. The leader of critical realism Roy Bhaskar was to re-visit the ancient Eastern Ways in his later work, to the consternation of some of his early followers, who tended to be Marxist materialists (Bhaskar, 2000).

Harrison's lyrics hinted at three aspects of non-dualism. First, there was the artificial divide between individuals. This has a profound ontological implication about our common humanity and inter-connectivity. Social psychologists and those doing process-outcome research in psychological therapies, all develop theories that put *relationality*, not intra-psychic events or individual conduct at their centre. This disrupts one foundational idea in our culture that psychology means understanding the experience and behaviour of us as *separate individuals*.

Second, the relationship between the ego and its restriction, along with our deeper subjectivity or conscious and unconscious aspects of experience, are explored in the lyrics and the spiritual tradition it honours. This implies that inner reality combines aspects that might be knowable or unknowable, as well as known and unknown. In principle, this is no different from external reality and the relationship between **the empirical, the actual** and **the real** in its totality (see Chapter 1).

Empiricists, since the introduction of behaviourism in psychology, tend to overstate their ambitions in relation to external reality and understate the possibility of legitimate inner exploration, or they might, at times, express anxious embarrassment about its scientific legitimacy. In fact, external reality too has a plurality of unknowns and even 'unknowables' (most of outer space, the deep-sea bed and sub-atomic particles) but its actuality tends not to be queried, in principle, by naïve realists. To single out inner reality alone as being 'off limits' to science is an unwarranted implication of positivism. It will though require particular epistemological caveats and methodological innovations, beyond empiricism, which are likely to be a source of contestation (see below). The human mind is part of an open not closed system and so has to be understood accordingly in its complexity across time and place (see Chapter 2).

Third, Harrison points to the constant interpenetration of inner and outer reality. As with other mammals, we perceive and apprehend in order to relate to our shared outer reality in an adaptive way, even if our inner reality might distort our understanding of the outer as well at times. Our perceptual apparatus is physically imperfect and our cognitive competence is fallible. Moreover, our previous experience shapes how we both apprehend and comprehend each new situation, with more or less accuracy. Notwithstanding those imperfections and idiosyncrasies, we navigate the world most of the time with functional competence. If we fail, it becomes noteworthy as some culturally coded form of mental abnormality (see Chapter 10).

In that constant interplay of experience and situated contexts, which shapes all mammalian behaviour, humans have elaborated language. Accordingly, thought processes and meaning attribution add a very important emergent layer of reality to our more general inherited primate mental dispositions, such as reasoning and memory. This point is made here to remind us that other animals have inner realities (at times manifest in their behaviour), not just humans. However, the emergence of elaborate verbal communication, with its wide variety of native linguistic codes, creates a much greater possibility for us to share our inner worlds with others, with attempted frankness, coherence and insight. The psychotherapy client taking the opportunity seriously and the skilled novelist or poet exemplify these prospects. The opposite side of the same coin is that we are deceiving and self-deceiving beings at times, which warrants some form of psychological understanding.

Language is critical to the emergence of our agency, manifest in our conduct. It reflects our capacity to be intentional, and our ability not only to make statements but also meta-statements. The latter are statements about statements, such as 'Maybe I could have phrased the sentence I have just written in a different way in order to better convey the same meaning'. Statements and meta-statements can be codified and transmitted beyond our immediate proximal connections and even our earthly existence. Our messages can be received instantly on the other side of the world and can resonate profoundly after our death.

Non-human apes (and pre-verbal children) use a series of gestures to communicate desires and intentions but they are limited in number and require direct proximity to the receiver, in order to be functionally effective (Carpenter et al., 1998; Hobaiter and Byrne, 2014). A residue of seemingly unconscious and automatic non-verbal gestures persevere in adult humans as well. Watch how football supporters in unison put their hands on their heads in a signal of social defeat, when a penalty is missed. See how in very hopeless situations we tend to hold out our palms in plaintiff despair.

These human gestures in very broad terms hint at our evolutionary history as primates. However, because gestures have been overlain with language-mediated cultural norms, there are large variations in their meanings in human societies across time and space. Consequently, decoding gestures in humans may actually be *more* challenging than when studying other primates, despite the latter being unable to speak. Moreover, as I noted above, gestures are about the here and now, whereas codified language can also be about the 'there and then'. We can do both, not just the first, with all the advantages and disadvantages that double possibility brings. We might be tortured by nostalgic longing or terrified by the prospect of death, whereas other animals might stay more readily in the here and now. Language mediates both high-level mental operations and self-deceit. The metaphors used by Buddhists about 'beginner's mind' and seeing the world simply and directly through the eyes of children and animals makes this same point about the mixed blessing of being language users (Suzuki, 1970).

Behaviourism and putting inner reality off limits

The rich complexity of cognitive, conative and affective life introduced above was of interest to philosophers before psychology emerged as a separate discipline (more on this below). And when it did emerge, a plausible elimination of inner life on scientific grounds could never be completed. The most self-assured rejection of subjectivism by radical behaviourists could never be a matter of erasure but only of re-framing or explanation. B.F. Skinner had to provide some sort of account of what he called 'inner events', for the very reason that they *existed* and he knew it (Skinner, 1974).

This was a contradiction: purist positivist science was evangelically rejecting inner life but accounting for it at the same time in a second-rate, degraded and externalised form of measurable behaviour alone. Thinking *could* be reduced to small muscle movements around the larynx ('sub-vocal speech') but arguably it was more sensible to simply ask people what was on their mind. Generally they would tell you and certainly give you a more meaningful account than would sensory electrodes placed on their throat (Kelly, 1955; cf. Watson, 1913). *Ipso facto* behaviour without meaning is meaningless.

Journalists, detectives, judges and market researchers used this method of account seeking, so why was 'scientific' psychology being so haughty and contemptuous? And as these tried and tested interrogators, reporters and interviewers knew, most of us are canny enough to approach personal accounts with a mixture of credulousness and scepticism. An acculturated competence we learn is to spot liars and cheats, even if we fail some of the time. A study of that imperfect competence is legitimate material for psychologists. It would be a study of our **judgemental rationality**.

Probably, behaviourism was appealing to many psychologists, mainly because of the scientific respectability it seemingly gave to their newly emerging discipline (see Chapter 2). However, that ideological appeal did not necessarily make it philosophically unchallengeable. A philosophical default to behaviourism was a professional convenience for psychology but it also reflected a lack of intellectual imagination.

Moreover, it was deliberately putting itself out of touch with one domain of reality that does not go away simply because we opt dogmatically to consign it to silence.

We do not, naïvely, have to take speech acts as a direct read-out of an inner reality but they are a good enough starting point. Just because we might distort and deceive ourselves and others, at times, does not mean that all of our communications are worthless or that our testimonies are always without veracity. And if projections and cognitive biases might mean we get other people 'wrong' at times, the very opposite is also true of our capacity for accurate empathy, even if some of us are better at the latter than others.

Before we even enter the debate about human agency and language use (Skinner, 1957; cf. Chomsky, 1959), we can identify the weakness of Skinner's account of S-R psychology explaining all behaviour, even in non-human species. The work on primatology noted above indicates that other apes experience and communicate their intentions. In apes, gestures signal the need for example for food sharing, social distance, sexual contact, the need to be picked up and carried, and grooming, amongst other things. This suggests that apes are *purposeful* communicators; they signal their desires and striving for something.

Philosophically, this goal-directed striving is called 'teleology' and it has a mixed pedigree. For example Aristotle thought that acorns had an intrinsic telos to become a grown oak tree. It is less contentious in human affairs because we are language-using and rule-following animals. We can readily see that if we learn rules, we also then become mindful of their infraction. This renders us as moral agents, who know right from wrong. Our emotions of fear and anticipated guilt or shame may not always follow that knowledge, as a confident brake on rule infraction. For example the criminal breaks laws despite knowing very well that they exist. Nonetheless, the rules are known to everyone socialised in a particular society at a moment in time. To comply or defy is a choice, even though some of us are in more of a position to take the first route easily.

Also language allows us to throw ourselves in our minds back and forth in time and so we can plan our actions and anticipate their consequences. We can imagine the future and recall the past. We are proactive agents, not just reactive organisms. It is only in those we judge to lack mental capacity (following J.S. Mill, traditionally this meant children, 'lunatics' and 'idiots') that we create the exception that proves the rule about being fully accountable moral agents. This graduated process is readily demonstrable in children: an average three-year-old is less of a moral agent than a ten-year-old.

So when behaviourists say we lack freedom (Skinner, 1971) they are only partially correct. It is true that we are not free to do anything we want, because of bodily and situated material constraints that are beyond our individual control. The blind cannot choose to see and the homeless must live on the streets and cannot choose to live in a palace. Nonetheless we *are* determining not just determined beings and, to a lesser extent, this principle does apply to other animals as well. Of course language use has massively expanded the agential dimension to human action. Humans do not merely behave, they also *conduct* themselves.

Thus we do have freedom, even if it is limited in its aspirations by real constraints. For this reason, we can demonstrate that teleology connotes what it is to be a human much more accurately than does S-R psychology (Taylor, 1964; Porpora, 1980; Archer, 2000). If we were *not* knowing and self-conscious purposeful moral agents then we would have no recurring societal requirement for ethical and legal codes, although it is important to concede their variation across time and space. Without being knowingly purposeful we would never be correct to hold ourselves and one another to account for our actions. Quite understandably, we do this routinely and so it is an aspect of human reality that requires description and explanation. Forms of social psychology, aligned with critical realism, have already achieved that task to various degrees (Antaki, 1981).

To summarise, not even the most radical of radical behaviourists would argue that inner events do not exist, only that they are beyond legitimate scientific scrutiny. So if they exist, then this is an acknowledgement of their ontology. And if they exist then we may be unwise to ignore the **generative mechanisms** that underlie their **emergence**. If behaviourists wanted to place inner reality off limits that does not mean that a case cannot be made, on both rational and humanistic grounds, to defy that advice. Instead we might create systematic and credible ways of exploring inner reality via personal accounts in addition to the interpretation of visible conduct.

At this point we need to address then the competence of both phenomenology and depth psychology in that task. Before that we can note the role of empiricist philosophy in the 19th century, prior to the squeamishness of radical behaviourism about inner life, which emerged in the wake of logical positivism in the 1930s (Moore, 1985).

Naïve realism and inner life

The amalgam of empiricism with positivism was discussed in Chapter 2. As I noted then, in the 19th century before psychology emerged as a distinct academic discipline, empiricist philosophers were not at all opposed to examining inner reality seriously. Not only was the ontology of memory, perception and aesthetics addressed by them, their preference for defining truth via the senses inherently contained subjectivity. Empiricism *ipso facto* relies on sensory experience and so has a subjective component, albeit one that then seeks to build an inter-subjective consensus on *what* is experienced.

In addition to this point about the role of sensory encounters with the world, philosophy recurrently discussed inner life. Philosophy began, and often also ended, with pure logic, introspection, reflection and speculation. Indeed this was seen as a shortcoming by the early psychologists (see my citation of Ward and Rivers from 1904 discussed at the start of Chapter 2). It is not surprising then that a prestigious traditional philosophical journal is called *Mind*. It is also little surprising then that behaviourism would not triumph in perpetuity in psychology but the discipline would return instead to empiricism with different clothes: cognitivism. Dogmatically ignoring an aspect of reality, as behaviourism tried to do, does not make it go away. If psychologists were to really compete with the older and highly practised custodian of 'the mind', philosophy, then there really was little point proceeding in a mind-less manner. This would have left the ancient parent supposedly left behind but still in charge of matters psychological.

Our inner lives make their presence felt at every turn in human existence. Our motives, our creativity, our imagination, our intentions, our amoral desires, our interpretations, our mental arithmetic, our inner tunes and eidetic images, our empathy or sympathy, our perceptions, our memories, our day and nocturnal dreams, our intuitions, our rapid risk calculations, our fantasies, our infatuations, our sense of nostalgic reverie and our reflective musings all play out without the presence of any external witness. They mix **intransitive** and **transitive aspects of reality**. When we remember a dream on wakening, the former is confirmed and if we *interpret its meaning* then the latter is confirmed.

Moreover, these cognitive and conative aspects of inner life are bathed in forms of emotion that wash to and fro in our embodied experience over time and place, sometimes intelligibly, sometimes mysteriously. They are in the realm of the actual but are not always readily quantified in the realm of the empirical. Their dynamic flux, partially in sight and partially out of sight, reminds us of Heraclitus and his foundational river metaphor for critical realism. What cognitive science has done is return to the earlier concerns of empiricist philosophers and endeavoured to quantify experience and discover mental **covering laws**, within the tradition of positivism. As such, this still reflects the legacy of Parmenides, not Heraclitus.

Thus, if behaviourism is not a sustained alternative to subjectivism in its different forms, that does not mean that cognitivism can successfully objectivise subjectivity and convincingly secure *permanent laws* related to inner life. This is because studying experience means inevitably dealing with *both* the transitive and intransitive aspects of reality in constant and often unpredictable interplay in open human systems. The impossibility of covering laws was discussed more in Chapter 2; judgemental rationality about the contingencies of emergence was offered instead as a plausible and sensible philosophical alternative. Here I give an example of this in the organoleptic judgements made at moments in time and place in the food and drink industry.

Olive growers in Southern Italy pride themselves on the quality of their extra virgin oil. One empirical dimension to ensuring that it is good is *both* the laboratory testing of its components *and* recorded testimonies of its very early pressing. For extra virgin oil this means within hours of the olives being shaken from the tree. However, these producers are more than aware that this systematic checking is a necessary *but not sufficient* guarantee of good quality. In addition, a panel of experts is employed, who actually taste the oil. They do this blind in relation to the source and type of olive and might wear dark glasses, so that they cannot even discern the hue of its oil. They leave the oil on their tongue for around 30 seconds and wash it around their mouth before then sucking air into it between their teeth. It should then leave a bitter aftertaste and not be bland and its nuances can be described richly then by the expert taster. The ratings and rich descriptions of the blind testers are then added to the laboratory findings and guarantees of rapid pressing. A batch of oil may seem perfect according to the latter criteria but not good for the market, according to the former. It is only when *both* empirical thresholds of quality are achieved that a batch of oil is approved for sale.

This example reminds us that the empirical domain of reality in human affairs (even something as seemingly simple as approving that extra virgin olive oil is right for the market) is complex. It contains mind-independent aspects of reality (the olives and the machine-generated findings of laboratory analysis of their oil) and mind-dependent, culturally specific, value judgements about taste and interpretations of the lab findings. In the latter regard, olive oil experts are aware that what is to the taste of one generation may not be to the next.

Accordingly, the judgement of good quality using this mixed method is a form of contingent objectivity but not of permanent judgemental neutrality. Taste in its literal and metaphorical sense changes across time and space in human societies and, in the latter regard, may even be a symbolic marker within a society of dominant and subordinated social groups (Bourdieu, 1984). Taste reflects not just what is but what ought to be; such subtle aesthetic judgements are then an aspect of **axiology**. Human scientists cannot investigate differences in taste unless they defy two positivist conventions. First, it requires the acceptance of the inevitable coupling of facts and values, which positivism seeks to separate. Second, it must concede fluxing open systems (changes of values, in this case taste, across time and place). This undermines the possibility of a covering law about human value-judgements and the fixity of reality.

The hardy perennial of deep and complex subjectivity

What the more subjectively orientated psychologists from the traditions of psychoanalysis, phenomenology and existentialism have agreed upon is that the contingent meanings that we bring to our lives are important. We find and make meaning because we are reflective agents but at times meaning is shaped or even imposed without our awareness, from primary socialisation in our families and schooling through to political propaganda, advertising and nudge technologies in our adulthood. In whichever way meaning might come to emerge in our lives, if psychologists do not reject inner life in principle, then an option and even obligation is to develop a coherent rationale for its description and understanding.

Psychoanalysis, phenomenology and existentialism have offered variants of such rationales. They reflect a competing approach traceable to the 19th century to that of empiricism, which imposed the rules of the natural sciences (*naturwissenshaften*) prematurely upon the discipline of psychology (see Chapter 2). Instead, different rules of enquiry were implied from the study of culturally determined meanings in time and place, studied in the arts and humanities (*geisteswissenshaften*).

I noted in Chapter 2 that a false confidence in the first part of the 20th century had arisen from the pincer movement of empiricism and positivism. This had seemingly resolved what a scientific psychology was to look like; the complexities of meanings, made, found or imposed upon us contingently in our lives, was to be ignored, held in suspicion or expelled. However, the crises in psychology that then emerged in the second half of the 20th century, created an intellectual space and opportunity for concerns of the *geisteswissenshaften* from the previous century to be rehearsed once more.

By the 1960s, psychoanalysis was considered pretty much beyond the pale for most research and applied psychologists but this was not the case for phenomenology, which was making a credible fight back against behaviourism as a rationale for legitimate research (Wann, 1964). The dominance of behaviourism at the time relied upon the claim that psychology like all forms of proper science should be explanatory (*erklären*). However, the phenomenologists argued that meaning exploration by human beings and its study by psychologists is not an exercise in explanation but instead in fine grain description and interpretation (*verstehen*). This more modest ambition is consistent with the critical realist stricture of **epistemic humility**.

The phenomenologists posed a fundamental question: how can we systematically explore consciousness, in terms of its content, structures and processes? Their answer lay in a careful and credulous approach to people's reports of their inner lives (their thoughts, feelings, memories, perceptions melded into preferred narratives), without any presuppositions from the psychological investigator. In American psychology probably the best-known advocate of this approach was Carl Rogers and, probably known more in Europe than his homeland of the US, George Kelly, with his psychology of personal constructs. The latter focuses on how we all construe the world differently and how we can also re-construe our worlds. The roots of this approach lay at the turn of the 20th century in the work of the philosophers Edward Husserl, Franz Brentano and Carl Stumpf.

The study of personal accounts and conclusions drawn from them about human functioning was now posited as the most important path for a credible version of psychology. Moreover, this opened up possibilities about not only turning objects into subjects (to reverse the logic of positivism and empiricism) but also how to understand *interpersonal conduct*. If we are language-using and meaning-attributing agents, who construe and re-construe our worlds, then this shapes how we engage with others and how they engage with us. Inter-subjectivity not just subjectivity becomes the focus of psychological enquiry. This once more brings us back to common sense. Not only if we want to understand someone could we start, quite reasonably, by asking them about themselves and then listening credulously, we might be able to get to grips with the complexities of how we understand one another (Laing et al., 1966). For example, we might examine how language impairment alters our experience and conduct interpersonally and that might give us a window into the mediating role of meaning attribution in everyday conduct (e.g. Gillespie et al., 2010).

The phenomenologists did not have the same weighty baggage as the psychoanalysts, who had become target practice for positivists and critical rationalists (Bud and Bunge, 2010; Popper, 1962; Eysenck, 1985). Their methods were close to those of the empiricist philosophers, even if they were averse to the objectification of human subjects it implied. The fact that phenomenology was, by and large, a *methodology* derived from philosophy, and not an overly ambitious version of deep philosophical subjectivism, probably permitted it some extra legitimacy.

Existential psychologists, like their psychoanalytical colleagues, were held in some suspicion on the margins of academic respectability. They used terms that made those in mainstream psychology feel uneasy, such as 'authenticity', 'love' and 'will' (for example in the work of Abraham Maslow, Rollo May and Viktor Frankl). That intellectual queasiness about existential psychology reflected the positivist assumption that facts and values must be kept separate and that objectivity meant neutrality. These emotional and emotive aspects of existentialism threatened the value-neutrality being claimed by positivists. By contrast, phenomenological methods could, in principle at least, bracket their consideration and thereby accrued some credibility.

Moreover, existentialism explicitly pre-empted positivistic claims about fixed psychological covering laws by emphasising contingent and unique experiences: how does this particular person living in this particular social context make sense of their particular life? Existentialism and phenomenology emerged as well in dissenting psychoanalytical texts (e.g. Laing, 1960) and became misleading as a common hybrid (the 'existential-phenomenological' approach). However, they were and are different. One is a method for investigating the content of consciousness, whereas the other is about how we view our own unique existence and the implications of doing that honestly or dishonestly before we die. Put differently all existentialists are phenomenologists but not all phenomenologists are necessarily existentialists. As a method, phenomenology might be adopted by psychologists, whereas the larger philosophical expectations of existentialism might be a bridge too far for some.

We can see here then that the role of *methodological credibility*, rather than the nuances of competing theoretical claims, became the main political concern when modern psychology created its favoured naïve realist rhetoric of justification. Although phenomenological methods still dealt with the dubious realm of inner life (according to behaviourists), they were at least *credible methods*. Whereas the psychoanalytical method in its various manifestations insisted on the hermeneutic authority of the analyst, phenomenology was concerned with clarifying direct accounts of experience; one was expert-centred the other was (or tried to be) person-centred. Maybe this appealed to the spirit of democratic individualism, especially in the USA, with the work of Carl Rogers and George Kelly supporting this point.

This matter of credibility, based on methodological prowess within the positivist mainstream, became evident in psychology, with its enthusiasm for the repertory grid offered by Kelly's personal construct theory (Neimeyer, 1985). Another example, in the qualitative methods wing of psychology, was the Q-sort methodology, derived from psychoanalysis, but modified and adapted for pragmatic assessment purposes (Stephenson, 1953). This adaptive interest in methodological prowess was aligned with empiricism's interest in confidently securing the facts (in a narrow way that obscures the actual and the real) and the sort of disciplinary rhetoric laid out so explicitly by Ward and Rivers that I cited at the start of Chapter 2. It was also aligned with the disciplinary interests of psychology as a young discipline, trying to justify its legitimacy in the academy, when squeezed from two sides by the confident and mature disciplines of philosophy and medicine.

What we might call 'methodologism', which I return to in Chapter 12, increasingly defined what was and was not mainstream psychology in the past century. Qualitative methods were just 'in' (even if quantification was preferred). Existentialism and psychoanalysis were highly distrusted. Phenomenology as a method was retained but kept on the margins of disciplinary legitimacy. Nonetheless, mainstream psychology had given itself early permission for the investigation of inner processes in the 19th century. For this historical reason, the study of say memory or reasoning had been conceded by empiricists at that formative stage of the discipline. Behaviourism was *not* then the default form of empiricism or positivism for a while. Moreover, the reality of inner life has not gone away for positivists, as the emergence of 'cognitive science' has demonstrated.

Behaviourism was an implausible philosophical dogma that developed in the wake of logical positivism in the 1930s and afforded psychology some self-confidence as a 'proper' science. By casting inner life 'off limits', it was burying its head in the sand and trying to close down an important implication of **ontological realism**. For example, the *interpretation* of dreams is a transitive matter but our dreams simply *exist* as mental events, whether we interpret them or not (an intransitive matter). This reminds us that the intransitive does not always mean 'stable and permanent'. It can also allude to transitory but still real aspects of our experience. What that experience means and how it arose might then be a matter of hermeneutic speculation but the experience is simply there.

These inner events may come and go privately and without consequence. On the other hand, they may be very consequential when inner events become causally efficacious. For example, Kekulé famously linked his day dream about a snake biting its tail to his insight that triggered swathes of research into benzene-based research in organic chemistry. In another example, when Martin Luther King made his famous 'I Have a Dream' speech he was crystallising eloquently his whole ideology about human rights that drove his life project and eventually triggered his premature death.

However, the behaviourist objection to such descriptions and speculations about inner life pointed to two fair cautions. First, inner reality is by no means easy to investigate and a wide range of options is available to us (from depth psychology, existentialism and phenomenology). A substantial tolerance of uncertainty is required, when and if we embark on making sense of the subjective and intersubjective aspects of being human. It is not for those psychologists who find the interpretive ambiguity that comes with efforts at *verstehen* discomforting.

Psychologists schooled in positivist aspirations seek routines which, *ipso facto* are about the identification of *positive presence* and thereby exclude a wider and more uncertain domain of absent reality, which is permanently unobservable or maybe yet to be observed. This preoccupation with what is positively present in order to justify disciplinary legitimacy was exemplified by the quotation I used from Ward and Rivers in Chapter 2. The problem for psychologists following their lead in the past hundred years is that such an emphasis creates the erroneous assumption of **ontological monovalence**. The absent is excluded and yet it is part of reality; indeed absence massively exceeds presence.

The second prompt from behaviourism that has been useful is the reminder that *pure* subjectivism is itself a dubious project. The radical behaviourists were at least correct about one thing: the importance of behaviour and its contingent context. By not conceding the importance of understanding the actual manifestation of agency in our conduct and actions, subjectivism creates the risk of becoming a vacuous exercise in conversations or unending situated 'narratives'. Our human agency can only be properly investigated by taking the relationship between experience *and* behaviour (praxis) seriously. One or the other in isolation will not exhaust our responsibility as human scientists.

Where does this leave social constructivism? The answer, as is clear in Chapter 7 discussing child sexual abuse, lies still in the risk of denying ontological realism. **Epistemological relativism** without reference to this produces a distorted account of reality. How can we deconstruct reality without at least provisionally operating some common-sense agreement about its character at the outset? This is a parallel and complimentary process to Skinner and his need to account for inner events, while also disallowing their proper exploration on their own terms. Similarly, social constructivists deny the ontological legitimacy of facts (with constant allusions to them in 'speech marks', thus) but then pick them up and drop them arbitrarily in order to defend the mantra that 'everything is socially constructed' and their contempt that 'essentialism' is the original sin of academic discourse (see Chapter 3).

For example, biological types are simply there, they are not constructed. Our genes determine what sex we are, many of our physical characteristics such as eye colour and that we are humans and not giraffes. Testosterone levels in the bloodstream inflect aggressive conduct in human beings not just rats. We, like giraffes and rats, salivate at the smell of food. And like giraffes and rats, the death of our bodies and their biological frailty and vulnerability to sickness before that are certain, not a matter of construction. Our **four planar social being** entails us being part of the natural world, just like everything else beyond us. Our emergent and elaborate use of language has come from that natural world and so social constructivism *itself* is part of that emergence.

Conclusion

I began this chapter using George Harrison's song as a starting point. Its words were profound in two senses, one certainly intended and one maybe not. First, life does indeed flow on inside and outside of us. Both aspects of reality deserve serious consideration, especially the relationship between them. Second, life flows on without us: reality does not require our personal existence, nor even that of the human species. While we are alive, aspects of inner reality, such as consciousness and its constituent processes, as well as the unconscious dimension to our interiority warrant our considered interest, as do the specific and general meanings we attribute to our unique but temporary existence. This chapter has pointed up ways in which forms of psychological theory and practice have either avoided or embraced that challenge. More on this in Chapter 11 when I address the marginalisation of psychoanalysis.

7

IS CHILD SEXUAL ABUSE A MORAL PANIC?

Introduction

This chapter addresses the above question in order to illuminate the problem of relying on social constructivism in social science. In Chapter 3 I noted that the earlier version of social constructivism, based upon symbolic interactionism, was more respectful of ontology than its later radical version. Nonetheless, both are prone to the error of over-valuing ideas and language use. A case in point that I explore in this chapter is the way in which symbolic interactionism shaped the notion of 'moral panics' (Waller, 1936).

Though largely the domain of sociology and criminology, moral panic reasoning is also used at times by psychologists, for example when researching sex offending (Brooks-Gordon, 2010; Quayle, 2015) and the hostility towards asylum seekers (Pearce and Charman, 2011). For reasons to be made clear below, I would argue that child and forensic psychologists need to reflect critically on the plausibility of moral panic reasoning and its relevance to their own work. The enactment of child sexual abuse (CSA), the complicity of third parties and the personal impact on victims are all psychological matters, which we might fail to take seriously if we are persuaded that any concern about adult-child sexual contact is merely a moral panic.

Those using the concept from any disciplinary background, when discussing child protection, fall into a taken-for-granted mode of argument: it is taken as a given that CSA is, in whole or part, reflecting an irrational reaction from the general public. I will demonstrate below that this requires a response of **judgemental rationality**. That is we need to step back and reflect critically on the wisdom of applying moral panic claims in the field of CSA.

To be clear at the outset, I am not saying that the moral panic concept has no utility for us understanding irrational reactions from ordinary people, from time to time, in modern societies. Below then is not a wholesale critique of moral panic theory, though I would encourage a general caution that it is very easy to confuse a *controversy* (in which strong feelings are held) with a *panic* (implying mass irrationality). Such a confusion or conflation emerges readily when we are in the thrall of social constructivism, a point that was illustrated well by Eide (2012), when taking the life stories of people in chronic pain seriously.

At the start of the study, in her search for literature on the topic, Eide came across an internet pro-paedophile site. What struck her was not its existence (we now expect these sites) but the convenient intellectual rationalisations used by paedophiles, when deploying social constructivist theories. The site put forwards the stories of victims of abuse as being 'constructions', which in turn became synonymous with 'fiction'. The slippery interchangeability of the meanings of the words 'narrative', 'construction' and 'fiction' permitted the dismissal of the ontological referents in the accounts, i.e. reports of actual crimes against children. As Eide (ibid.: 140) correctly put it, constructivist theories and their 'obsessive focus on epistemology' lead to a mystifying retreat from social justice for victims. Their accounts were not 'fictions' but testimonies as witnesses to actual events that were crimes against children. In sexual crimes typically the victim is also the only witness, making it easy for perpetrators to deny the charge against them.

In line with Eide's disquiet, in this chapter I want to demonstrate that social constructivist research may not expose injustice or a threat to human welfare but instead it may do the very opposite. I have explored this topic at greater length elsewhere (Pilgrim, 2018a, 2017c), so this is a compressed essay on why we should reject moral panic reasoning, when researching child sexual abuse (CSA), despite moral panic claim makers advancing counter-arguments (e.g. Jenkins, 2004; Zgoba, 2004; West, 2001; Beck, 2015).

Conceptually 'moral panics' emerged as a serious focus in criminology after the Second World War. Two key writers on the topic were Jock Young, who studied illicit drug use, and Stanley Cohen who became interested in warring working class youth gangs ('Mods and Rockers') (Young, 1973; Cohen, 1972). I use their work as a starting point because they set out the criteria for a moral panic. This then invites an **immanent critique**, when and if the notion of moral panic is used to account for a social problem. In this case we can set out those criteria and then check whether they do indeed account for how we understand child sexual abuse accurately.

If, as I a demonstrate below, CSA is *not* a persuasive example of a moral panic, then why do so many intelligent people cling on to that misguided notion? Answering that question then is an **explanatory critique** of CSA as a moral panic. In turn this raises a wider question about multi-layered and dispersed adult complicity in society about CSA. It is an example of what Stanley Cohen himself went on to admit was a collective 'state of denial' characterised by the 'bystander effect' (Cohen, 2001). Accordingly I then move to an **omissive critique** but the first priority here is the immanent critique.

An immanent critique of CSA as a moral panic

An immanent critique about any theory or knowledge claim looks at whether it 'walks the talk' or 'does what it says on the label'. What then is a moral panic according to its proponents? Cohen and Young were concerned about threats to contemporary values and norms posed by some people or their actions. In response, the 'moral majority' were offended and the mass media responded to and amplified such emotional reactions. Formal definitions of this point can be found in Cohen (1972) and Goode and Ben-Yehuda (1994). They pointed up the following five general criteria to define a moral panic:

1. Some transgressive social group creates moral offence in society. Thus moral panics are not invented from thin air but begin with some *actual* social concern to the moral majority in a society at a moment in time.
2. This triggers an emotional reaction of fear, anger or disgust.
3. That reaction is disproportionate and amplified by mass media reporting.
4. These reactions tend to come and go quickly.
5. A moral panic serves the interests of preserving the norms of the *status quo* via a condemnatory and repressive response to expressions of deviance in society. This protects the dominant interests in society of current elites and provides daily security to ordinary people who typically conform to social norms.

In accordance with an immanent critique, we can now examine the degree of fit these criteria have in relation to CSA and the evidence we have about it to date.

1) A moral offence to the great majority

This box is ticked for certain. Adult-child sexual contact is universally condemned, though a key exception to this is the tolerance of men taking child brides in some societies even today (including some parts of the USA). The depth of feeling about CSA is such that in some countries it warrants the death penalty, even though it is not about homicide. Despite the note on child brides, more generally in the USA any sexual contact with a minor is considered statutory rape.

2) There is an expression of fear anger or disgust

Yes this too is typically the case in relation to CSA. It seems then that as far as the first two expectations of moral panic are concerned, then CSA is a legitimate case. This is why it has attracted the attention of moral panic theorists, which I return to later. However, as we move now to the other expected features of a moral panic, we find that CSA is not at all a good example.

3) The offence expressed is disproportionate

This is not the case in relation to CSA. Indeed many of those investigating its scale suggest that we are not concerned *enough* about protecting children and are in a range of ways complicit in their victimisation (Cheit, 2014; Salter, 2017). Stanley Cohen himself later in his life began to concede this point about CSA and argued the problem may not be moral panic but 'moral stupor' or 'chilling denial' (Cohen, 2002). A genuine challenge when appraising this criterion is methodological. CSA offending entails the offender avoiding detection and, as with torture (see Chapter 8), they seek to suppress evidence of the offence; typically offenders are devious and furtive.

The emergence of the offence in family systems (most abuse occurs in the home) means that there is also pressure on the victim to keep incidents secret. Some very young children are not aware they are being abused and older ones may be reliant on the security of their relationship with their abuser. An exposure of the offending may jeopardise the family, a point that abusers may communicate to manipulate the victim. This has led to a scenario where official enquiries into incidence (first cases) and prevalence (accumulating cases at a point in time or across time) have offered estimates, which are provisional but with the caveat that they are probably *underestimates*. We now know that only about a third of cases of CSA are reported to the police and analyses of reported cases suggest a nine-fold underestimation of incidence (Finkelhor et al., 2008; Children's Commissioner's Report, 2016; Council of Europe, 2007; Pereda et al., 2009; Radford et al., 2011).

Not only is CSA under-reported and underestimated, its short-term and long-term harm are now well established (Kendall-Tackett, 2002; Cutajar et al., 2010; Hillberg et al., 2011). This evidence points to why survivors of CSA are over-represented in their chronic healthcare contact (Jonas et al., 2011; Del Gaizo et al., 2011). Moreover, the health economic toll on mental health, criminal justice and drug and alcohol services combined is now documented (Saied-Tessier, 2014).

All of this evidence is relevant because one defence used by child sexual offenders is that their actions were not harmful to the child. A similar case, denying harm, has been made at times as well by moral panic theorists, when offering CSA as a case example. Whilst some *individual* victims of CSA may survive with no apparent adverse psychological consequences, it is clear now using health economic assessments across data sets (a form of retrodiction) that CSA increases the probability of a range of personal problems, including higher risk of the re-victimisation of survivors in their intimate relationships (see above and Filipas and Ullman (2006)).

Thus the harm of CSA is to society not just to the individual victims of CSA and this point extends to the consequences for detected perpetrators, who are processed through the criminal justice system. They may spend repeated periods in prison and efforts at rehabilitation or 'treatment' there have had a poor outcome (Hanson and Morton-Bourgon, 2005).

Poor treatment efficacy has consequences for re-offending. In relation to the latter, estimates vary from 8 to 150 victims per perpetrator across their life span (Lockhart et al., 1989; cf. Beckett et al., 1994). Perpetrators too may suffer career damage and alienation from their relatives, reporting mental health and substance abuse problems. Thus the personal and social impact of CSA goes far and wide. CSA is not just a socio-psychological conundrum (is it or is not a moral panic?), it is also a major public health problem confirmed by a range of evidence about its costs to victims, perpetrators and society more generally.

4) Moral panics are ephemeral

Apart from the universal incest taboo, for over a century in most countries there has been a persistent and enlarging policy of child protection. The latter has been applied to both family and external settings. Not only are their policies to protect children and checks on those working with them, backed up by laws criminalising adult-child sexual contact, there is no evidence for the foreseeable future that this trend will change. This aspect of a typical moral panic is therefore inapplicable in the case of CSA.

5) Moral panics protect current elites by demonising low-status social groups

This is not true in relation to CSA. Investigations of CSA in church settings show that clerical authorities protected their own and suppressed a moral panic they did not whip one up at all. Moreover, the classic moral panics described by Young and Cohen identified low-status or already stigmatised groups in society as 'candidates' for a moral panic. For example, working-class youth (girl gangs, Mods and Rockers), homosexuals (the 'Gay plague' of AIDS), immigrants etc. are suggested as being typical. But in the case of CSA, the perpetrators are ordinary people (typically men) such as parents, teachers or academics. Some are even high status such as pop stars, politicians and TV celebrities. This list is not consistent with the traditional focus of a moral panic, which are people who are distrusted or stigmatised on an *a priori* basis. In the case of CSA, perpetrators are only stigmatised *post hoc* after their discovery or prosecution.

This criterion then is not aligned with or applicable to CSA. Moreover, in this case what we can say is that the *victims* not the perpetrators are low status in modern societies. Children lack social, economic or political power. In addition many victims of CSA are situationally vulnerable and powerless; trapped in families or institutional settings isolated from scrutiny. In the latter, children in the care of state or religious institutions have typically been of low social class and may be there because of their waywardness or delinquency. In that sort of context perpetrators could treat their victims like 'moral dirt'. Powerlessness then is relevant in CSA but it relates to victims not perpetrators. In the example I gave of child brides in some parts of the USA, the girl tends to come from a poor background.

A final point that cuts across all of the above is that in a classic moral panic the mass media are central to its amplification. As Cohen put it pithily 'no media – no moral panic' (Cohen, 2001: 3). However, in the case of CSA the mass media have been highly inconsistent in the reporting and framing of the social problem. Some reports focus on the animalistic ('beasts') or sub-human qualities of perpetrators (making them 'folk devils', to use a term from Cohen). At other times though, the folk devils are state employees, such as social workers, child psychologists and paediatricians (agents of the 'nanny state'), who are accused of intruding, like meddling busy bodies, in the lives of ordinary and innocent families. At other times the reverse might also be reported: why did the state authorities *not* intervene earlier or at all?

Thus child protection workers are 'damned if they do and damned if they don't' from one report to another. In other cases, investigative journalists have calmly collected evidence about perpetrators and passed the information on to the police. Thus mass media involvement has been highly contradictory in, or ambivalent about, the reporting of CSA. This reinforces the conclusion that CSA is not a moral panic but a *controversy*, which is not logically or empirically the same.

Controversies can reflect legitimate moral or political concerns about human welfare. For example, children in general are powerless compared to adults and some children are particularly vulnerable (the poor, the disabled and the entrapped). Strong feelings about this scenario do not have to be connoted as a panic at all, because they are based upon a form of judgemental rationality and compassionate concern. This inconsistency in the mass media undermines the case of CSA being a moral panic. However, the main problem is that unlike classic moral panics, CSA is clearly underreported, the harm it creates has been under- not over-estimated, and elites in society have benefited from news of it being suppressed not whipped up.

Thus an immanent critique concludes emphatically that CSA is *not* a moral panic. If moral panic claim makers were to limit their claim to the fact that CSA is indeed an emotive public policy *controversy* (which it clearly is) then that would be legitimate. However, to stretch that claim to argue that CSA is a classic moral panic is totally implausible. Our fair-minded judgemental rationality, when faced with the above evidence, confirms that conclusion. This then raises the question about why such a claim is maintained as being plausible by some lobbyists. I turn now to an explanatory critique.

An explanatory critique of CSA as a moral panic

For those new to this topic, they may be surprised that in the light of the above immanent critique, anyone would still try to claim that CSA is a moral panic. This would be an understandable reaction. However, such a surprising position has remained a recurrent, albeit minority, contrarian stance in social science and in child protection work (Pilgrim, 2017c). When researching my book on this topic (Pilgrim, 2018a), I came across four overlapping groups, which have continued to promote a moral panic claim about CSA, namely:

1. Sexual offenders trivialising harm and arguing for their right to have sex with children (Mihailides et al., 2004).
2. Libertarian political lobbyists arguing for sexual freedom across the life span, for example when a groups of French intellectuals lobbied their government in 1977 – see below (Krizman, 1990).
3. Libertarian sexologists emphasising natural variations in sexual expression, which encourages judgemental relativism at the expense of judgemental rationalism (Plummer, 1991; Constantine and Martinson, 1981; Rossman, 1985; Sandfort, 1987).
4. Social work re-professionalisers resenting criticisms of their failures and restrictions on their daily discretion (Clapton et al., 2012; cf. Shaw and Kendrick, 2017).

These groups occasionally overlap. Although the first of these are usually identified for their cognitive distortions, when special pleading that their individual contact with children was benign and beneficial not harmful to the child, some of them have published formal political arguments to justify the abolition of an age of sexual consent (O'Carroll, 1980). Beyond these politicised paedophile activists, there have also been academics seeking a liberalisation of the law on the latter, who were subsequently found to be offenders against children.

For example in 1981 the Australian criminologist Paul Wilson produced *The Man They Called A Monster: Sexual Experiences Between Men and Boys*, which contained the libertarian tropes of the time: the boys are participants not victims; it was a fulfilling not harmful experience for them; and there is a moral panic about paedophilia and so we must campaign to overcome social and political barriers to its legalisation (Wilson, 1981). In 2016 he was convicted of a sexual assault on a 12-year-old girl in the 1970s.

In the UK two high profile academics, the social worker Peter Righton and the child psychiatrist Morris Fraser, had extensively published material on adult-child sexual contact. Subsequently the first was found in possession of indecent images of children and the second prosecuted for molestation of boys. In the case of Fraser he continued to write on paedophilia after his convictions for sexual assaults on boys in the 1970s. Both were members of the Paedophile Information Exchange, which existed in the UK between 1974 and 1984.

An important collection *Perspectives on Paedophilia* edited by Brian Taylor appeared, which included contributions from Righton and Fraser (Taylor, 1981; Righton, 1981; Fraser, 1981; Plummer, 1981). Taylor (a sociology lecturer at the University of Sussex) under the pseudonym 'Humphrey Barton' was the Research Director for PIE, which lobbied the British government to liberalise policies on adult-child sexual contact, although this declaration was not made in the 1981 collection he edited. Arguments under the name 'Barton' were virtually identical to those he rehearsed under his real name of Brian Taylor (Barton, 1976; cf. Taylor, 1976 and 1981). The gist of the arguments from these published academics has been that adult-child sexual contact is harmless and that sexual expression in all its forms is a healthy, not pathological, human right.

Libertarian intellectuals in France including Michel Foucault, Jean-Paul Sartre, Simone de Beauvoir, Jacques Derrida and Roland Barthes also lobbied unsuccessfully in 1977 for their government to abolish the age of sexual consent. Thus we can see a direct parallel process between the individual rationalisations for their actions preferred by child sex offenders (their 'cognitive distortions') and the wider ideological justifications by some libertarian intellectuals about adult-child sexual contact.

This sort of research and lobbying from the 1970s began to peter out but never disappeared completely. For example, Ken Plummer, a prestigious UK sociologist and researcher of sexualities (who note has no criminal record), reported his ethnographic findings about PIE in the 1981 Taylor collection (Plummer, 1981). Plummer, who joined PIE to access his material and subjects, continued to publish material that argued that paedophilia was a human right and that children were not harmed; accordingly CSA for him remained a moral panic.

More recently Plummer has apologised for his earlier work, if it might have been used to do harm to children, and he has removed all of his earlier publications about this topic from his website (Plummer, 2014). In 1991 he was still defending paedophilia as a legitimate sexual orientation akin to being gay. He invoked the logic of moral panic theory in this article: 'As homosexuality has become slightly less open to a sustained moral panic, the new pariah of the "child molester" has become the latest folk devil to orchestrate (sic) anxieties over the moral and political life of Western societies' (Plummer, 1991).

Over the past 40 years other academic writers have chipped in occasionally to propose CSA as a moral panic and to argue for a liberalisation of laws about the age of sexual consent. These have included libertarian critics of excessive state surveillance, such as Frank Furedi, who argues that this undermines the labour rights of professional social workers and the confidence of ordinary parents to look after their children. He goes as far as arguing that unreasonable concerns about child protection actually put children at more not less risk but he offers no evidence for this claim (Furedi, 2013, 2015).

The work of Ken Plummer in his role as the ethnographer of PIE in the 1970s was replicated in part, in a later study of continuing paedophile advocacy groups at the turn of this century, with the research of Richard Yuill. However, now the latter libertarian academic defences were also co-opting postmodern contributions of Foucault and Queer Theory, not just the moral panic tradition from symbolic interactionism (Yuill, 2004). These sympathetic portrayals of paedophilia form part of our collective denial of the scale and adverse consequences of adult-child sexual contact and this has not gone unnoticed or unchallenged (Greer and McLaughlin, 2015; Salter, 2017).

A final couple of relevant points to note in this section need to be made for readers new to this topic. First, paedophilia is a sexual orientation and only becomes an offence when enacted. Also many non-paedophiles, especially inside family systems, sexually assault children and so it is important not to crudely conflate paedophilia and CSA. Paedophilia is a persistent and general sexual interest in pre-pubescent children, whereas many intra-familial assaults are opportunistic and targeted on particular children, including teenagers, living at home. Moreover, the mass media are prone to call

all sexual offending against children 'paedophilia', when most of the victims are mid-teenagers (under the age of consent). In the sexology literature, the desire for this post-pubescent group is instead dubbed 'hebephilia'.

A second final note of clarification, in relation to explaining our collective failure to face up to the full scale of CSA, is the false negative picture created by the criminal justice system in relation to historical cases. I mentioned that only a third of cases of CSA are reported to the police. Not all of these reach court and the attrition rate for sex offences (against both adults and children) is high. At times this means that the perpetrator may be dead or too old to face trial because of impaired mental capacity. Given the principle of presumed innocence, a proportion of the latter who were actually guilty of crimes against children, would be on record as being 'innocent'. This highlights why there is a discrepancy between the actual prevalence of CSA and its empirically recorded prevalence (Connolly and Read, 2006; Fitzgerald, 2006). A false negative picture is driven then both by incomplete original reporting and subsequent attrition rates in the court system. This contributes to a complicit culture about the scale and harm of CSA because non-offenders in the general public may wrongly assume that it is a very rare crime.

An omissive critique of CSA as a moral panic

The ambivalence of Stanley Cohen about CSA ('moral panic' or 'moral stupor' and 'chilling denial'?) offers our clue about an omissive critique. There have been active attempts by some in the academy to trivialise the adverse psychological impact of CSA at the individual level and its social and economic costs to society. The lobbying from those intellectuals in PIE, and the libertarian philosophers in France during the 1970s, sought to formally reject any legitimate critique of adult-child sexual contact. Trivialisation about harm has been interwoven with claims that adult-child sexual contact is a human right and that the only harm done to victims emerges because of the drama of criminal investigation and subsequent prosecution. Those in the Taylor collection, along with more recent moral panic claims from Furedi, Yuill and Cree and her colleagues have sustained this contribution to a body of knowledge, which minimises adverse consequences and maximises the assumption of a moral panic.

But these libertarian academics (some but not all of whom proved to be child sex offenders) are only part of the picture. In addition, elite groups in political parties and religious organisations have also worked towards suppressing evidence of the scale of CSA in their midst. This cover up mentality was also evident at the BBC, when its managers failed to control the sex offending of Jimmy Savile, who is now on record as the most prolific sexual offender against children in British history. After Savile died it became clear that it was common knowledge in the BBC that he routinely had sex with children but this was ignored by both his managers and his peers.

In the early chapters of my book, *Child Sexual Abuse: Moral Panic or State of Denial?* (Pilgrim, 2018a), I look at the evidence about the role of elite groups in society in suppressing evidence of CSA, as well as describing the challenge of exposing its scale in child care organisations. Those with the power to do so will at times protect their own colleagues and organisation by suppressing evidence of CSA. Those trying to expose this process are accused of being 'conspiracy theorists'. However, if we are to take seriously the social psychology of CSA and its denial then, just like the notion of a moral panic, any claimed 'conspiracy theory' invites judgemental rationality (Pigden, 2007; Bale, 2007).

Those committing crimes *can and do conspire with others*. For example, look at the planning of a bank robbery or gangs involved in online scams. Given this, we can look carefully at the circumstances in which conspiracies occur rather than preemptively deem such an investigation to be irrational. When used for rhetorical purposes both of the terms 'moral panic' and 'conspiracy theory' may discourage critical reflection case by case and encourage unwarranted generalisations about social processes. The presumptuous rhetoric built from them can deflect us from rational judgements. We do not know *in advance* whether a conspiracy did or did not occur in a particular circumstance. Each case needs to be appraised in its particular context as a **concrete singularity**.

This active suppression of, or laziness about, critical reflection has joined wider social processes of complicity. When we look across of all of the case studies of CSA, whether they are about families, in schools and childcare sites, by politicians and pop stars, on the streets or in religious institutions, there is a consistent theme: non-offending third parties fail to report the abuse or take corrective actions. Thus Cohen was correct (eventually) to conclude that we must address the 'chilling denial' and 'moral stupor' of ordinary people, who themselves are not sexual offenders. Cohen called this the 'passive bystander effect'. The psychological conundrum here then is not about the perpetrator but the onlooker: it is not what people do but what they do *not* do. This reminds us of Burke's homily, 'The only thing necessary for the triumph of evil is for good men to do nothing.' Complicit inaction in a wide range of settings maintains a denial of the occurrence and impact of CSA. This wide and recurrent matter of complicity has to be at the centre of any omissive critique. I return to inaction in Chapter 9 when discussing that we often do not protest when its need is fully justified.

Discussion

We can see from above that the resources of immanent, explanatory and omissive critiques from critical realism enable us to understand CSA in a clear way. It establishes that CSA is not a moral panic, explains why some people mistakenly hang on to that assumption and provides a window into a range of matters that distort our understanding of the scale and impact of CSA, via contrived or unwitting ignorance. Inaction and complicity are common psychological processes to understand in their context.

This case study of CSA alerts us to the pitfalls of social constructivism; even the less radical version of symbolic interactionism favoured by the early moral panic theorists. Later moral panic theorists looked to postmodern philosophy to justify their cause. Even more blatantly, that intellectual cadre of leftist libertarians like Sartre and de Beauvoir and postmodern mischief-makers like Foucault and Derrida in 1970s' France made their (unsuccessful) case to permit adult-child sexual contact. The intellectual anarchy of postmodernism I discussed in Chapter 3 has been linked to progressive and liberating ways of thinking. However, as I noted in that chapter this is not a straightforward matter at all: such forms of radical demand have turned out to be part of the problem, not the solution, to the global challenge of CSA.

This challenge is enlarging since the innovation of the internet. This is an example of how the **transitive aspect of reality** and the **intransitive aspect of reality** can mutually affect one another in society. Whereas, prior to the internet, indecent images of children were produced in printed form for circulation to a restricted group of offenders, now those indecent images have become easily accessible. Offenders can even now be involved in the online *in vivo* abuse of a child in another country. In the past decade there has been a year-on-year increase in the use of the internet to sexually abuse children. This takes two forms. The first is the distribution of indecent images and the *in vivo* involvement just described. The second is the use of the internet to groom children as a stepping stone to physical contact with them.

The internet has been a game changer for CSA. Accordingly, research into the scale of CSA implicating both perpetrators and victims has utilised online data to answer new questions about the sexual interest of adults in children (Wurtele et al., 2014; Dawson et al., 2014; Seto, 2012). Another impact of a shift to online offending has been that it has triggered new forms of vigilantism, which seemingly confirm a moral panic for those still taking that contrarian position. However, as a sign of a proportionate reaction from citizens about sexual offending against children, an irony is that police forces are struggling, for resource reasons, to detect all online offenders and prosecute all cases requiring it. Some forces have now co-opted vigilantes in their assiduous, albeit overly zealous, detective work to compensate for a lack of police resources to deal with the scale of online offending.

Conclusion

This chapter has been an opportunity to demonstrate the pitfalls of social constructivism by examining the case study of CSA as a purported moral panic. The latter position has been around in social science in the past 50 years, although I noted that a seminal leader in moral panic theory, Stanley Cohen, slowly changed his mind over time. By the end of his life he raised questions about 'moral stupor' and 'chilling denial'. That ambivalence did not prevent some in the academy continuing with their contrarian line of reasoning about CSA. Although symbolic interactionism has been the main social constructivist reasoning underpinning moral panic claim making, we also need to countenance other contributory mechanisms, including the power of postmodern influences in the academy.

Using the resources from critical realism of immanent, explanatory and omissive critiques, I demonstrated why CSA is not a moral panic but also which social processes might have accounted for the specious belief to the contrary. I finished by looking at a web of complicity operating at different levels in society. Elite groups have suppressed information about offending, not whipped up a panic at all.

Some of those offering intellectual justifications for liberalising laws about the age of sexual consent turned out to be sex offenders.

Any psychologist now wishing to understand CSA today has to begin by reflecting on the plausibility of it being a moral panic. If the contrarian position is still appealing, then the immanent critique I began with would require a list of evidence-based counter-arguments. To merely note that CSA is something many people get upset about is not a sufficient case to defend it being a moral panic. Not only is a public controversy or concern not necessarily a collective panic, in the way those like Cohen and Young portrayed the social groups and events in their research at the end of the 1960s, but it also requires that we look at Cohen's later interest in 'the passive bystander effect'.

Finally, I noted how human thought and activity has changed the technological character of CSA. Prior to the internet emerging, offending was limited to sexual contact inside and outside of families, along with the production and distribution of indecent images of children in print. Now the internet affords the possibility of the online distribution of such images to a much larger audience. Moreover, *in vivo* sexual assaults on children can now involve paying consumers. The latter may consider themselves 'non-contact' offenders but of course every online indecent image of a child has entailed the actual abuse of that child. Not only has CSA not been magically abolished by dubbing it a 'moral panic', the scale of its occurrence and the adverse consequences for victims and society this brings have actually increased, not decreased, over time. Moral panic claim making obscures our understanding of CSA, when encouraging judgemental relativism at the expense of judgemental rationality.

8

HOW DO WE KNOW IF A PERSON HAS BEEN TORTURED?

This chapter considers a practical challenge facing some applied psychologists when they are asked to assess people who report being tortured. In particular this illuminates the distinction between **the actual** and **the empirical** from critical realism. Naïve realist criteria for truth (whether in applied psychology or in legal proceedings) mean that there will be a bias to be suspicious, or even dismissive, of actual events that were unobserved, in this case because they were deliberately obscured from view. If they were obscured from view then they cannot be positively verified (the fetish of positivism).

Given that some crimes such as torture and many sexual offences are overwhelmingly about private events, and perpetrators wish to avoid the legal consequences of their actions, this typically renders the victim as the sole witness and reporter of what has occurred. I will return to this core point but first a brief description of torture will be provided for those new to the topic.

Torture: a summary of the topic

In pre-modern times, the use of torture to gain confessions, or simply to inflict pain for wrongdoing for an actual or claimed wrongdoing, was commonplace in many societies. Today it is considered a hallmark of a civilised society that any government should condemn and not use torture but much hypocrisy is evident still about this matter. Torture can also occur outside of sanctioned settings of confession and punishment of those deemed to be enemies of the state. For example, the word in its everyday sense can be applied to the cruel treatment of animals and children. The infliction of physical and/or emotional suffering is also found in sexual life in the game playing of consensual adults ('BDSM') and the actions of sexual offenders. The line between these can be blurred when some offenders can claim consensual activity, when facing charges of rape or homicide.

Psychologists have a legitimate interest in torture for a number of reasons. It is a recurring aspect of human conduct entailing an extreme interpersonal event. The motivation and role of the perpetrator and the vulnerability of the victim are important to understand within the latter events and their dark form of temporary intimacy. Also, psychologists recruited by the state to advise on interrogation techniques have a moral responsibility about supporting or resisting governments promoting and enacting torture. Psychologists have not always covered themselves in glory in protecting human beings from cruel and degrading treatment when offering their advice.

The prerequisite of dehumanisation

A useful social psychological process for understanding torture is that of dehumanisation (Viki et al., 2013) or 'infrahumanization' (Leyens et al., 2000). Recently this has also been described as 'othering', which is a necessary but not sufficient condition for torture to emerge. It is part of a **generative mechanism** of torture, with other parts including the personal characteristics of the torturer, the ideological and political setting of the host society that dehumanises some groups but not others, the required social isolation to ensure privacy for a crime, and the contingent availability and vulnerability of the incipient victim. At times victims may be blamed for their own victimisation: assaulted children are accused of defiance or seduction and political opponents are accused of violating the security of the nation state. These people, the argument goes, 'deserve what they get' because they (not those abusing power) are morally inferior or even not really human at all.

In the context of say sex offending, the perpetrator uses their victim as an object to manipulate, dominate and assault, thereby failing to respect their consent and autonomy as a fellow human being. Cruelty to children entails adults using their power alongside their sense of entitlement to inflict pain to punish or control those deemed to be less than human. For example, studies of child abuse in institutional settings (the isolation factor enabling secret crimes) illuminate how a particular form of power can operate in which one party is deemed to be worthy of pain because they are not fully human but merely 'moral dirt' (Ferguson, 2007).

This was the case when religious staff were cruel to children in Catholic Ireland in the middle of the 20th century. Here is a testimony of a woman who was beaten by a nun (a member of the so-called 'Little Sisters of Mercy'): 'She would beat you with the leather strap and count to 100 as she was beating … If you cried you got worse, so I learned not to cry' (Ryan Report, 2009: 144). The latter official enquiry reported this as an example of physical cruelty but the obvious connotations were also of sexual sadism. The girl beaten was tied down with ropes on a bed and other victims reported the nuns stripping them and inserting fingers and objects into their vaginas.

Another example of this pattern of dehumanisation being interwoven with domineering power brings us closer to the main text below, about state-endorsed cruelty, which can also extend to murder. In 1941, as Germany occupied Soviet territory in its military push eastwards, the SS leadership encountered a challenge, when its men were expected to kill monotonously one after another person by shooting them in the back of the head. Day after day thousands of Jews and communists were killed in this way and it began to have its toll on the SS foot soldiers, despite them being committed Nazis. They were shaken and demoralised and they resorted to excessive alcohol use to make their task bearable.

Faced with this crisis of morale in the ranks, in a speech to his demoralised troops in Minsk, the leader of the SS, Heinrich Himmler, made this stirring point by reminding them of the truths of 'Social Darwinism'. He told them to: 'look at nature, there was struggle everywhere, not only for humans, but in flora and fauna as well. Those who didn't fight simply perished … we humans were in the right when we defended ourselves against vermin.' The Hitlerian 'kill or be killed' approach to politics was predicated on the assumption that Jews were intent on enslaving or killing Aryans. Thereby the victims of Nazi persecution and murder were blamed for their own demise, which mattered little because they were sub-human.

This example of dehumanisation (the Jews were recurrently depicted as 'vermin' in Nazi ideology) was extended to other groups including Slavs, 'Gypsies', disabled people, communists and homosexuals. Millions of these groups of people were starved or worked to death in labour camps, shot or destroyed industrially in the death camps of Poland after 1942. In the case of psychiatric patients they were victims of medical killing centres; persecutory agents of the state at times can wear a white coat, not just a military uniform.

Himmler went on in his speech to counter any risk of sympathy for their fellow humans undermining the task of mass murder by holding firm to Nazi ideals, implying not immorality but moral rectitude. This flimsy hypocrisy was highlighted by other recorded war crimes in Poland and occupied Soviet territory, which entailed the rape of Jewish women before they were murdered. Pregnant victims were shot, face on, through the belly. These gratuitous acts of cruelty were not functionally required, given that murder was the goal intended and politically formally justified by Nazi ideology. However, infrahumanisation affords the possibility of actions requiring no moral restraint at the point that a cruel act is committed. Nor does it necessitate any subsequent remorse and regret. War crimes involving sadistic beatings, without or without murder, and the use of rape as a weapon are now well documented across a range of settings (Patel and Mahtani, 2004).

Thus a clear pattern is one of the victims of sadistic power being cast in the role of being less than human. This usually entails a whole group of people being designated as sub-human (Jews, Muslims, Mexicans, asylum seekers, children etc.) and thus not worthy of personal recognition as individuals with names (see Chapter 4). It can be partially accounted for within social identity theory by reference to in-group and out-group membership (Leyens et al., 2000). However, other factors might be included in a formulation of complexity in particular cases, such as our variable conformance to authority, our ideological zeal to defeat and humiliate enemies and our occasional aesthetic or sexual delight in seeing others suffer.

I use the word 'our' here to signal that the willingness to be cruel or to condone torture are commonplace. However, the relevance of contrived experimental scenarios (often entailing the unethical practice of deceit) to the real world has also been noted by critics. For example, what appears to be a demonstration of the widespread capacity to carry out cruel and degrading treatment by ordinary citizens in the famous Milgram experiment (Milgram, 1974) has transpired to be flawed in a number of ways. In fact, the majority of duped subjects *resisted* the demands of the experimenter to inflict pain and so Milgram inflated the depiction of this propensity (Fromm, 1973; Reicher and Haslam, 2011; Gibson, 2019). Nonetheless, a minority of the subjects were indeed willing to proceed to shock others maximally and needed only the very *minimum of encouragement* to do so. We seemingly are a species that shows a capacity to *both* obey *and* to disobey our fellows from context to context, with some of us more than others being open to persuasion from those in authority.

In the Milgram study, what started as a seeming demonstration of human obedience to authority in a dyad (the duped subject and the deceitful experimenter) transpired to be an ambiguous and complex scenario. The context of the experiment (in the authoritative setting of Yale, the encouraging technology in the scientific setting of the laboratory and the changes of compliance levels, when the play-acting confederate assumed to display pain was actually in the room in conversation with the 'shocker' rather than behind a screen) all provided a contrived setting of persuasion. Milgram's experiment was really an implicit demonstration of rhetoric rather than one of direct obedience and so the face validity of his headline findings was undermined substantially by the fine grain of what actually happened in context.

Accordingly we should be wary of the error of **transduction**, as his critics noted above demonstrate well. In open systems, such as the one I described above with Himmler, rhetoric was important, even with those ideologically committed to the Nazi cause. Also whilst the majority of conscience-driven citizens are not at all prone to torture others, they do often evade the evidence of it in their society. The 'passive bystander effect' suggested by Cohen, which I discussed in Chapter 7 in relation to widespread complicity in child abuse, is an example of this point.

Thus, it is as important to consider our widespread complicity in wrongdoing, as it is the presence of a minority of willing sadists in our midst. The latter, like narcissistic power-seeking politicians, will always be there but they require a normative context of permission or encouragement to enact their impulses. This point about acquiescence or non-protest is picked up again in Chapter 9. Conformance is important to consider but it is a social phenomenon in the main. Social norms, group processes and rhetorically infused settings cannot be reduced credibly to individual characteristics. With these conclusions in mind about a minority of us being ready to torture others but a majority of us being passively willing to be complicit in its occurrence, I now turn to the psychological assessments of those reporting being its victim.

The psychological assessment of individual reports of torture

Some psychologists are involved in the assessment of asylum seekers who report being tortured. Critical realism provides us with a framework to make sense of their challenge (Patel and Pilgrim, 2018). Torture is prohibited in international law and the UN Convention Against Torture and Other Cruel, Inhuman or Degrading Treatment of Punishment (UNCAT) has been ratified by 147 countries. However, despite this international consensus, torture is not unusual (Amnesty International, 2011). Article 1 of the UNCAT defines torture as:

> any act by which severe pain or suffering, whether physical or mental, is intentionally inflicted upon a person for such purposes as obtaining from him or a third person information or a confession, punishing him for an act he or a third person has committed or is suspected of having committed, or intimidating or coercing him or a third person, or for any reason based on discrimination of any kind, when such pain or suffering is inflicted by or at the instigation of or with the consent or acquiescence of a public official …

As with the example given of the Nazis above, it is commonplace today still for the governments of many nation states to define all political opponents as legitimate targets of imprisonment, torture and summary execution (Joseph, 2007; Bowring, 2008). Both the US and the UK have been accused of either using torture or being complicit in the transportation of political prisoners ('extra-ordinary' or 'irregular rendition'). This has been described by critics as 'torture by proxy' (Weissbrodt and Bergquist, 2006) and sometimes psychologists have been involved in this process despite it being unethical (American Psychological Association, 2005). The hypocrisy of the Nazis was noted above, but such a trend continues today, given that some countries violate their own policy declarations about torture (Gray and Zielinski, 2000; Harper, 2007).

In Chapter 1, I noted that critical realists constantly steer a middle way between the certainties of positivism and the nihilism or linguistic reductionism of strong social constructivism. I also noted in Chapters 3 and 7 that the latter introduces the risk of deriding the seriousness of harm done to people, which is real and obvious. As I noted in Chapter 7, one social constructivist who eventually conceded that risk was Stanley Cohen, who admitted that his idealist philosophical premises may have led to injustice. Cohen admitted that his favoured social constructivism led to the assumption that it was impossible to make truth claims. He then regretted that position when his own report on torture appeared in Israel and it was dismissed using his very own constructivist arguments (Cohen, cited in Taylor (2007)).

However, the inverse of this problem of judgemental relativism is offered by some positivists writing on torture who take modern norms about torture to be universal (e.g. Kelsen, 2002). Torture for such investigators is what some modern states do, which can just be simply described and measured in a 'disinterested' manner. This tick box approach to events, which avoids the complexities entailed in examining the underlying generative mechanisms of torture and the value engagement required to understand them, is likely to lead to both false negative and false positive assessments, because of the false premise from positivism of **empirical invariance** (Bhaskar et al., 2018). Given this difference of philosophical starting points, the legal context in which particular cases of torture are assessed by psychologists and then adjudicated upon by immigration judges is important.

Lawyers, like psychologists under the sway of positivism, may believe that their views are 'disinterested' but such a position is precarious when dealing with torture.

The matter is further complicated by the ontology of the crime of torture. When it occurs it is done in private and isolated from witnesses. Torturers are skilled in leaving no marks and so formal physical signs by medical examination tend to be missing (Burnett and Peel, 2001; Patel and Granville-Chapman, 2010). This is particularly the case given the typical timing of such an examination, which is often months or even years in the wake of the alleged event. Sexual torture using rape, electrocution or forced insertions of objects will often leave no evidence *post hoc.*

Traditional positivism would be challenged by this scenario because torture cannot be measured directly. For example, a person who was *actually* 'water boarded' or beaten on the soles of the feet or had their genitals electrocuted (all favoured methods) would appear unscathed in a later medical examination. The weakness of empiricism here is revealed: absence of evidence is not evidence of absence.

A second impact of positivism in medical–legal settings is that both law and medicine tend to operate digital judgements of 'absent or present'. By contrast, psychological formulations are more likely to be probability statements of a 'more or less' type (analogue reasoning). However, this distinction is not hard and fast for two reasons. First, despite their scepticism about diagnostic judgements and a preference for formulations, psychologists on pragmatic grounds for communication may offer a view about the former. For example, DSM criteria might be invoked in such a way as to argue that a person examined is presenting with first rank symptoms of 'post-traumatic stress disorder', a taken-for-granted condition fairly well understood by lawyers, who also may use the term 'nervous shock'. Second, judges themselves are well experienced at comparing and contrasting case law and appraising the credibility of witness statements in context. So what over-rides or modifies their digital reasoning is *phronesis* (wisdom borne of experience).

Thus, in practice, both the assessing psychologist and the immigration judge deciding upon the merits of an asylum application, arising from an alleged crime of torture are committed to a process of **retroduction** because *phronesis* cautions that each case is unique and has a particular context (they are each a **concrete singularity**). All parties look at the case before them and try to trace the antecedent conditions that might account for the presentation, taking many factors into consideration. Both lawyers and psychologists are particularly mindful of their obligation to ensure there is no false negative in their assessment. This is because a person who has been tortured should be protected and given refugee status in the country they are being assessed according to the 1951 Geneva Convention on the Status of Refugees.

A false negative decision would compound the violation of a human being, who has already been violated. This might lead to the applicant being returned to the very country in which they had been tortured; a process called *refoulement*. Thus all concerned with making fair and accurate judgements in a process of **judgemental rationality** carry a heavy moral responsibility. In the case of the psychologist's assessment, their report may contribute to a decision with potential life-changing consequences.

For their report to be coherent and persuasive when presented to court authorities, there are three main considerations:

1. Is the psychological presentation of a person claiming they have been tortured consistent with what we already know about the crime in general and its common personal impact?
2. How consistent is their narrative as the sole witness to the reported crime of torture and is that account understandable psychologically?
3. Can the psychological assessment enable the judge to discern the veracity of the witness's account and therefore is confirmatory of the crime reported? In the British legal system, the matter of veracity of the witness account is ultimately the concern of the judge receiving their report. For this reason, any opinion from the psychologist must be offered diplomatically and it must be cogent. If the report is overly focused on the aspect of veracity of the testimony then the judge may be dismissive of the psychologist's opinion. We can note here that this matter of credibility may be prioritised in psychological reports elsewhere, such as risk assessments in the mental health system, but in the Immigration Court it has a different salience and standing.

These three main considerations for the psychologist occur in a normative context that invites critical reflexivity for the psychologist. Torture is an emotive topic, but so is immigration in many countries receiving those claiming asylum. Whilst judges focus on their independence from State interference, they are also human and part of their native society. The same is true of all other parties in the deliberation about torture, from immigration staff at national borders to human rights advocates and expert witness, including psychologists. In some jurisdictions asylum seekers may be viewed as burdensome and suspicion about their motives for migration may be common in the general population. Migrants from countries with high rates of torture may also be associated, in the public imagination, with being potential terrorists or of cynically seeking economic benefit. Those responsible for making decisions about refugees may be prone to mirroring a 'culture of disbelief' about migrants (Independent Asylum Commission, 2008).

In this normative context, the ethical responsibility and interpretive challenges for the psychologists, given the focus on an account of the complainant as the sole witness to alleged torture, are extensive. There is no prospect in this setting of an applied psychologist being 'disinterested' (the preferred mantra of naïve realists – see Chapter 2). Their assessment inevitably will be both value and theory engaged. Their own gender or class origin may inflect their assessment as will their political viewpoint. Like the judges receiving their report, they are human beings not decision-making automata.

From a critical realist perspective values are ontological (they are not simply relative), and that therefore we can make judgements about appropriate and inappropriate values, given the objective here of a psychological assessment. In the case of fairly assessing the likely truthfulness of a witness to a reported crime and the coherence of their narrative then some values are more facilitative than others. An *a priori* suspiciousness of asylum seekers would not enable good judgement. However, being overly credulous and superficial in accepting an account would also have little value. Not only would it not be a sophisticated version of judgemental rationality expected of an expert witness in the legal system to confirm this failure, it would be dismissed understandably by the immigration judge.

Paradoxically, attempts at 'disinterested neutrality' undermine rather than strengthen the credibility of the psychologist's assessment. The practitioner is not neutral because no one is. Their values of cautious credulousness and fair-mindedness are important to guide their assessment. The report of the latter to the court should then reflect a consideration of a range of evidence. It needs to provide an honest contextualised understanding of the person's experience of reported torture and of the personal consequences.

Psychologists assessing allegations of torture and presenting their opinion to court authorities have to weigh up the following.

1) Tactical complicity in medical positivism

This is a glaring dilemma. The legal system is more aligned with medical categorisation than psychological formulation because of its digital tradition of reasoning. The presence or absence of abnormality from medicine aligns with the presence or absence of a crime according to judicial reasoning and focus. The psychologist could accept this digital tradition by simply reporting their findings according to their fit with psychiatric diagnoses provided by the Diagnostic and Statistical Manual of the American Psychiatric Association (American Psychiatric Association, 2013). Instead, a non-diagnostic formulation could be offered or some combination provided. We can see here that the psychologist will come to a position entailing their own judgemental rationality about the likelihood of the complainant being actually tortured. They then are faced with their knowledge of how that view will be received in the particular legal context of their host society. Psychologists are expert witnesses; but they are not the ones making the final judgement because the latter resides with the court.

2) Reflexivity about values

Axiology then is a consideration because the assessment of any claim of torture is a serious ethical matter. The psychologist strives to be objective (i.e. to be true to the object of their enquiry) but they can never be impartial, nor can any other party in this context of assessing the accounts of those complaining of being tortured. They are concerned not only with what is the reality of the case, according to the facts and their interpretation in their psychological report. They are also of a view and preference about the needed outcome. If they are persuaded that they have assessed a genuine victim of and witness to torture, then they will be concerned to influence a judicial outcome in that person's favour. The latter outcome from the perspective of the psychologist will be a 'true positive'; this would be at odds with a 'false negative' if the judge were to dismiss the case as being one of likely torture.

3) Versions of retroduction

If lawyers have a socialised commitment to digital forms of reasoning (present or absent), whereas psychologists are socialised more in analogue logic (more or less) and can report their viewpoint as formulations not diagnoses, then what they do share is a commitment to the principle of retroduction. They are both concerned, when considering cases of alleged torture with the same challenge. We have the evidence before us now, in as complete a form as has been possible in the light of practical constraints, and we must now trace the best explanation for the evidential picture. This is not an easy exercise for anyone. The crime reported occurred months or even years in the past and in another country. Forensic evidence from the crime scene is typically missing.

As for the psychological outcome of torture, post-traumatic symptoms predominate, but this broad picture requires caveats. Some actual (not purported) victims of torture may at the time of interview not be obviously distressed. In the other direction some distressed people may be in the state they are for reasons other than torture in their past. Also the standard description of PTSD is very broad; some victims of torture may not manifest all of the symptoms expected (Patel, 2012). The psychologist's task then is to report the presentation of the person and their history in order to piece together whether the latter did or did not contain torture. They do so in the knowledge that the ultimate judgement about the latter is not their own but that of the courts.

The judgemental rationality deployed in good faith by both psychologists and judges, when faced with this uncertainty requires particular forms of fine-grained and contextualised decision making. They draw upon their knowledge of witnesses in asylum-seeking scenarios and their degree of confidence in the veracity of complainants. These decisions are uniquely human: they could not be made by computers as they entail '*ad hocing*' procedures, common to most forms of human decision making, given the unique context of each case (Garfinkel, 1967).

Both judges and psychologists need to be mindful of different factors in play from case to case. These include for example knowledge of the political situation in a particular country at a point of time relevant to the alleged torture. These might include: known patterns of systematic persecution in relation to particular social groups or political opponents of the state; multiple losses of family members, friends and colleagues; sustained material deprivation; homelessness; racism; and other difficulties experienced by torture survivors in their country of origin or at reception in their current place of residence.

These then are real-world considerations and they reflect the focus of critical realism on open systems. Moreover, although the starting point of legal systems may be characterised by digital not analogue logic, in practice situated judgements are made by flesh-and-blood judges. The standard of proof in asylum law is 'a reasonable degree of likelihood'. This refers to whether it is more likely than not that the difficulties identified are the result of the torture, inhuman or degrading treatment experienced. These then are probability statements, i.e. is it *more or less* probable that the appellant's account of their experience is true? The law broadly may prefer digital reasoning but in a *particular case* analogue reasoning has to be applied.

Discussion

The above description reveals points about ontology, epistemology and ethics. As psychologists, do we believe in principle that torture *exists* in the world? If so, then how do we clarify validly when it occurs in concrete and actual events, which are being deliberately obscured from our view by cruel agents of a state apparatus and their governments? In attempting this very difficult exercise, what is the best way to proceed in any assessment that is a rigorous form of judgemental rationality but is also persuasive to others, who have the ultimate power to adjudicate on the truthfulness of the complainant?

If torture exists as part of our world then its accurate identification, via the accounts of its victims, is important as an ethical imperative. To justify torture, as some psychologists have done to their shame, is quite correctly condemned by our disciplinary leaders. To ignore our role in its assessment because of our anxieties based in naïve realism (offering a view about unobservable events) is not shameful but it is unwarranted. The above has explained how to proceed cautiously in the task.

The retroductive emphasis of case formulation in psychology is consistent with that of critical realism and in the case of considering torture, it is also consistent with forensic investigation in principle. Torture is both a traumatic event and process for its victims but it is also a crime. Accordingly, retroduction provides a common logic for both the proper understanding of a psychological presentation in a particular case and the fair judicial understanding of criminality.

By building up a detailed case study from the testimony of the complainant, the psychologist is considering the ontology of torture (it certainly happens in the world but did it actually happen to this person?) and the meanings they are presenting about their experience (an epistemological matter). In turn the formulation of the psychologist in their report to the court draws on both ontological and epistemological considerations to produce their opinion, in the full knowledge that they are not the adjudicator about an alleged crime but they might influence those who are (the court officials).

Thus an important consideration here is about power in the relationship between the witness, the psychologist and the court. The last of these is the most powerful and the first the least and so psychologists are an important intermediary, leaving them with an onerous but important role in the assessment of torture in those countries receiving asylum seekers. (Note that the latter do not all report being tortured. Torture victims are a sub-set of asylums seekers.)

To summarise the role of judgemental rationality, the psychologist builds up a biographical fragment that contains the alleged torture. They make sense of this in relation to the person, their life and the political and social conditions extant in their country of origin at the time of the alleged crime and known to the assessor. The psychologist must be cautiously credulous but not naïvely gullible. If they do not report gaps and contradictions in the testimony, then the judge assessing the case is likely to spot this shortcoming and may then dismiss the opinion of the psychologist in its totality. Thus the psychologist is not an advocate for the witness but a mediator and interpreter of their testimony. Accordingly they must balance scepticism and credulity in their honest exercise in judgemental rationality and its eventual translation into a written report for the courts.

Judges reviewing cases also exercise their own judgemental rationality. They look at the primary testimony and consider the psychologist's report (and maybe medical evidence if any is available). Judges in this work are used to dealing with uncertainty and they become *au fait* with the political context of cases from countries known for their reputation for torturing citizens. A ruling is then made in the light of all of this, which is a probability statement and fallible. The outcome then is a product of a social negotiation, with the psychologist playing their part.

Although neither psychologist nor the judge are value-free, they can work within a framework which understands or has a consensus about the existence of torture in the world. This could be thought of as a form of objectivity, borne of *phronesis*, about torture. The latter really does exist, and has done for centuries in human societies, and so some people will be inevitably at some point its real victims. When they are, despite it being a crime entailing systematic denial and deceit from its perpetrators and their state employers, it is the role of the judiciary in democracies rejecting the practice to identify its occurrence accurately when considering those reporting it.

This complex challenge about a crime and human rights violation entails a consideration of trust in personal accounts in society. Whilst the witness is the main focus of doubt in that regard (i.e. are they telling the truth?), the good faith of the psychologist and judge are open to critical reflection. Their credentials and respectability increase the chances that the witness will be dealt with fairly but they are both fallible and are not impartial, despite their attempts at consensus building about an objective picture of the case.

This reminds us that a positivist expectation of separating facts from values is untenable. For example, psychologists working in this field may be prone to holding political views that are sympathetic to the plight of refugees in general. Judges specialising in the field also will have their own particular views about migration and human rights. So while rigour and cogency will attend the work of both lawyers and psychologists acting in good faith, they are also human agents holding particular views. They are also citizens, affected by the norms of their time and place and they will exercise variable degrees of critical reflexivity about their personal impact.

Conclusion

To answer the question in the title of this chapter in its simplest terms, we never know *for certain* whether those reporting their torture are telling the truth. The role of psychological opinion in the specific legal setting dealing with asylum seekers is about providing a second order account from the primary testimony offered by the complainant, who is also the sole witness to the crime being alleged. They must balance credulity with scepticism and then report their views honestly. It is not their job to make a decision about the veracity of the complainant's account. However, the rigour and cogency of their report is the basis for their report being taken seriously by immigration courts, which are responsible for such a final judgement.

The complexity of the psychological assessment of those reporting torture provides us with much to reflect on critically in relation to the role of retroduction/ retrodiction and judgemental rationalism in psychological formulations about people in the real world (i.e. in open systems not the psychological laboratory). It also illustrates the need for psychologists to be mindful of their own values, and linked motives, and for them to work with the tension between the empirical and the actual in the world they inhabit, along with those they study or investigate.

That honest recognition separates a critical realist approach to this work from those who wish to adhere to an empiricist and positivist approach to torture. To only focus on the lack of evidence attending the complainant's account and to assume that their legal assessors are value-free in their viewpoint may lead to a bias towards false negative decision making in the legal system. If that is so then it may reflect a residue of positivist assumptions.

A critical realist position on torture is also different though from a strong social constructivist one. As I noted early in this chapter, those like Stanley Cohen was hoist by his own petard within that idealist tradition of social science. Torture is not merely a matter of perspectives (people offering views, and views about views). It has an ontology: it has actually occurred in many human societies for centuries and is ongoing. Sadly that remains the case today and so psychologists will be called on as researchers and expert witnesses in the field of torture and its implications for human rights, for the foreseeable future. Philosophical clarity about the character of their work is important and critical realism is a useful resource for them.

9

WHY DO WE PROTEST (SOMETIMES)?

Introduction

I begin with the work of a psychologist, little known in academic circles, but important for the purpose of this chapter. In 1959 Emory Hestus Holmes (1924–1994) bought a house in the San Fernando Valley. This unremarkable everyday event became significant though because Holmes was black and the neighbourhood at the time was wholly white. He and his family encountered a sustained campaign of harassment. Rocks were thrown through their windows, their car was vandalised and the symbol of the Ku Klux Klan, a burning cross, emerged on their front lawn. In a two-week period Holmes recorded over a hundred incidents after he and his family moved in.

The white vendor (an engineer recorded for posterity, known only as 'Mr. T') fared little better. He was tracked down by racist vigilantes and was forced out of his job for his perceived betrayal of white folk. Holmes successfully sued a neighbour involved in the violent harassment. This was the first legal success of its kind in California. Holmes went on to become a leading figure in the local group of the National Association for the Advancement of Colored People (Barnes, 1960).

After 1960 the US civil rights movement was to set a trend for diverse protest groups in Western liberal democracies. Sociologists soon dubbed these emergent groups 'New Social Movements' (NSMs). They could be distinguished from the older labour movement, with its focus on structural aspects of society (working conditions and low pay) and the first wave of feminism at the turn of the 20th century (focusing on suffrage and property rights). Now the personal was political and for some the political was personal.

Since the 1960s the NSMs have focused on civil society and on personal rights of citizenship and free expression. They have largely been linked to leftish or progressive causes but not wholly. For example, in recent years white supremacist groups have emerged and have been linked to the 'Alt Right' and its alignment with the aspirations of Donald Trump. Another example of this contradiction is the emergence of the social movement of Incels (heterosexual men who cannot find willing sexual partners). Their online campaigning is misogynistic and promotes violence against women and even against men who readily form consensual relationships. Identity politics and its permission to special plead for sexual minorities can thus be extended to Incels and paedophiles (see Chapter 7).

Another example to confirm protest, which is not necessarily a reflection of leftish ideologies, was the destruction of Jewish property by Nazi paramilitaries and their civilian sympathisers on 9 November 1938 (*Kristallnacht*). Some other movements have had an ambiguous claim to progressive credentials. For example, the trans movement is judged to be liberally progressive by some but deeply reactionary and bullying by others (Pilgrim, 2018b). As a further confirmation that protest comes from *both* the left (with its overall goal of changing the world to a new order) *and* the right (with its overall goal of preserving the *status quo* or even returning to an old order), the case of Professor Holmes I offered at the outset makes the point. Reactionary racists protested against his presence and in turn this politicised him about racial discrimination.

Relevant concepts from critical realism

Critical realism provides us with three main guiding considerations for this chapter:

1) *Master-slave relationships* were discussed by Hegel and picked up and elaborated by Bhaskar (1993). Human history and current social relations have been replete with examples of power asymmetries, in which the dominant party has authority without any necessary responsibility and the subordinated party has responsibility without authority. Both outcomes diminish our humanity. The first party will seek to maintain their power and the second may or may not resist it, from circumstance to circumstance. Whereas Hegel envisaged that the dialectical relationship between master and slave would lead to a resigned acceptance or compromise of some version of it in our lives, Bhaskar (in the tradition of Marx) envisaged it leading to a form of struggle for liberation for human beings. Bhaskar's focus then is on the recurring human desire for freedom.

2) *The ubiquity of power.* In tandem with the matter of human freedom is that of power. Bhaskar (1993) drew attention to three versions in human life. 'Power$_1$' is the present but variable capacity of people to think, communicate and empathise with others, which is a function of human agency I discussed in Chapter 4. 'Power$_2$' is contingent upon our particular relations with others and our biographical position within in a web of social structures in flux. It is this second feature of power that Bhaskar called 'generalised master-slave-type relations'. Bhaskar's third and underlying version of the reality of power in our lives he called Power$_0$, which is about the human potential for expressing ourselves freely (as in being creative) or in being together to overcome oppression and injustice (as in our tendency to seek solidarity with others). The failure of us to realise the potential of Power$_0$ is, following Marx, what Bhaskar explores as a feature of our current alienation.

In critical realism the word 'power' recurs often because it is used to describe both the general processes of stasis and change in the world (causal powers in potential or actualised) and the particular expressions of power in the way we relate to one another. The asymmetries of power in human affairs are evident in relation to intimacy (sexual partners, parents and children, teachers and pupils, healthcare professionals and patients etc.). They are also relevant in relations between social groups; hence the discrepancies in power between the rich and the poor, men and women, whites and those of colour, adults and children, those in the labour market and those outside etc. It is little surprising then that so much of sociology has been about studying the process and outcome of these asymmetries of power between social groups, especially in relation to social class, sex, sexual orientation, disability, race and age. These discrepancies of power and their consequences are the material conditions in our social structures that prompted old and new social movements.

3) *Emancipatory axiology*. In light of the assumed alienation to date of our relationship to ourselves, one another and our planet, critical realism offers itself as a resource to consider its reversal or rectification. The research focus of critical realists in any discipline, or when considering any field of enquiry or specific topic from an interdisciplinary perspective, begins with these layers of alienation. Critical realists are then concerned to make a contribution to the illumination of a topic (in this case protest) and to make recommendations in the interests of human welfare.

Evolutionary origins

Protest is not always judged to be in pursuit of social justice, even if that trend does seem to predominate. But *what* social justice is may at times be open to argument and *who* are the identified oppressors and oppressed can be a matter of ideological dispute. Accordingly protest might reflect a deeper, diffuse and ubiquitous psychological proclivity in us all to simply object to what displeases us or what we construe to be offensive about the world or those around us.

One obvious developmental possibility is that we all survive from infancy by protesting; it may simply be an inherited survival mechanism. The cry of a baby signals a mixture of distress and anger about some unfulfilled need. A trick of successful parenting is to decode efficiently that pre-verbal form of communication. This generalisation, linking infantile protest to positive parenting, frames it as an interaction between parties, with a strong evolutionary component. By the time we meet adolescence, resistance to parental and other forms of authority is an unremarkable feature of differentiation or individuation. That separation to create autonomy (i.e. finding and then standing 'on your own two feet') is clearly important for our survival within, and adaptation to, the world.

The development of attachment theory by the psychoanalyst John Bowlby, which I return to later, placed that relational element to individual and collective survival centre stage in animal life, so this is not a uniquely human consideration. If this is in doubt, witness the plaintiff bleat, part distress and part anger, of the disconnected lamb from its mother on a country walk in spring. Bowlby was as reliant on ethology as he was on psychoanalysis for his theory to work in order to describe how parenting works well, when it does. However, protest is not always well received. Some parents assault or kill their crying babies in frustration (and again note this happens in other species).

The roots of the affective dimension to protest might then reflect an embodied evolutionary legacy but in addition there is the matter of the means of collective survival. When our ancestors were hunter gatherers, the emotional attachment learned during childhood in recent times in advanced societies to *specified territories* was absent. Once we settled to grow crops and raise animals for food, the physical boundaries of our existence became important for our security. This shift of the mode of survival altered our psychological position about others, from enjoying mutual tolerance to one of being, and in anticipation feeling, threatened by others.

More generally we know from primatology that territoriality is a key trigger for attacks on intruders or out-group members (James and Goetze, 2001). A good comparison here is the aggressive chimpanzee and the pacifist bonobo (Hobaiter and Byrne, 2014; Wrangham and Peterson, 1997). The first group is highly territorial and patriarchal, whereas the second is matriarchal and relies less on territory. These differences are afforded by habitat differences, even though these species do not live that far away from each other. In primates more generally then we can trace a link between territoriality and aggression to others, prompting the capacity to distinguish in- from out-group membership. Thus, maybe just like other primates, when our habitat is under territorial threat we will instinctively identify enemies and attack them. In our case this is codified in language as hostility to out-group members, which triggers the dehumanisation of 'foreigners' (Smith, 2012).

That recurrent tendency of dehumanisation is real enough and is expressed ultimately in the cruel treatment of others (see Chapter 8). However, as critical realists we need to accept these embodied tendencies, such as the ones implied by these writers on evolutionary psychology, and put them in the wider context of our emergent human agency and capacity for **axiology**. Our species is marked out from other primates in a number of ways, namely:

1. We have migrated purposefully to a greater extent than other apes. We now have very widespread intra-specific phenotypical variations in appearance, with the selection pressures created by climatic adaptations (Gibbons, 2014). This has culminated in the legacy of ethnic and regional differentiation of skin colour, hair type and height. Out-group members are often then identifiable in inter-group power struggles, simply by their immediate outward appearance.
2. There is a strong historical consensus in philosophy that the cognitive competence elaborated by complex language use is what makes us humans and differentiates us from other apes. This view afforded us souls, according to both Aristotle and Descartes, and was the basis for both Kant and Hegel marking out our unique character as a rule following moral species. We have developed language to codify the experience of individual and collective identity about kith, kin and place and we have elevated preferred forms of

normativity (norms, mores and role expectations) into distinctive societal or cultural types. The latter include assumptions about religious and ethnic difference and superiority, as well as us defining power relationships and property rights. In-group and out-group distinctions can be made by humans according to a linguistic identifier in speech, even including the accent we use. Accordingly, we may find parochial, not just nationalistic, suspicious and hostile sentiments about outsiders. This differentiation of others adds to the aspects of physical appearance noted in (1).

3. Whilst we are not unique tool users (this capability is evident in all apes with an oppositional thumb and even in some birds), this is a matter of degree. There has been a qualitative shift at a point on a continuum that has characterised our species. In particular we have developed the use of tools to alter our capacity to defend and extend territoriality (weapons and modes of transport) and to ensure food and water supplies. The means of production of these then became a matter of possession and then a source of dispossession: we can by force steal the property and territory of others. The shift from hunter gathering to agriculture was a turning point and the creation of fire and tools were 'game changers'. This moved us from being mere users of tools to their elaborate systematisation in modes (how not what) of production, which were fit for purpose when adapting to differing environments. Moreover, the domination over other species extended from them being used as a food source and for clothing to their domestication and use as a source of labour for work and transport. With settlement came defensive territoriality. Our elaboration of weapons to kill impersonally at increasing distances (including today with the use of drones) reduced the feedback to us about violent domination, commoner in other intra-specific disputes. In the latter, defeat does not have to necessitate the death of the opponent, only that they take flight or concede submissively. By contrast, mass murder comes fairly readily now to humans.

4. In light of the above, we have witnessed intra-specific power struggles, culminating in varying forms of hierarchy and domination across time and place, especially but not only in relation to controlling the means of production noted in the previous point. In particular we can reflect on power differentials within and across our **four planar social being**. For example, we have been in a struggle with nature to ward off its powers (e.g. its floods, droughts, disease and pestilence) and have sought to dominate it for our own benefit (e.g. the exploitation of its minerals, flora and fauna). This has now culminated in ecological disruption and an existential threat to our species – see below. At the intimate relational level of our being there have been struggles between men and women and adults and children, within families. At the structural level, power has been disputed between classes and social groups. At the individual level we struggle with our life-affirming and life-denying tendencies variably in our lives affecting ourselves and those around us (our 'demons' and 'personal neuroses'). All of these examples might at time implicate expressions of protest. While, for the bulk of us as adults, linguistic competence and its linked expression of our agency are expressed at the individual

level, they are not the whole picture at the structural level. Instead, the latter is characterised by powers beyond our individual control (for example the patterned power of the rich compared to the poor or the patterned power of men compared to women). As individuals we may or may not be aware of those powers of social structures operating in our lives contingently from moment to moment. Thus evolution has afforded us some power (agency) at the personal level but we are embedded in societal structures, which are not of our individual making and of which, for much of the time, we are not even conscious. Thus domination, oppression and the perpetuation of, or resistance to, them can operate at both levels of our existence (personal and societal). More on this below.

Critical reflexivity about the evolutionary roots of protest

For human science, the above points raise the need for constant critical reflexivity and **epistemic humility**. On the one hand we can appeal to phenomena which are unambiguously **intransitive aspects of reality** because they have been and gone (time is an arrow that only travels in one direction). For example, we have migrated across swathes of land, leading to legacies of colonialism. We have made tools that can kill others dispassionately at a distance, creating folk memories of defeat and maybe an ongoing desire for revenge and reparation. We have settled and created defined territories (private property and claims to national boundaries). These in turn have created loyalties, which invoke indignant aggression if threatened, as in reactionary post-colonial nationalist movements. Politics and human protest then emerged from a combination of material conditions, power struggles and the ideological justifications attending them. This led to differentials of power and wellbeing, with the experience of oppression and injustice then following from these ideas put into action; what William Blake called 'mind forg'd manacles'.

This evolutionary context of our species might though risk **reductionism** if we rely narrowly on primatology as our guide to understanding human experience and conduct. For example, sex differences in testosterone and the aggressive appetitive behaviour it encourages may be one factor in explaining strivings for domination, competitiveness, patriarchy, rape or domestic violence but it is not the only one. If we need, quite properly, to attend to the role of evolutionary legacies within a process of **retroduction** of current power differentials in human relationships, then this needs to be done comprehensively. For example, human agency afforded by complex language use means we are not merely 'naked apes' (see below). The opposite side of the same coin is that human agency emerging from our complex language use may seem like our 'trump card' but it is not the only card.

The ambiguities created by us being primates (i.e. part of a real biological type) but us not being other apes or monkeys (i.e. a specific difference within that type) has led to necessary debates. These have focused on how we might make sense of our current politics in the light of a primate history that is *both* shared *and* differentiated by our separation from other ape species around six million years ago (Engels, 1902; Lerner, 1986). Within our four planar social being we are clearly in part a product of our relationship with the natural world, which includes our inherited primate biology, subsuming the physiological differences triggered by our sex chromosomes during our individual development. The caution, for emphasis though, is that this relationship is *one plane amongst four.*

Compared to other primates, we have extensive intra-specific empirical variance in phenotypical appearance, nuances of language use, artefacts and art, power hierarchies and social, cultural and sub-cultural norms. Only we bury our dead, make necklaces and can leave words to be read after we are gone. For this reason, any psychological theory that claims that we are no more than 'naked apes' in its explanations will be a form of crass reductionism (cf. Morris, 1967). Our shared primate ancestry is a necessary, *but not a sufficient,* condition to explain human complexity. Whilst we share some common tendencies, in relation to our fight or flight reactions to conflict, the fluxing balance between cooperation and competition or the assurance of our sustenance and our biological reproduction, there have also been enormous differences in forms of human organisation.

Such empirical variance brings with it wide variability in how we understand ourselves and others (a **transitive aspect of reality**). However, in addition, we are born into a world in which social structures, norms and mores are *already present* and are not to do with our construal of them. Social structures are an intransitive aspect of reality, even if in human affairs the blurring of the boundary between transitive and intransitive aspects of reality needs constant attention (Porpora, 1993; Richards, 2018).

When we are born, we are thrown into a particular world that is structured physically by nature, psychologically by those immediate to us and socially by our species as a whole to date. However, we have the power as human agents individually and collectively to either preserve the social *status quo* or to endeavour to alter it. We have the power to codify, via language use, rationales for those capacities to resist, or insist upon, social change. Those codifications might be about political ideology (e.g. socialism, neo-liberalism) or theological certainties and preferences (e.g. Christianity, Islam). These then furnish others with conditions of loyalty to collective causes and individual motives to act and they are sources of potential and actual conflict between both individuals and groups.

One form of action emerging from these tensions created by power differentials then is *protest* but another is *acquiescence.* These then are psychosocial processes and so implicate *both* psychological *and* sociological examination (see below). When we consider protest and acquiescence all the above is relevant. The shift from a hunter gatherer form of survival (the great bulk of human history) to relatively recent agricultural settlements and animal domestication formalises boundaries, with their assumed property rights, and inflects the sexual division of labour and the need for stable sexual pair bonding (Power and Aiello, 1997). Protest can (and does) emerge then at times about sex and territorial defensiveness in human relationships, even if these do not explain everything about our complexity in general and the reasons why we protest in particular. (See Chapter 11 on sex and aggression in psychoanalytical thinking.)

If the matter of territory does not explain all bases for protest or aggression to out-group members, and competition with in-group members, which would be a form of reductionism, we can clearly identify its role in the politics of protest. Apart from wars being recurrently triggered by territorial boundary transgressions, the tension between aggressive forms of nationalism and the countervailing trend of internationalism or globalisation is evident today. Populist reactions against 'globalism' are evident at the time of writing in Europe and the USA. These are characterised by a combination of pride in, and a wish to preserve, national identity and opposition to immigration (more on this to follow).

At this rudimentary level of human interaction protest seems to contain an important *affective* component both for the protester and those receiving it driven by impulses of individual and parochial collective survival. Our emotional security and our anger and anxiety about that being threatened (actually or in our imagination) might arise then for what we might consider very simple and basic reasons (in relation to our embodied attachments to others and our attachment to place). This then is where protest is rooted. It is embodied and it is located in space and time and is a product of our four planar social being. We are not merely particular moral agents acting in a social context situated in time and space, we also exist in nature (our embodied evolutionary history and our current particular ecological context). However, given our capacity for language use noted earlier, we have developed secondary but very important sentiments (such as hope, loyalty and nostalgia), which elaborate our evolutionary history of primary affect (such as fear and anger) shared with other primates (Leyens et al., 2000).

Apart from our genetic material and the primate history it contains, our material conditions of nature (say climate change at present) shape who we are and what form of struggle that exists for us contingently. Our interpersonal settings, as we develop and network with others, shape whether we are aggrieved or happy with our lot (for example, benign friends and relatives enable our sense of security). Our wider social context affords us varying degrees of constraint and opportunity (for example life in a war zone is certainly distinct from peace time and it is easy to rejoice in the tent of plenty, whereas 'poverty sucks'). From the contingencies of our lives (our **concrete singularity**) we develop or embrace ways of thinking (ideologies) and we produce our particular personal meanings that inflect our tendency over time to protest about, or acquiesce to, the *status quo*.

The biopsychosocial complexity of protest and acquiescence

Thus protest and acquiescence have both contextual and personal elements, some affective, some cognitive, some conscious and some unconscious. Experiences such as national pride, religious zeal or football fanaticism reflect this mixture of biopsychosocial features. That mixture takes place in variable natural not just social conditions, which inflect the probability of protest. For example, angry protests against fracking tend to take place in a context of adverse impacts on the natural world in the *locality* of the protesters.

By the time we reach adulthood, the affective dimension to protests is overlain with complex cognitive or ideological components and becomes the stuff of martyrdom. Here I give a few illustrative examples. In Otranto Cathedral in Italy, the main altar contains a dramatic glass backdrop, which is filled with the sculls and the bones of hundreds of Catholic men who, in 1480, were slaughtered by the invading Turks. They had stubbornly refused to convert to Islam. The 'Tolpuddle Martyrs' were six Dorset agricultural workers, who set up a trade union to campaign for decent work conditions in conditions of rural poverty. In 1834 they were punished for their efforts by being deported to Australia in penal servitude. Martyn Luther King predicted his own assassination and Nelson Mandela told the white apartheid court that he was prepared to die for his cause of a post-racialised democracy.

Thus the intertwined affective and cognitive aspects of protest can literally be a matter of life and death. The leaders of old and new protest movements have been prepared to die for their cause or, short of that, suffer the privations of imprisonment and torture. Protest does seem to increase in probability the more that the daily living conditions of people are considered not just to be harsh and demanding (which might arise, for example acutely, as a result of extreme weather events) but also to reflect forms of obvious and prolonged social injustice. Moreover, those conditions of life may be a threat to survival or they may be dealt with by governments in ways that produce unequal outcomes.

Take the example of the 'Community Charge' in the UK in 1990. The Prime Minister, Margaret Thatcher, had altered a system of local property tax in the UK, which had been in existence since the 17th century (then called 'rates') and was correlated with house size. The new 'poll tax' no longer taxed properties by size but was now a flat rate *per capita.* This meant that a rich person in a mansion would now pay exactly the same amount as a poor person in a small flat. The consequence of this tax to favour the rich at the expense of the poor was that it became immediately unpopular. Large scale riots ensued in a range of British cities. As a consequence, Thatcher resigned and her replacement, John Major, abolished the new tax.

Rioting and physical protests, which might be either peaceful or violent, emerge when individual motives become causes for personal action or when collective ideology becomes collective action. Those ideologies might be political or religious and as I noted above, may be labelled as left or right wing from context to context. Occasionally protest reflects collective grievances but is enacted by only a few people or even individuals. Public suicides exemplify this point, such as suicide bombers in the Middle East in recent times and, during the Vietnam War, when the Buddhist monk, Thich Quang Duc, set himself on fire in public, in protest at the persecution of his faith by the South Vietnamese government. Hunger striking in prisoners is another favoured method of protest, which may or may not culminate in death (examples here were of IRA prisoners in Northern Ireland in 1981 and the suffragettes in England in 1909).

Insights from the Frankfurt School about negativity in politics

Critical realist writers have drawn upon the insights of the Frankfurt School about power and its expression in protest and acquiescence (Porpora, 2015; Sayer, 2011). This is little surprising given that the roots of the two currents of thought are shared (the dialectics of Hegel and Marx). At the structural level the focus was then on Marx's emphasis on the history of humanity being about the history of class struggle (Lukács, 1968). The Frankfurt School writers extended that interest to its implications for the cultural and psychological life of humans from context to context.

For those new to the Frankfurt School here is a summary of its concerns. It emerged before the Second World War in Frankfurt but was relocated during the war years to the USA. At the end of the war some members stayed in the USA and others returned to Germany. The writings of figures relevant in that tradition, which is ongoing, for our understanding of protest and conformity are its early members Max Horkheimer, Wilhelm Reich, Theodore Adorno and Erich Fromm, and then later Herbert Marcuse, Jürgen Habermas and Axel Honneth. (These were all men, leading some to speculate that feminism would have added a dimension to their work, which would have provided it with more relevance and impact (Jeffries, 2016).)

From the outset its theorists were *anti-positivist*, rejecting positivism for similar reasons to those of critical realism, which I laid out in Chapter 2. Although driven in the main by Marxism in its early days, it completely rejected Soviet Communism for its authoritarian and anti-democratic character, flowing from Leninism, and it became increasingly concerned, given the time and place, with critiquing and resisting Nazism. Thus a focus on authoritarianism in society came from this twin frontal attack on dominant political ideologies of the time (communism and fascism). The most transparent claim from the group that protest, as a precursor to positive social change in order to steer a path towards a humanistic and socialist future avoiding capitalist alienation and authoritarian communism, was offered by Erich Fromm. For example, see his classic essay on 'disobedience as a psychological and moral problem' (Fromm, 1963), which was extended later with the subtitle, 'why freedom means saying "no" to power' (Fromm, 2010).

Just as the Frankfurt School focused on the political and social conditions of possibility of protest and conformity, those affording conditions of its time and place (the twin towers of communism and fascism in the first part of the 20th century) also account for the emergence of the School itself. The overlapping feature with critical realism was that of *criticality*. The Frankfurt School writers' focus on the experiential aspects of human alienation in modern societies meant that they were concerned to understand the relationship between inner and outer reality under specific social conditions. Accordingly, this anticipated many concerns of critical realism, including: open social systems in flux; inner and outer ontology and the relationship between them; the value-saturated character of human affairs; and the prospects of, and impediments to, human flourishing.

For example Max Weber, who focused more on status differentials and power hierarchies than the oppositional approach between capital and labour of Marx, also saw conditions of adversity as important for human progress. With that adversity and oppression came human suffering and that stimulated what Weber called 'charismatic needs' and political imagination about better futures for ourselves (Weber, 1968). This chimed with the view of Adorno that we can imagine better futures and we might be galvanised into political action in order to create those alternatives (Adorno, 1982). The problem for Adorno was that given such an opportunity in the face of suffering and adversity, why do we conform to the present and the given, rather than being provoked into critique and radical action for change? That theme was picked up then by Marcuse (1964) in his study of conventionalism in modern American society, *One Dimensional Man*. This theme of acquiescence and social conformity limiting the potential of human beings, as I noted above, was also developed by Fromm (1941) in his *Escape from Freedom*, which takes the potential for human agency in a leftward direction; the opposite one offered by Ayn Rand (see below).

Apart from Marx and Weber from sociology, the other important influence within the Frankfurt School was Freud. It was psychoanalysis then that was being relied upon as an authoritative psychological resource when mapping the dialectical relationship between outer and inner reality (Reich, 1946; Adorno, 1982; Fromm, 1966). This allowed them to try to understand the emergence of authoritarianism as a personal tendency at the individual level (priming compliance with strong and dogmatic political movements), as well as what Fromm called 'the pathology of normalcy'. Our *failure* to rebel or revolt is part of the latter, in the view of the Frankfurt School.

If anyone is in any doubt about negativity in politics and the current relevance of the Frankfurt School, take the state of US and UK politics in the past decade. During that time many poorly paid and unemployed white people have offered their support to conservative anti-immigration policies. During exactly the same period, life expectancy in those very groups has decreased, with 'deaths of despair' from alcohol and suicide being particularly marked in middle-aged men (Barr et al., 2017; Dickman et al., 2017). The paradox of this mortally injured group supporting conservatism (the poor Trump supporter or the working-class Tory) invites a psychological account because they seem to be like 'turkeys voting for Christmas'.

The psychological insights of the Frankfurt School are still important for that task. Apart from the traditional trope of scapegoating out-group members (see below), poor white people in the US and the UK have lived with multiple insults to their egos. Neoliberalism has encouraged consumerism and strong individualism, creating a trajectory that both seduces and impedes them, engendering anger and shame about personal failure. Comfortable elites in our political class, of all hues, are seen by them as distant and unconcerned about their plight. That anger then encourages an attraction to radical solutions that turn against other social groups. They have become 'Strangers in Their Own Land' and they are angry (Hochschild, 2016).

Structured and contingent power differentials

If the Frankfurt School largely focused on the history of class struggle and its psychological implications in modern societies about why we *do not* protest when there are clear grounds to do so, then this does not exhaust the topic of grievance and acquiescence. Power imbalances, and the disputes they create, may be structured as general tendencies, but they also may be contingent as concrete singularities in individuals. The structured tendencies refer to power differentials related to social group membership, i.e. social class, race, gender, age, disability and sexuality. When alone or together, these are embodied in, and experienced by, individuals.

We all know from our social networks that some in our midst are more prone to protest than others. Today explanations from within social psychology, about this spread of activists and non-activists, fall into two main camps (van Zomeren, 2014). In the first is a traditional individualistic account of motivations for involvement say in the ecology movement: we understand protesters by their individual motives about survival. A fear of a gloomy future for themselves and those they care about drive the motivation to protest. The 'rational actor' model of motivation underpins this tradition (Becker, 1976). The second is a collectivist account, where people come to recognise their *shared* grievances with those in a similar position to themselves. This is reflected in the varied campaigns from left and right I noted in the introduction to the chapter. Rather than using a rational actor explanation, these collective forms of action are explained using social identity theory (Tajfel and Turner, 1979). The accounts of protesters will be characterised by a shared set of values and aims operating in solidarity with other group members.

These can be reconciled, according to van Zomeren, by adopting a relational approach. By drawing upon both the attachment theory of John Bowlby and the relational models theory of Alan Fiske, we can appreciate how all forms of protest and acquiescence reflect our *relationality* (Bowlby, 1957; Fiske, 1992). Relationality and its particular contingent meanings are learned from infancy (and, according to Bowlby, from an inherited orientation). The communal sharing aspect of relationality in Fiske's work explains why the *content* of the group's aims might reflect ideological differences, which are afforded by the particular contexts of our socialisation. For example, it could be about international cooperation and socialism ('one race, the human race') or alternatively white supremacy and nationalism ('blood and soil'). Thus the *meaning* of what we do or do not protest about is derived from the concrete singularity of our biographies. We carry our learned view of values about justice from one context to another as we age, but each new context over time invites new appraisals or applications of those values that we learned and reflected on in our particular lives.

The four planar social being framework allows us to reconcile these understandings of group experience and conduct. The social ontology of the group (Toumela, 2013) implicates our embodied experience of emotions, our shared relations with others in solidarity and our particular individual experience of connection with others. Our social context (the particular embedding social structure) affords or prevents such concurrent layers of experiences in groups in particular ways across time and space. All four planes are relevant to understand in relation to group activity, whether that is about singing in a choir, attending a street protest or enjoying a mass sporting event (e.g. Sullivan, 2018).

And then came identity politics ...

Beyond these conceptions from social psychology about individual versus collective explanation of group experience and action, we live in a particular historical period when identity politics has come to the fore. The intersecting impacts and identities of class, race, sex, disability, sexuality and age have created that new political form of identity politics. If the Frankfurt School was interested in the relationship between external and internal realities created by the opposition of capital and labour in modern times, these other sources of power asymmetries extended that concern. For example, within second-wave feminism, we find it applied to the experience of being a woman in modern societies (Eichenbaum and Orbach, 1982). Other writers focusing on the experiential aspects of oppressive or alienated social conditions in advanced capitalism include Richard Sennett and Christopher Lasch (e.g. Sennett and Cobb, 1973; Lasch, 1978).

Although more recently identity politics has drawn us towards the experiential aspects of oppression and away from the structural roots of inequality, and is criticised accordingly (e.g. Benn Michaels, 2006), it has encouraged our critical reflection on power differentials in everyday life, which reflect variants of the master-slave relationship. These experiences are real and routine and can be subtle. They include for example a woman being expected to do the domestic labour in an intimate relationship and the 'micro-aggressions' experienced by black people (e.g. whites avoiding eye contact and showing wariness about them). These contingent points might also be the source of resistance to power. Take the example of a customer being kept waiting at a long serving counter and being told by an underpaid worker to move to a till nearer for the convenience of the latter. This reflects a minor resistance about their alienation by controlling their environment and the customers whose buying power and personal demands they have learned to resent. Service industries (which often entail poorly paid work) create some opportunities to reverse power relationships contingently in such minor ways.

Identity politics has opened up a whole range of fluxing contingencies about the enactment of domination and resistance to it, complicated even further by varying understandings of the implications of 'intersectionality'. The latter at times refers to interacting social forces, at other times it is limited to experienced identities. At the time of writing, an interpretive consensus about the very complexity this has created has not been resolved. For example, a major challenge is that of *epistemological privilege*. The latter refers to the claim made by an oppressed person that their account of reality is sovereign and it debars competing claims being warranted by those not in their position in life. This creates both a logical and psychological challenge of understanding. How do we establish who is more oppressed than someone else (or indeed oppressed at all)? And what if there are competing versions of epistemological privilege? This is the case in relation to the currently unresolved stand-off between transgender activists and gender-critical feminists (Pilgrim, 2018b). My point here is not to dismiss our psychological consideration of epistemological privilege but to argue that, case by case, we need to work through what it means in each context.

Emancipation and axiology

The range of examples given above largely focuses on human freedom, even if the content of that is defined and prioritised in different ways by different people across time and place (the matter of **epistemological relativism**). However, sometimes there have been protest movements about our relationship to other species (Animal Rights campaigns) and the planet we exist on (the Ecology Movement). The very existence of these non-anthropocentric forms of protest suggest that we need to dig deeper than immediate contingent self-interest, as a species or individuals within it (Jakobsen, 2017). Whether the latter is subjectively warranted, as in the recent preoccupation of identity politics with individual expression, or it is objectively explained, as in the anger created by social inequalities, anthropocentric forms of protest do not exhaust our field of enquiry. The emergence of New Social Movements in the recent past throws into relief the complexity of the topic of protest, so before returning to its psychological aspects, I will introduce some relevant philosophical questions about values, power and human alienation.

Protest in large or small ways implies that there is something wrong; we see the way the world is and we want it to be something else, which reminds us of the importance of axiology within critical realism. Our lack of concern for ourselves, one another and the world around us has brought us to the edge of our collective demise, with nuclear war, even today, being a greater and immediate threat to our existence than the incipient ecocide we are all experiencing, year on year. We, or our children and grandchildren, may now be witnessing, not the end of the world, but the end of the human species and the fractional phase of geological time in which we have inhabited this planet: the 'Anthropocene' (Schwargel, 2014). During that period not only have we jeopardised the existence of our own species but many others as well (Ceballos et al., 2017). I return to this point for emphasis at the end of Chapter 12.

Our arrogance in relation to this contemporary ecocide may come in part from our sense of superiority bolstered by our language use and our individual capacity to outwit one another and other species, as well as to dominate nature. A by-product of that power struggle has been intra-specific: some groups, and individuals within them, seek to dominate and enslave others. The latter in turn at some point and in some cases will resist their oppression. It is at this point that protest emerges empirically. Our only brake on anthropocentric arrogance has been our invention of God or the gods in order to create a form of seeming humility when looking outwards in awe at a projected higher power. Unfortunately the balance sheet for the world religions has been a zero-sum game, with an apparent consensus on the rhetorical importance of universal love being negated by the violence and domination each at some point justifies to itself, when straining towards theocratic authority in politics.

Implications for the psychological study of protest

It is this wider social and historical context that is the starting point for exploring psychological aspects of protest. Reflecting on this relationship between context and concrete instances of protest, we can explore its motivational and experiential aspects. However, a health warning is that protest cannot be *explained* by psychology (that would be a form of disciplinary reductionism) but clearly those involved in protest, individually and collectively, have motives and experiences, which are important to document and understand as part of reality. Ideas are real and they can be causally efficacious (**generative mechanisms**), when enacted, or as a process towards the latter (Bhaskar, 1997). These motivational and experiential aspects of the praxis of protest are of special interest to psychologists but we need to be aware that they always emerge in particular contexts. The latter require forms of understanding, which are not psychological but instead are social, political and economic, i.e. they implicate the expertise of other disciplines.

To focus only on understanding the (true enough) tendencies of some individuals to seek and enjoy power over others, or to *only* investigate the motivational and experiential aspects of protest would blinker us from important aspects of context and complexity. Power relations between groups is a sociological not psychological matter. Material inequalities are an economic and political matter. Our fragile earth is a matter for a range of disciplines concerned with ecology. Psychologists then can make a contribution to a complex topic but they must also exercise epistemic humility and respect the need to join an interdisciplinary project of understanding (see Chapter 12).

If we are alienated from ourselves, one another and our planet, then the recognition and experience of that alienation will lead to a range of affective outcomes from despair and depression to anger and agitation. We may also react against that alienation by seeking comfort in diversionary activities such as consumerism, which keeps us in a permanent infantile state of precarious and illusory security (Barber, 2007). We may also seek security by conforming to and reproducing, rather than protesting against and seeking to change, the *status quo*. In doing so we may develop ways of thinking that direct our anger at scapegoats.

A consistent pattern in this trend of out-group hostility is the anger at minority groups that threaten our traditional sources of ideological confidence and social norms, which in turn afford us one form of ontological security; hence the immediate psychological comforts found in religious sectarianism and ethnocentricity. Ethnic and sexual minorities are the recurrent focus of distrust and animosity that *inter alia* serve the function of preserving current power relationships and traditional social norms. They are the ready target for a moral panic (see Chapter 7). We may be convinced that some groups, such as immigrants or indigenous ethnic minorities, are particular blameworthy for their role in the demise of our status and security.

For example, during the Nazi period Jews were held responsible for *all* threats to the pride and prosperity of Germany and were considered to be organising a world conspiracy between Bolshevism and finance capitalism. When Germany began to lose the war against the Allies, Hitler even blamed the Jews for the scenario. That insistent reductionist scapegoating culminated in the 'supreme tragic event of modern times' (Sontag, 1961: 124), with six million European Jews being murdered industrially. Thus if hatred against others is elevated to a political ideology *and* it finds a route to hard power then it can end in genocide. The word 'can' here also points to failed human agency. At every stage of the rise of Nazism, with its particular brutal processes and outcomes, many ordinary Germans, as well as State bureaucrats, chose to play their part, prompting the controversial phrase 'the banality of evil' (Arendt, 1963). The counterexamples were those who resisted that regime, with many of that minority paying with their lives.

Turning to peace time and the capitalist economy, fears of collective forces might also prompt forms of practice based on selfish individualism, such as the moral philosophy underpinning neo-liberalism in recent decades (Rand, 1964; Hayek, 1944; Friedman, 1962). This may seem to solve the problem of alienation from ourselves because it emphasises the need for our immediate personal freedom, free from state constraint, and our absolute individual responsibility as moral agents to face the consequences of our actions at all times. However, it negates or obscures wider responsibilities about our fellows and nature and it decontextualises our choices.

Any form of selfish individualism denies the ontological reliance we have on one another and our natural world. Becoming very rich, whether that is from inheritance or personal effort and good opportunities, endorses the necessary existence of the very poor. The exploitation of others and the natural world are necessary and inevitable practical outcomes of fetishising and acting out the needs of the atomised self. In terms of our four planar social being, it is based upon the (false) assumption that freedom is *only* of operational relevance in the final plane (our unique personality).

Reflecting on structure and agency in relation to protest

An emphasis on human agency without reference to its varying social contexts is misleading, both factually and morally. Apart from the limitations of the egoism encouraged by the intellectual leaders of neo-liberalism just noted, the alternative compassionate version of individualism also has its limits. For example, liberal politicians in recent times, such as Barak Obama, have placed an emphasis upon empathy for our fellows, as an experiential vehicle to encourage progressive social change. However, although empathy seems at first glance to be available for this role in social change, it has two inherent impediments for the task.

First, empathy may, in its selectivity, simply reinforce group solidarity. For example, the white supremacist might empathise with the existential plight of their white fellows, which will then confirm their shared continuing need to hate black people. Second, the affective focus of empathy may encourage us to rest on our laurels and evade a cognitive opportunity and moral obligation to analyse and appraise the social structures, which afford the emergence of injustice and the experience of oppression. For example, feelings of horror and compassion for migrants putting themselves at risk in flimsy boats (a scenario in Europe in recent times) cannot be a substitute for an analysis of a post-colonial context of warfare.

As we begin to reflect on the range of theories or ideologies about what is wrong with the world, we can see why enacted protest may be reactionary, not just progressive. It might be about seeking to return to a previous state of an actual or imagined better life, or clinging to what is familiar, rather than seeking to reverse current forms of alienation for a better future. All of these possibilities have a psychological dimension to them, with both cognitive and affective features, when and if they are expressed as protest.

Finally, the four planar social being framework from critical realism helps us to keep in mind the complexity of protest. Our transactions with our natural world involve dealing with the evolutionary outcome of our primate tendencies, when balancing cooperation and competition and its emotional apparatus, but also responding as human agents to the conditions of the natural world that now exist around us (including the crisis phase of the Anthropocene). Our relationship with others can affect our tendency to protest or acquiesce under particular contingent conditions of social influence or conformity – we can choose to conform or rebel. Our relationship with our embedding social structures affects our actions as well. For example, we can seek to change or retain the type of social conditions we see around us and so we can opt for either conservative or transformative allegiances to forms of political ideology.

If we acquiesce without question or affirmatively to the *status quo* then this too poses psychological questions (see **omissive critique**). For example in Chapter 7 where I examined child sexual abuse, I noted that a more important question than understanding its perpetrators is understanding its complicit non-perpetrators: the 'passive bystander effect'. The questions about acquiescence and blind conformity, or the *absence* of protest, then are unending but here are some examples: Why do some people blithely ignore the ecological impact of their actions? Why do some people stay in relationships that make them unhappy? Why do some people blame the homeless for their plight rather than the economic policies creating homelessness? Why do some of us resent or hate immigrants, coming to us in flight from places blighted by bombs that our own country manufactured? Why do we conform to and support norms that dehumanise others; for example, why was apartheid supported by most white South Africans and even their allies abroad?

These types of questions will never be answered in the psychological laboratory using experimental methods seeking the false hope of transferring discovered constant conjunctions using positivist methods. We need to replace **transduction** with a range of methodologies that contribute to a holistic understanding of the ways in which protest and acquiescence emerge in the contingent social contexts.

Thus the overarching psychological conundrum, as the Frankfurt School writers emphasised, is not why we protest about social injustice but why we do *not* protest about it, or even support its new forms. Protest as a precursor to both social progress and personal change has served the survival of the species well to date. Standing by and doing nothing has at times impaired our survival and flourishing. However, at times protest has been adopted for hateful and life-negating purposes. The psychological aspects of that complexity can only be grasped by being sensitive to our four planar social being.

Conclusion

I have explored the reasons why human beings protest and placed that tendency in the context of alienation from ourselves, one another and the planet we inhabit. By the end, when considering the work of the Frankfurt School and some later political and social theorists discussing consumerism and narcissism under late capitalism, I raised the opposite side of the same coin: why we do *not* protest. To protest implies we want to bring about or to resist change, but clearly much of the time people do not enact that desire or it does not enter their consciousness.

Because protest exists in an open social system, with particular contingent natural and social characteristics, it cannot be understood in the psychological laboratory. Each case will be different and needs to be addressed cautiously and curiously by attending to our four planar social being. Psychologists have a role to play understanding protest but the insights of many other disciplines are also implicated.

10

HOW HAS PSYCHIATRIC DIAGNOSIS *BOTH* FAILED *AND* SURVIVED?

This chapter continues an exploration started in Chapters 2 and 4. It provides another opportunity to demonstrate three linked key resources from critical realism: **immanent critique; explanatory critique**; and **omissive critique**. For readers needing a longer exploration of the topic, I have provided that elsewhere (Pilgrim, 2013, 2015a).

Background to the emergence of psychiatric diagnosis

When we consider psychiatric diagnosis, then **epistemological relativism** is immediately implied. How has psychological difference in various times and places been described and dealt with accordingly (a **transitive aspect of reality**)? When considering this question though, we can also note that no society seems to have been indifferent to those in its midst who are sad, scared or unintelligible or, in some other way, transgress everyday expectations of psychological normality, according to the particular norms of a time and place.

The fact that being profoundly sad or scared or unintelligible seem to reflect recurring human experiences and conduct, could indicate a demi-regularity of what we might broadly call 'distress and madness'. This being the case, then we are maybe also exploring the contested claims about an **intransitive aspect of reality**. As will be clear below, even the most ardent critics of psychiatric positivism do not deny the reality of people actually being distressed or mad in their experience and presentation to others. Indeed it is *because* of these actual events that each society had developed both informal and formalised responses, from adoring curiosity to authoritarian repression, when faced with distressed or mad people. Sometimes those responses have been highly elaborate and enshrined in dedicated legal measures to paternalistically control those deemed unfit to care for themselves.

The recorded concerns from antiquity about psychological difference largely refer to unintelligible conduct; in the modern vernacular, 'madness', 'lunacy' or 'insanity', rather than *distress*. The latter is now used as a generic euphemism, by some, for all unwanted psychiatric descriptions. However, it is misleading because it does not exhaust descriptions of the wide range of deviant conduct and utterances that falls within the remit of diagnoses. Madness is not only about distress and when it is, then *who* is distressed varies contingently, as those around the diagnosed patient are often frightened and despairing. Some voice hearers are distressed by their voices but not always. The hallmark of madness is not distress but unintelligibility and what is to be done about it in rule-following social orders. The societal value placed on it does vary though across time and place.

For example, Socrates (who himself heard voices) was of the view that the gods had provided an equal value to all existential states and so madness and sanity should be granted equal value. He pointed up the positive aspects of mad rapture. These included the capacity to prophesy (what he called a 'manic art'); a special competence in mystical initiations and rituals; a talent for poetry; and the mad ecstatic state of falling in love (Screech, 1985). It was not all good news though, despite this Socratic endorsement. Rosen (1968) notes, in ancient Greece and Rome, people who wandered around aimlessly and might become violent were considered insane. Today in English this is reflected in the word 'mad', referring to both wild fury and insanity.

The theme of madness and greatness being at times linked was also common in premodern times. Socrates was not alone in hearing special voices not audible to others. This experience was also reported by Pythagoras, the Prophet Muhammad, Joan of Arc and Martin Luther. Jesus and the Buddha could both be accused of being deluded in their grandiose strictures about the meaning of life. All of these religious and philosophical figures now might be thought of as being 'schizophrenic'.

When faced with these unusual experiences there was a division of view about recording and speculating about the particular source of madness (beyond it being, like everything else, simply given by the gods). Socrates and many of the Greeks saw it as a disturbance of the heart and diaphragm – the *phren* (the source of our words 'schizophrenic', 'frenzy', 'frantic' and 'frenetic' today). However, Hippocrates the Greek physician eschewed explanations and suggested that we should simply record carefully the detailed conduct of the mad person, maybe anticipating behaviourism, as well as a 'single symptom' approach. The latter was also favoured by the Roman physician Galen who was interested in separate descriptions of sadness, excitement, confusion and memory loss.

With the emergence of modern medicine and the new-found desire to create taxonomies of pathology, in the 18th century the Scottish physician Cullen began to describe the 'neuroses', which subsumed a wide range of conditions today called 'mental disorders'. This very wide notion began a key trend of biological reductionism in psychiatry today: psychological difference is a product of neurological damage or dysfunction. Terms like 'neurasthenia', 'nervousness' and 'nervous shock' then flowed from this framing. Also in 18th-century France, de Sauvages provided ten broad categories of disease. The eighth of these was 'insanity'. Just prior to the French Revolution, Pinel, following the strictures of Hippocrates, on close observation, delineated categories such as: mania with delirium; mania without delirium; melancholia; confusion; and idiocy.

Further categorisations then were offered by German psychopathologists. Kahlbaum argued psychological dysfunction could be reflected in unbalanced judgement ('paranoia'), bad moods ('dysthymia') or a failure of the will ('diastrephia'). This increasingly empiricist approach to taxonomy was championed ultimately and most famously by Kraepelin (1883). Today systems like the Diagnostic and Statistical Manual from the American Psychiatric Association and the International Classification of Diseases from the World Health Organization, reflect that tradition and so are sometimes called 'neo-Kraepelinian'. The positivist assumption is that mental disorders are *naturally occurring categories*, i.e. nature is 'carved at the joints', ready for and awaiting diagnosis in particular cases. The premise that carbon is essentially different to silver in nature is quite correct, but the question is whether the categories invented at a moment in time to describe psychological deviant from normative expectations are logically equivalent. In truth taxonomies like DSM and ICD are only *seemingly* like the periodic table. Accordingly, this is a misleading and pretentious exercise from psychiatric researchers.

An immanent critique of the diagnosis of schizophrenia

Turning specifically to unpacking the concept of 'schizophrenia', it was connoted first as 'dementia praecox' by Arnold Pick in 1891 and then developed immediately by Kraepelin. Both Pick and Kraepelin viewed it as an early form of dementia and product of degeneracy. Presently, in 1908, Bleuler rejected the term in favour of 'schizophrenia' ('splitting' of the 'phren', from the Greek noted earlier). Bleuler did not query the surface empirical clinical descriptions of Kraepelin but challenged his idea that this was about an immutable form of early dementia (Bleuler, 1911). He focused upon an underlying splitting of the psychological functions (thoughts and feelings) culminating in the fragmentation of the personality.

Using the initial claims in this Kraepelinian tradition, we can offer an immanent critique of schizophrenia following our expectation of how a medical diagnosis works successfully:

1. Ideally, there should be *aetiological specificity*. In the case of schizophrenia this is simply missing. Indeed, for all functional psychiatric diagnoses (i.e. those without a proven organic cause), this absence is the case. The only exception to this is the diagnosis of post-traumatic stress disorder (PTSD), which requires a specifiable ('pathognomonic') trauma in the patient's history.
2. Ideally we should be able to track an *intermediate causal chain* connecting aetiology to current signs and symptoms. This is an account of the 'pathogenesis' of the latter. Signs refer to bodily indicators of disease (detected by examination or in laboratory testing) and symptoms the patients report of their illness. In the case of 'schizophrenia' and other functional diagnoses (including PTSD) there are no signs, only symptoms. It has no blood test or physical signs to be observed on the body. However, the patient's actions are sometimes used by psychiatrists as signs not symptoms (a debatable shift of logic). There are no reliable and valid

indicators of the pathogenesis of schizophrenia. There are though diagnosis-independent indicators of a history of childhood adversity. That is, the latter predicts a range of symptoms across diagnostic boundaries but not specific to 'schizophrenia' (Read and Bentall, 2012; Galea et al., 2011). For emphasis, we need to keep in mind that childhood adversity is predictive of becoming distressed, unintelligible or dysfunctional in a range of ways; it does not predict *particular* diagnostic outcomes.

3. Medical diagnoses should be *categorically different* from one another in terms of their defining features. This posed an early problem for those following Kraepelin, because in the case of psychosis he had differentiated 'dementia praecox' from 'manic-depression' (today dubbed 'bi-polar disorder'). In practice asylum doctors encountered patients presenting with a mixture of symptoms from both categories. From necessity, this led to the invention of a third category, 'schizo-affective psychosis' (Kasanin, 1933). This ambiguous category posed a problem for the Kraepelinian tradition, which assumed a distinction between mood-driven expressions of psychotic conduct and another version reflecting a disintegration of the personality. An additional problem about claims of unique symptoms, within one category, is that the same specific symptom might be included in another. For example, patients with a diagnosis of schizophrenia are deemed at times to have 'negative' symptoms (a passive non-engagement with others in daily life). One of these is called 'anhedonia' – a listless, apathetic loss of interest in life and its pleasures. However, this might also be described, understandably, as a symptom of 'depression' not 'schizophrenia'. The diagnosis thus lacks concept validity, which can lead to it also having poor inter-rater reliability. Psychiatric categories have porous boundaries and so, as it were, 'bleed into one another'. As a consequence, psychiatric patients can find themselves being subjected to a variety of diagnoses over time and when being assessed by different diagnosticians.
4. The *legitimacy of prognosis* is a key part of the medical holy trinity. In the case of 'schizophrenia', predictions at the individual level are impossible. Whether treated or not, about a third have a one-off episode, a third have intermittent episodes and a third are chronically disturbed and impaired in their cognitive and emotional functioning. Subsequently functional diagnoses such as 'schizophrenia' may be changed when patients have episodic service contact. Accordingly, the diagnosis has poor predictive validity and poor test-retest reliability.
5. A confident diagnosis should guide *treatment decisions and, optimally, treatment specificity*. However, in psychiatry there is no single treatment used to treat those in one diagnostic group from another. Biomedical or medicinal psychiatry is drug-centred not diagnosis-centred (Moncrieff, 2008). For example, so called 'antipsychotics' are used to treat a range of problems, including anxiety and agitation in older people, not just 'schizophrenia'. Also, those with the latter diagnosis have been treated at different times using opiates and anxiolytics.
6. A good diagnosis should be *helpful to the patient* and in the case of 'schizophrenia' it is ambiguous who gains from the label. Some patients accept it but

many do not and they consider it unhelpful and stigmatising. It is not uncommon for patients to be unware of their diagnosis, which signals its dubious utility (utility to whom and about what? – see below).

Discussion of the immanent critique of schizophrenia

If we consider the six criteria in the round, this immanent critique suggests that 'schizophrenia' is a very poor diagnosis. I would go further and say that it is totally inadequate. A caution here is that other diagnoses are vulnerable on a range of counts, across the six criteria. Most of the functional psychiatric diagnoses could be subjected to a very similar damning immanent critique.

Thus 'schizophrenia' is illustrative of the weakness of psychiatric diagnosis in general but it is not uniquely inadequate. Also, physical medicine is by no means perfect when supplying common diagnoses (Pilgrim, 2007). For example we understand the pathogenesis of type 1 diabetes but we are still not clear about its aetiology. In the case of poor treatment specificity, rheumatologists treat musculoskeletal problems with analgesics, anxiolytics, anti-inflammatories, opiates and even anti-cancer agents at times.

What makes 'schizophrenia' particularly vulnerable to an immanent critique is complex and implicates *both* its six counts of failure *and* their context of emergence. This double failure has exposed the diagnosis to extra scrutiny from its critics (Bentall, 2010; Ciompi, 1984). A core problem is that if we rely on DSM or ICD to tell us what schizophrenia *is* then this is an **epistemic fallacy**. To complement this problem if diagnosticians point to the presence of individual 'schizophrenic' patients as *evidence* of the disease category then this in an **ontic fallacy**.

Thus, DSM and ICD do not validate the existence of schizophrenia, they only *describe* what it is, according to a contemporary medical consensus. That would be fine if the description was coherent by the criteria of an optimal medical diagnosis: maps can be helpful. However, as I demonstrated above, this is not the case here. The description of 'schizophrenia' affords clinicians poor concept and predictive validity, does not guide specific treatment decisions and often is not experienced as helpful by the identified patient. The map then is fairly useless and so it is misleading.

The epistemological relativism implied by psychiatric diagnosis is reflected in a form of consensus building that alters over time. DSM and ICD keep changing, revised in one-after-another editions. Reality is reformed by committee and some diagnoses are dropped and others introduced afresh. At any point in time, peers, patients and the rest of the world are expected to accept that *this version of reality* is to be welcomed and accepted unquestioningly. However, a modicum of critical reflexivity should reveal that if the previous edition of the taxonomy was deemed to be inadequate or flawed then why should we have confidence in the current one? This is the corner that medicine paints itself into when reducing statements about the purported ontology of 'schizophrenia' to statements about medically preferred knowledge about the latter.

Psychiatric and other medical diagnoses are normative, they imply not merely empirically detached descriptions, but also value judgements about what ought to be (see **axiology**), according to a mixture of stable and shifting social norms. Psychiatry is more interested than physical medicine in rule transgressions, whereas the latter is more concerned with impaired role competence. However, there is an overlap, this is not a dichotomy. Both entail value judgements about the optimal functioning of individuals in society.

Because of psychiatry's over-reliance on symptoms, rather than signs, what the patient says and does is its narrow pre-occupation. This reflects the everyday concern of lay people about distress, dysfunction and unintelligibility in particular social circumstances. Accordingly, the detached behavioural checklists for the categories of DSM or ICD are only *seemingly* objective. In truth they are predicated upon norms about psychological difference in their current host society. Hearing voices not obvious to others becomes 'an auditory hallucination', a fixed and strange belief becomes 'a delusion' etc. This is merely a medical codification of what lay people describe, whether or not the troubling incipient patient is diagnosed by a psychiatric expert (Coulter, 1973). We also learn in our natal culture the particular 'emotion rules', which apply in daily life and how to comply with them; we expect others to do likewise. The sad or frightened patient knows that they are not supposed to act in the way they do in the presence of others but the psychotic patient may not know or not care about these expectations. Thus emotional deviance is partly self-ascribed and partly ascribed by others (Thoits, 1985).

Psychiatry thus rubber stamps and codifies daily lay judgements and seeks to enforce rule compliance via its interventions ('treatments'). Psychiatric diagnoses using operational definitions provide the kind of 'meaning empiricism' that I discussed in Chapter 2. However, these medical codifications offer little or no epistemological clarity, beyond that of ordinary language descriptions. After all, they are *descriptions not explanations*, as I showed in relation to the tautology of the diagnosis of schizophrenia in Chapter 2. We do not need medical training to spot when we are anxious or sad or when a fellow citizen is acting unintelligibly. However, this invites a question about why we continue to rely on the authority of diagnostic psychiatry, despite its weak plausibility as a form of applied science. This is a cue for the next section.

An explanatory critique of the diagnosis of schizophrenia

What did the world have to look like for the diagnosis of schizophrenia to emerge and be maintained despite the above inadequacies? The key political context of the emergence of the diagnosis was Western European eugenics at the turn of the 20th century. Like many of his colleagues from a middle-class background, Kraepelin was adamant that madness was one amongst many expressions of degeneracy. The continuing salience of the diagnosis for eugenicists during the 20th century meant that it shaped the beginnings of psychiatric genetics. Despite Nazi eugenics, including the murder of 'schizophrenic' patients in medical killing centres endorsed by the German Medical Association, the degeneracy assumption persevered after the Second World War (Pilgrim, 2008; Joseph, 2005).

The linkage of authoritarian state politics to the creation and control, or even elimination, of 'schizophrenia' in modern rationalistic industrial societies was a prompt from a key critic of the diagnosis: the psychiatrist and psychoanalyst, Thomas Szasz. A refugee from the Stalinist eastern bloc migrating to the USA, he combined a general attack on psychiatric diagnosis in his seminal text, *The Myth of Mental Illness* (Szasz, 1961) with a specific critique of 'schizophrenia' as the 'sacred symbol of psychiatry' (Szasz, 1976). He argued that if the totemic role of 'schizophrenia' tumbled, then so did the professional credibility of the profession. His overall concern was not just to score epistemological points (by saying that minds can be sick only in a metaphorical sense, like economies) but to demonstrate that this misconception, which he called 'the myth of mental illness', was a medical rationalisation ruthlessly to control non-conformity.

Szasz described the psychiatric patient as the modern witch and psychiatrists as the modern witch-finders (Szasz, 1970). However, and this is important, he did not deny the ontology of what he called 'problems in living' (distress, dysfunction and unintelligibility). This is mentioned as it might be assumed that he was unconcerned with the latter as serious existential challenges, connoted possibly by his choice of the word 'myth'. His moral focus was on the amelioration of psychological problems *but without coercion.* This reflected his sensitivity about involuntary psychiatry acting on behalf of its employing state to crush non-conformity, but then describing that process in the mystifying language of caring and curative medicine.

His epistemological analysis was bound up with his libertarian distrust of the state. Accordingly he had a lop-sided interest in the power of human agency and so he was preoccupied with adult citizens being responsible for their own actions at all times. He had no objection at all to any of us seeking the help of others, when and if we struggle with the latter overarching moral obligation. However, that negotiation of help should be voluntary and not imposed. Thus his critique of mental illness as a metaphor was bound up with a more general moral distaste of coercion by the state.

The emergence of the Szaszian critique in the 1960s was aligned with other internal critics of the profession of psychiatry from different political 'stables', including the Scot Ronald Laing, the Italian Franco Basaglia and the South African David Cooper, but only the last of these accepted the description of being an 'anti-psychiatrist'. The others were psychiatrists who considered that their profession had taken the wrong turn in being more concerned to label problems and treat them chemically than by responding to madness compassionately and supportively.

What they were all concerned with though was the coercive role of psychiatry on behalf of the majority in society, who were sane by common consent. Diagnostic labelling codified offensive rule transgressions and this was used as basis for involuntary constraint and physical medical interference (using drugs or shock therapy). That process of the codification of rule transgression attracted the interest of sociologists, who began to use the labelling and treatment of mental illness as an illustrative exemplar within the sociology of deviance.

Those sociological authors too were to receive the attribution of 'anti-psychiatry' from conservative defenders of the psychiatric orthodoxy, who even attempted at times to depict the problem as being about those with envious motives conspiring from outside the profession (Roth, 1973). The conservatives tended to 'shoot the messenger' rather than exercising critical reflexivity about the inadequacies of their own Kraepelinian legacy. The problem for them was that their enemies were not simply without but many were within. This was to lead to the profession remaining rife with hostile factionalism to the present day. Those factions were in an ongoing power struggle during episodic revisions of the DSM within the American Psychiatric Association (Wilson, 1993; Bayer and Spitzer, 1985).

What had happened in the first half of the 20th century to prompt or trigger this contention about 'anti-psychiatry', so called, and to lead to subsequent movements such as 'critical psychiatry? The Kraepelinans had not had it all their own way in the academy. An important minority position was adopted in opposition by the Swiss psychiatrist Adolf Meyer, who worked for the bulk of his career in the USA at Baltimore. He had suggested that diagnosis was less important than posing and answering a different question. Rather than merely discerning what was wrong, the doctor might ask instead variants of 'why is this particular patient presenting with this particular problem at this time in their life?'.

Such an alternative approach was to reappear later in the *Power Threat Meaning Framework* developed by a group of British clinical psychologists (myself included) and which is considered further below (Johnstone and Boyle, 2018). That framework gives agency back to patients: what meanings do they attach to their experiences, how do they cope with life and how might they be supported to change? Personal agency (along with real enough constraints in our lives) has to be a key expectation of a critical realist approach to mental health problems and this is at odds with the Kraepelinian tradition of biogenetically determined afflictions that denies the personhood of the patient. For a longer critical realist discussion of this point about agency and madness see Mooney (2016).

The Kraepelinian trajectory for the profession faced another problem because of its commitment to the assumption of degeneracy. During the First World War, the shellshock doctors noted that 'officers and gentlemen' and working-class *volunteers* were breaking down with predictable regularity in the prolonged stalemate of trench warfare. They were being psychologically wrecked by the entrapped horrors, witnessing the daily death and gory injuries of their comrades. In this context, a degeneracy thesis was tantamount to treason. The casualties were, after all, 'England's finest blood'; the officer class was actually *more* prone to psychological breakdown than the men they led (Stone, 1985).

After the 'Great War', other evidence emerged to undermine the Kraepelinian current of thought. Suicide rates rose and acute distress became common in the face of the downturn of capitalism, with the Wall Street Crash of 1929. A degeneracy thesis would suggest mental disorder was genetically caused and so its incidence should be predictably stable and independent of environmental conditions. Warfare and economic crises disrupted this eugenic logic. Genetic explanations in psychiatry, still favoured by many today, are an attempt at a **covering law** within psychiatric positivism. They fail though because *what happens to people* inflects the probability of developing a range of mental health problems, including psychosis. Adverse childhood conditions and trauma later in life disrupt the tramline logic of psychiatric genetics.

The psychological outcome of a traumatic war and economically insecure post-war socio-economic environment boosted the arguments of those at odds with the assumption of degeneracy. The Meyerian line of reasoning became more plausible and attracted academic psychiatrists who appreciated the complex interaction of biological vulnerability, psychological differences and social setting. This movement towards social rather than biological psychiatry was to culminate formally in a position within psychiatry to defend a 'biopsychosocial model' during the 20th century (Engel, 1980).

By the end of the Second World War, the formal legitimacy of old-fashioned categorical diagnosis was to receive an important new boost in the face of the latter shift towards the alternative of biopsychosocial formulations. In 1948 the World Health Organization was formed and it inherited the International Classification of Diseases (ICD) previously under the jurisdiction of the health committee of the League of Nations. By 1949, two overlapping changes occurred in this tradition of medical taxonomy, which had begun in the European public health associations of the late 19th century. First, the ICD, now in its sixth edition, incorporated morbidity not just mortality data (i.e. the earlier editions recorded only causes of death). Second, for the first time psychiatric categories were included in the system. Until then psychiatric knowledge had enjoyed both a low profile and status within scientific medicine, which was cautious or even dismissive of its subjectively based focus on symptoms and the lack of evident true signs to defend diagnoses.

This change in the epistemological status of psychiatric knowledge accompanying ICD-6, was a fillip then to diagnostic psychiatry in the Kraepelinian tradition and it displaced the more environmentalist legitimacy of the Meyerian tradition, despite its academic adherents. The resurgence of diagnostic psychiatry after the war was the context then for a new generation of doubters within the medical specialty. Notably this came from psychologically orientated psychiatrists, such as Szasz and Laing noted above, both of whom were medical psychoanalysts.

Apart from the post-Second World War shift away from social psychiatry and psychoanalysis, and towards biological psychiatry, another process was to reinforce the legitimacy of psychiatric diagnosis. The organic chemistry industry, which had sold its over-the-counter potions (including opiates), along with hair dyes and paints, in the drug stores of the US by the end of the 19th century, was emboldened after the Second World War. If psychiatric categories permitted and legitimised under ICD-6 were grouped together (today called 'Diagnostic Related Groups' or 'DRGs'), then this afforded opportunities to develop and market drugs that would target them *en masse*. The nuances of the patient's biography and social context were then rendered irrelevant to psychiatric practice.

The profits of the pharmaceutical industry then became a driver of neo-Kraepelinian resurgence, locking it into taxonomic systems like ICD and DSM. This idea of 'magic bullets' emerged and in the case of psychiatry this meant the marketing of 'antidepressants', 'anxiolytics' and 'antipsychotics'. These terms had curative connotations and pretensions but of course they did not cure anything. They merely suppressed some symptoms, some of the time, in some people. Moreover, their hit and miss blunderbuss effect on the central nervous system made them crude and 'dirty' pharmacological agents. They were addictive and patients habituated to their effects. Often their adverse effects offset any ameliorative advantage on offer. They were life diminishing and at times even life threatening. When critics of Soviet psychiatry in the 1970s showed political dissidents shuffling around like zombies under the influence of major tranquillisers there was understandable outrage (Bloch and Reddaway, 1977). But only a few at the time, or subsequently, asked the question why non-dissidents being affected in the same way by the drugs was considered to be benign and good medical practice.

Rather than stall the advance of diagnostic biomedical psychiatry, this widespread clinical iatrogenesis galvanised new pharmaceutical activity. 'New generations' of drugs could be developed to market fresh wares for the psychiatric industry for DRGs. This brought promises of reduced addictiveness, increased clinical effectiveness and patient safety; hollow claims repeated with each cycle of marketing new products. Rather than failures exposing a biomedical approach to diagnosis and treatment in principle being flawed and questionable, it provided an opportunity to maintain the research and development of new forms of profit by rendering the previously promoted generation of drugs obsolete. 'Old drugs bad, new drugs good' could be the guiding mantra by the end of the 20th century for the drug companies, guaranteeing an unending marketing cycle.

It is only very recently that this cyclical marketing formula broke down, as licensing regulations and user aversion to psychotropic medication prompted 'Big Pharma' to reduce its commitment to research, development and marketing within, and for, biomedical diagnostic psychiatry. For now though Western academic psychiatry remains enmeshed with the pharmaceutical industry. For now the profession has achieved a state of hegemony but this is precarious. It has though led to a set of dominant themes being taken for granted. These include the scientific validity of functional diagnoses, such as 'schizophrenia', and the progressive role of medicinal treatments in response: the unrelenting search for the 'chemical fix' to morbid psychosocial complexity. However, the challenges from a range of critics inside and outside of psychiatry imply a set of other lesser themes to consider, which have been less publicised or even supressed. This is a cue for the third and final section.

An omissive critique of the diagnosis of schizophrenia

Today, it is possible to listen to mass media reports of mental illness, or even read psychology textbooks guided by the naïve realist assumptions of DSM and ICD, and be unaware of the serious scientific and humanistic problems with psychiatric theory and practice. The immanent and explanatory critiques offered above point to a number of silences and suppressions that have maintained the spurious legitimacy of biomedical psychiatry today. Below I will note just a few of these, with a focus on the diagnosis of schizophrenia, though some would apply to any functional psychiatric diagnosis.

1) The eugenic origins of Western psychiatry remain implicit in the biomedical psychiatry

It is possible today to discuss 'schizophrenia' as a medical and policy conundrum as if it has no history of emergence within a medical and policy context. With that presentism comes an ahistorical ignorance of the powerful legacy in the Western world of eugenics during the 19th and 20th centuries. There could have been no 'dementia praecox' or 'manic depression' (now 'schizophrenia' and 'bi-polar disorder') outside of that eugenic context (Pilgrim, 2008; Joseph, 2005).

2) Biopsychosocial complexity has been supressed in favour of bio-reductionism

After the inter-war period when social psychiatry and Meyerian efforts to develop a biopsychosocial approach were in the ascendency for a while in the academy, the categorical approach of both the World Health Organization and the American Psychiatric Association prevailed about clinical practice and mental health service norms. This was boosted by an increasing investment of drug company money. The actual biopsychosocial complexity of mental health problems (and for that matter physical health problems) could be ignored now as a result of the collusive relationship between bio-reductionist psychiatry and 'Big Pharma'. The latter sponsored R&D and marketing and incentivised psychiatrists in their prescribing and research activity by offering free educational events and direct grants to investigate neurochemical mechanisms and the randomised controlled trials of new products. It was not until the 1970s in the wake of 'anti-psychiatry' that some psychiatrists resurrected a biopsychosocial approach in their profession (Engel, 1980; Double, 2007).

3) Non-medicinal approaches have been eschewed in psychiatric routines

An implication of assuming that mental illnesses reflect defective brain functions or structures (inherited or even acquired epigenetically) is that physical methods of treatment (drugs, psychosurgery or electroconvulsive therapy) are the default position of psychiatric routines. Since the Second World War, when diagnostic psychiatry and drug company interests became yoked, this has ensured such routines. This generalisation has been fair comment in the case of those with any diagnosis of psychosis. If a researcher today wanted to study people with a diagnosis of schizophrenia who had never been medicated it would be a nigh-impossible task. The trend is less clear cut with those diagnosed with 'common mental health problems', i.e. presenting with distinct or mixed symptoms of depression and anxiety. However, even in those cases antidepressants for now are the default position in primary care, with any form of talking therapy being on offer only some of the time.

4) User critics have demanded respect for biographical complexity

Because psychiatric diagnosis begins with the way that the doctor understands the world not their patients, then it is little surprising that their person-centred psychotherapeutic colleagues have at time protested at this priority. In addition there have been a number of patients receiving diagnoses that they find unhelpful, inaccurate or stigmatising who have also objected to the clinical practice and the assumptions behind it, such as bio-determinism. This user disaffection with psychiatric diagnosis has been one motive for collective opposition, which has been a form of New Social Movement or NSM (Crossley, 2006; Rogers and Pilgrim, 1991). NSMs are protest movements in civil society that demand rights of freedom and identity (e.g. Gay Liberation, black power, radical feminism) though some are about other species (Animal Rights activism) or even our collective survival (e.g. anti-fracking activism). I discussed these in Chapter 9 when discussing protest.

In the case of psychiatric patients, their resistance to psychiatry has taken various forms, from demanding service reforms to make them more patient-centred, to more radical abolitionist demands. One part of their critique has centred upon the inadequacies of diagnosis and the need to replace it with biographically sensitive and co-produced personal accounts as a starting point for helping patients (Clark, 2015; Rose, 2009).

5) The coercive role of psychiatry has been normalised but also resisted

An additional concern for the NSM of psychiatric patients has been the contradictions created by coercive psychiatry. Diagnosis is seen as part of a rationale to label non-conformist conduct as a prelude to its involuntary control. Given that coercive control existed in the old state asylum system well before today's ICD or DSM categories, we can see that diagnosis is not needed to control psychological difference in society, especially amongst the poor (Hunter and Macalpine, 1974; Cohen and Scull, 1983). However, today the link between psychiatric labelling and the experience of oppression from disaffected patients noted in the previous point have become yoked. Non-stigmatising and biographically sensitive accounts as an alternative to diagnosis have been bound up with campaigns against psychiatric coercion. This is particularly the case in relation to the imposition of physical treatments (mainly drugs but also at times electro-shock and psychosurgery). Thus any offence caused by diagnosis may have been offset by the pragmatic imperative to codify the rationale for detention (a diagnostic label from ICD and DSM).

These objections can be contrasted with the direction of travel of health policy in the past hundred years, which has tended to portray the existence of 'mental health law' as a *progressive* component of any developed society (Bean, 1986). We have then an NSM demanding citizenship on one side and being critical of coercion and traditional state paternalism promoting involuntary social control as a form of warranted *care* contained on the other. Diagnosis plays a role within the latter. For the first group diagnosis is a mystification and denial of a patient voice. For the second it is a necessary codification of what is wrong with patients to justify their involuntary treatment.

This puts mental health services in the paradoxical situation of forcing their wares onto identified patients, leading to complaints that they simply cannot be *both* kind *and* efficacious (Sedgwick, 1980; Pilgrim, 2018d). Kindliness can only be proven when patients experience their service contact as voluntarily sought and gratefully received. The presence of coercion undermines that outcome, though it may be effective at reducing risk on behalf of those who are sane by common consent. Given the greater power of the sane compared to the insane, mental health services are risk-driven in favour of the former at the expense of the latter.

A public policy challenge for now is that if coercion is used, then should it be within the penal or healthcare sectors, as far as risky psychiatric patients are concerned (American Psychological Association, 2014)? The oft-heard generalisation that one in four people suffer a mental health problem does not reveal the large differences in which of those will suffer coercive detention and treatment, according to their social group membership. Social class, race, age and sex intersect to produce a patterning of enforced detention (Audini and Lelliot, 2002; MHAC, 2009).

This point about aggregating and, at times, synergistic mechanisms generating the emergence of mental health problems alters our discussion of 'intersectionality'. In postmodern social science the latter tends to refer to mixed and contingent *identities* but for critical realism we should also think of ontology (Flatschart, 2017). Intersecting social group memberships have a *causal* dimension to their existence not merely one about experienced identity.

Conclusion

Functional psychiatric diagnoses have failed humanity. They do not work in the way that we expect good medical diagnoses to work. They are not an accurate guide to aetiology, treatment and prognosis. They are not found to be helpful by many of their recipients. I provided an immanent critique of 'schizophrenia' to demonstrate these points.

This leaves us with the conundrum of why they survive. I went on to provide an explanatory critique to answer that question and explored a range of conditions of possibility for their survival from eugenic origins to drug company profits. Those forces of maintenance have excluded and silenced other ways of understanding and responding to madness, misery and incorrigibility in society; what we might call 'psychological deviance'. Those other ways would be more objective than psychiatric positivism (because they would be aligned more sensitively and accurately with the complexity of their object of enquiry) and more compassionate (because the ethical dimensions to dealing with psychological difference would be rendered explicit). My omissive critique summarised the consequences of the dominance in service routines of a diagnostic biomedical approach to mental health work. Those routines at present deny that future of enhanced objectivity and compassion.

11

WHY WAS PSYCHOANALYSIS MARGINALISED?

Introduction

This chapter considers why many Anglo-American students of psychology either know little of psychoanalysis or they may have been exposed to it as a dire warning of scientific implausibility. Psychoanalysis is not held in universal contempt and even in Anglophone countries many clinical psychologists have embraced it as a guide to their practice. For a while it influenced our understanding of the psychology of organisations, within the interdisciplinary field of management studies (where we also find a fair share of critical realists). Nonetheless, it is fair to say that it has existed on the margins of mainstream Anglophone *academic* psychology, since the middle of the 20th century. This leaves many psychology graduates with little knowledge of it and vulnerable to making ill-informed dismissals of its merits, or of taking for granted its self-evident weaknesses.

Mainstream psychology has defied a wider trend of cultural understanding in Western intellectual life, in the past century, to look to the psychoanalytical current of thought for authoritative guidance. Despite this marginalisation within the discipline, more has been written by historians of the human sciences about psychoanalysis than any other form of psychology (Borch-Jacobsen and Shamdasani, 2008). The Freudian legacy, no matter how much disdain it has met from various sources (see below), has proved to be a major influence on modern culture in the past century, summarised in this view from W.H. Auden:

> ... if often he was wrong and, at times, absurd,
> to us he is no more a person
> now but a whole climate of opinion
> under whom we conduct our different lives ...
>
> *(Auden, 1940)*

As well as the skewed interest from historians and the cultural recognition, or even veneration, from some poets and the literati more generally, the philosophical appraisal of psychoanalysis has been extremely mixed. Both trained psychoanalysts and external observers have praised and damned it over the years at different times and for differing reasons (Jones, 1957; Roudinesco, 2016; Masson, 1985; Fromm, 1970; Gay, 1988; Eysenck, 1985; Thornton, 1983; Webster, 2005). In itself, such an extensive mixture of celebratory and critical histories should arouse our critical curiosity about the topic.

Some of the unease about the new discipline of psychology being under the undue influence of medicine may well have played into a wariness about psychoanalysis in the 20th century. However, medical dominance, though a political consideration, cannot fully explain that ambivalence. Whilst it is true that the emerging discipline of psychology could be seen historically as loosening itself from the constraints of both medicine and philosophy, medical psychology *per se* was not inevitably offensive. For example, the work of both Pavlov and Sherrington was readily incorporated because of its focus on experimentalism, which made it attractive to a discipline that was favouring this approach to human science in its bid for legitimacy.

The scorning of psychoanalysis came from two main philosophical sources: positivism and critical rationalism. The first of these was notably represented by Eysenck (1985) and the second by Popper (1962). However, these were different attacks with different motivations. Hans Eysenck was dealing with a body of knowledge that was a threat to a new vision of applied psychology. Psychoanalysis had already made inroads into clinical psychology practice in the USA, which he wanted to head off in the UK, where he was about to start the first course (Eysenck, 1949). At that juncture, his determined concern was to *delete* psychoanalysis permanently from psychology, as part of a professionalisation strategy to install his preferred version of science.

By contrast, Karl Popper was simply being consistent in his wider expectation about science progressing. Popper was not setting out for professional reasons to delete psychoanalysis but, instead, to query it because it could not be refuted or falsified (a point he made about a range of bodies of knowledge that he considered not to be feasibly scientific). By contrast, Eysenck had a self-interested axe to grind within the politics of his discipline. He was insisting that his version of positivism (an admixture of methodological behaviourism and psychometrics in the eugenic tradition) should prevail in professional psychology. Not only was Popper not concerned with these internal politics of psychology, but he was also critical of positivism, not one of its supporters.

As I noted in Chapters 2 and 6, critical realism diverges from both behaviourism and critical rationalism and so its particular response to psychoanalysis is now addressed. Critical realists have tended to find merit in psychoanalysis as an approach to human life because it takes *both* causes *and* meanings seriously. Not only does it endorse the relationship between **ontological realism** and **epistemological relativism**, it also emphasises that inner events can have causal efficacy (O'Mahoney, 2011; Collier, 1977, 1991; Clarke, 2008; Kran, 2010; Pataki,

2014). Psychoanalysis is an approach to human science that can gain interdisciplinary sympathy and is not restricted to the confines of academic psychology (Bhaskar et al., 2018).

Despite this respect in principle for psychoanalysis, critical realists have not explored it, or for that matter any other form of psychology, as extensively as they have varieties of sociology. To rectify that imbalance I return to a form of fundamental question for critical realism applied in this case: 'what were the conditions of possibility for psychoanalysis to first emerge *but then be marginalised* by mainstream psychology?' The rest of this chapter addresses that question, starting with an outline of the approach of Freud and his followers.

A relevant outline of psychoanalysis

1) The founding father of psychoanalysis, Sigmund Freud (1856–1939), was a working physician and so he was concerned *both* to make a living, by seeing fee-paying patients, *and* to understand the unconscious by listening to and interpreting their personal accounts. This is important to note because the twists and turns in his theory were in part because it was a form of *practice-based evidence, rather than evidence-based practice,* with a particular clinical sample (Brody, 1970). This reliance on clinical samples and the absence of separate testing out of the theory were to fuel later Popperian-type criticisms. But from a critical realist perspective, clinical case studies can be seen as detailed examinations of **concrete singularities**: stories of being this person in this particular biographical context. Moreover, for critical realism (contra critical rationalism), falsifiability is not the ultimate criterion to judge a good scientific theory (see Chapter 2).

2) *People as determined and determining beings* was an important working assumption in Freud's work and is aligned broadly with critical realist thought today. He emphasised the manifestations of the conscious ego in daily life in our visible actions. The latter were in response to the demands of outer reality and inner duty (a part of the super-ego) and goal seeking. For Freud the ego seeks to satisfy itself without feeling anxious or guilty. When this occurs successfully the action is 'ego-syntonic' but if it fails it is 'ego-dystonic'. This empirically visible aspect of our conduct contained an actual unconscious set of forces or mechanisms, which disrupt that balance and lead to us all being in our own way irrational. This is our personal form of neurosis; a psychological assumption in psychoanalysis is that we are all ill because we are out of touch with our inner depths and prone to a range of non-rational forms of conduct. For Freud those dynamics in our unconscious were **generative mechanisms** that determined our psychological functioning. They were, according to him, both ontologically real and intransitive. Therapy was aimed at enlarging the patient's and analyst's *knowledge* of those generative mechanisms (a transitive and epistemic matter). As Freud put it, 'where id is, there shall ego be'. By identifying the role of the dynamic unconscious, Freud was making a universal claim about the nature of our deep subjectivity. This suggests a positivist orientation in his claims about the ontology of the mind and its

intransitive features. These were rooted, according to Freud, in our commonly inherited and universally shared biological state: the 'push from behind' of our instincts (Sulloway, 1983). A less harsh judgement (about Freud's positivist pretensions) is that he was pointing to *tendencies or demi-regularities in nature* that would indeed be expected by critical realism. A sympathetic case could be made for either reading. If the emphasis on causal efficacy is retained but putative **covering laws** were to be dropped from early psychoanalytical reasoning, then this would align it unambiguously with critical realism. Definitive judgements about this ambiguity are made difficult because Freud himself moved between epistemological positions and not all of his followers were of one voice (see below).

3) *Our understanding of reality is suspect because the ego's functioning was distorted constantly by a mixture of internal and external threats.* Psychoanalysts invoked a position of superiority about ontological claims. Ordinary people were, as it were, constantly 'in the wrong' about reality because of their defence mechanisms distorting it in order to protect the ego from anxiety. This is put well here by one later analyst, Thomas Szasz, who noted that when there was a conflict of opinion between the doctor and the patient, the standoff was: '... not resolved by examination of the merits of the two views but rather the physician's autocratic judgment: his view is correct and is considered "reality"; the patient's view is incorrect, and is considered "transference"' (Szasz, 1963: 432). I come back to this point again below in relation to the **epistemic fallacy**. Despite these cautions, critical realism *expects* reality to be unfathomable at times and so a notion of 'the unconscious' and the fallibility of human cognition is in line with its assumptions. As Szasz pointed out, the issue here is not about the conceptual utility of 'the dynamic unconscious' but about the autocratic last word about it held by the therapist. This is about the power to define reality in an intimate relationship. At least some of the disquiet about psychoanalysis is that it was not a democratic and person-centred form of therapy; hence the reaction to it from some humanistic psychologists and more existentially oriented psychoanalysts.

4) *Psychoanalysis is not a unitary body of knowledge but a series of revisions and fragmentations.* This is important because often psychoanalysis is discussed, as if it is a single form of theory and practice, conflated with one version of Freudianism in the mind of the critic or advocate. However, this is inaccurate and so misleading. Within Freud's own lifetime he adopted three quite distinct and contradictory sets of epistemological positions. In the 1890s he accounted for psychological abnormality by actual sexual activity in childhood. He listened to accounts of sexual abuse at the hands of relatives from his patients and he noted that excessive masturbation and struggles with its guilty suppression combined to generate neurotic symptoms (Freud, 1895). After 1900 he altered his view, turning to the patient's fantasies and projections and ignoring actual events in the sexual experience of the child. For Freud these projections were re-enacted in the transference in therapy (Freud, 1912) and led to him elaborating the idea of defence mechanisms distorting reality for the unanalysed individual (Freud, 1935). Subsequently this led to his critics, who were analysts themselves, attacking Freud for betraying victims of incest (Masson, 1985; Miller, 1984). In the face of the unrelenting slaughter of the First World War,

Freud revised his theory yet again to the consternation of some of his early devotees. The focus on sex now shifted to one about aggression (Freud, 1920/1922). Only a few years earlier, some of his psychoanalytical contemporaries had already tried to point out the role of aggression in human functioning. However, Freud either parted company with them (Adler, 1912; Stekel, 1908) or tolerated them, before subsequently incorporating their insights (Spielrein, 1912). Because critical realism expects epistemological relativism, these variations in theorisation are also expected. Psychoanalysis is no different from other forms of psychology, where theoretical differences are common and come and go in fashion.

5) *The tension between instinctualists and environmentalists was bequeathed by Freud's legacy*. After 1920 Freud's followers varied in their elaboration of his variegated body of knowledge. Some focused centrally on the role of instincts, especially aggression. This was centre stage in the work of Melanie Klein within child analysis. Others shifted to a focus on what happened to the child to create their particular psychological strengths and vulnerabilities. For them, what actually happened to the child in terms of the quality of their parenting became central (Winnicott, 1965). This created major splits in the psychoanalytical movement, present still today. Some important variations attempted to meld psychoanalytical ideas with other quite different psychological traditions, such as ethology (e.g. Ainsworth and Bowlby, 1991). Other splits included the inflection by social conservatism on the one hand (e.g. Hartmann, 1939/1958), focusing on the adaption of the ego to daily life in capitalist society and, on the other hand, those looking to a hybrid of Freud and Marx to illuminate capitalist alienation. The latter coalesced in the early Frankfurt School, with writers such as Fromm (1970) and Adorno (1982). Psychoanalysis seemingly can appeal to social conservatives and revolutionaries in equal measure. Another important variation was the fusion of psychoanalytical ideas with those from existentialism (e.g. Laing, 1960; Lomas, 1994). I discussed the Frankfurt School in Chapter 9 and 'anti-psychiatry' in Chapter 10. Again we can note here that the uncertainty about 'nurture versus nature' is commonplace in psychology and not limited to the psychoanalytical tradition. The uncertainty is a product of an ontological point; our **four planar social being**. We are biological beings, sustained by our relations with others, living in contingent social structures and manifesting our unique personhood. Many of the disputes and divisions in psychoanalysis reflect epistemological preferences when journeying to and fro across these four planes of ontology. Even our relationship with the natural world was dealt with by Freud ('the biologist of the mind') differently than by a later psychoanalyst, John Bowlby, who was interested in the link between our embodied emotions and our relationality. Freud focused on the instinct of sex (and eventually aggression as well), but Bowlby prioritised the instinct of attachment in all mammals, shifting the relevant disciplinary focus from neurology to ethology.

6) *Epistemic fallacies can be found in the differing versions of psychoanalysis*. Those like Masson and Miller, noted above, who criticised Freud for betraying victims of child sexual abuse, complained that his insistence of asserting different versions of maps of the inner world implied his acolytes should now embrace new territories and readily discard the importance of past places visited. Of most importance, the ontology of

child sexual abuse was abandoned by Freud when, he shifted his focus onto projection and fantasy. The ontology of aggression was first discounted by him in 1912 but then embraced in 1920. This reminds us of the constant risk of any form of psychological theory to confuse reality with its preferred understanding or depiction of reality (the epistemic fallacy). Another example of this weakness in Freudian thinking was the invention of transference. Elaborating an earlier point, Szasz (1963) pointed out that the idea of transference emerged because of the challenge for *the analyst* of dealing with discomforting scenarios, such as the patient acting seductively or aggressively in therapy. The invention helped the therapist to deal with the immediate ontology of the raw and immediate feelings of temptation, embarrassment or hurt in the room, when patients 'acted out' in these ways. The transference (displacements from past relationships) may appear to *be* the patient's *actual* conduct and experience according to their analyst (an ontological matter). However, this is adjudged within the analyst's professional authority (an epistemic matter). It is an example of an epistemic fallacy. It might be expressed as an ontic fallacy when analysts incontrovertibly 'prove' the process of transference by citing and describing an example of a patient's actions from their consulting room.

7) *The strengths and weaknesses of forms of psychoanalytical knowledge need to be understood in their own socio-historical context of emergence.* Whilst British empiricism was never going to take kindly to psychoanalysis, a different context was present in Continental Europe at the turn of the 20th century. There a robust and valued engagement had emerged between the *naturwissenshaften* (the natural sciences) and the *geisteswissenshaften* (the cultural or 'spiritual' sciences). Freud's early meetings in Vienna contained enthusiasts from both traditions in many lively debates (Makari, 2010). The challenge for Freud was that he was vulnerable as a Jew in his medical culture. His ideas might be scorned by the majority of his Gentile colleagues. Jews were considered to be congenitally irrational by many doctors including Charcot (the French physician who mentored Freud in the 1880s) and psychoanalysis itself was seen as a dubious Jewish tendency within 'medical psychology' (Frosh, 2005). Were it not for the practical challenge of treating shellshock patients in the First World War, psychoanalysis may well have disappeared without trace (Stone, 1985). The anti-Semitism common in medical circles at the time helped to make Freud defensive and even dogmatic in order to protect his culture. With the rise of Nazism, with anti-Semitism at its core in Germany and Austria, the need for that guarded protectiveness became more pressing, as over 80% of the International Psychoanalytical Association's membership was Jewish. Freud's books were burned by the Nazis and many analysts were murdered or escaped that fate by fleeing to other countries. Helped by a loyal follower (the Welsh Gentile, Ernest Jones) Freud and his daughter, Anna, fled to that most empiricist of all countries, England. By a quirk of history, international debates about psychoanalysis were then to be played out in London and no longer in central Europe. The locked horns between Anna Freud and Melanie Klein, also reflected another abiding feature of Freud's legacy: its gendered character, which has left feminists with mixed views about psychoanalysis. Child analysis was left to the women, while adult analysis retained a

male-dominated character. Moreover, the contribution of female analysts such as Low (1920) and Spielrein (1912) were largely written out of the early psychoanalytical canon or appended as footnotes (Freud, 1920/1922). Psychoanalysis like all forms of psychology emerged in a particular social context and the latter needs to be considered when appraising its strengths and weaknesses.

Reflecting critically on the summary of the story of psychoanalysis

The above summary invites an understanding of a paradox. On the one hand, the arts and humanities, or *geisteswissenshaften*, in the past hundred years have embraced the variegated Freudian legacy, often adoringly. Despite some of its positivistic pretensions, the psychoanalytical tradition ultimately was a wide-ranging experiment in hermeneutics, with its focus on the interpretation of communications and its preoccupation with the non-rational aspects of human functioning. That interpretivism was aligned centrally with the concerns of the arts and humanities, where sense making, rather than laboratory-style proof, was the dominant way of working. On the other hand, because of this hermeneutic bent, it has been offensive to a conservative version of the natural sciences or *naturwissenshaften*.

If each variant of psychoanalysis was a descriptive and interpretive exercise, then its concern was largely with *verstehen* (an engaged understanding of human life). The positivist purism of early academic psychology aspired to go further and become an explanatory science (*erklären*) securing an understanding of psychological laws, in a spirit of aloof empirical detachment. There were elements of this though in Freud's thinking as well at times. For example 'defence mechanisms' explained our ways and means of avoiding aspects of our inner and outer reality; they were his posited mental generative mechanisms.

However, even at his most positivist, Freud never claimed a *comprehensive* explanation for all inner events and processes, only a framework for interpretations, which he was happy to weigh up and debate with trusted colleagues. The predictive power of the approach in particular cases was never boasted, despite some populist portrayals mischievously implying this claim. For example, in the early 1960s a British TV series, *The Human Jungle* starring Herbert Lom, depicted a psychoanalyst who could anticipate his patients' next moves in life with amazing accuracy. Psychotherapists, of any orientation, know that this sort of clairvoyant aspiration is, to say the least, very unwise in open systems. However, by lapsing at times into grander positivist claims about universal psychological processes, rather than staying firmly, but more humbly, within the domain of hermeneutics case by case, Freud exposed his theorisations to critical scrutiny and, in some circles, eventual ridicule. That ridicule needs to be placed into the wider context about whether *any* psychological theory developed in closed systems (say of the venerated laboratory, not just the clinic) *could be* predictive.

This raises the challenge of **transduction** across the discipline of 'scientific' psychology. Popper complained that psychoanalysis could not be tested as a proper science. Critical realists would argue that if that is the case then it also true in practice for *all* psychological theories being tested empirically because of the inferential weakness of transduction in principle. If the problem of transduction was not unique to Freudianism then this was also true of **reductionism**. Freud was an ambivalent supporter of psychological pre-eminence in human science. He rode two horses in his work, one as a hermeneuticist and the other as a neurologist. In the latter regard, he believed that eventually mental life would become explicable, and even predictable, more precisely, from within neuroscience rather than interpretive psychology (see Chapter 5). In this sense he was a 'hoped-for-reductionist' (Wolman, 1981).

Critical realism and the psychoanalytical defence of the ontology of our inner life

With this broad summary in mind, I will now say a little more about why critical realism is necessarily both critical and respectful of Freud and his legacy. I push on with this ambivalence now by looking at Freud's understanding about the ontology of inner life and how he altered his view of it, setting a trend for further disputes within the psychoanalytical community.

If the historical reconstruction of a patient's biography, via hours of careful listening to their personal account, characterised Freud's practice, then the theoretical speculations it prompted in him, which he shared in case discussions with his enlarging group of colleagues, was a different matter. The one-to-one focus of the first entailed empathic and in-depth story-telling, case by case. It was an early exercise in existential psychotherapy. However, the second was more ambitious because it involved Freud creating theoretical premises, which to his (fallible) mind *connected* those disparate patient accounts. And when he took that risk, what conclusions did he draw?

Freud counter-posed the unconscious part of the mind with that of the conscious part. His therapeutic challenge was then to use the agential capacity of the defensive, but note still reflective, ego of the patient to take responsibility for the hidden troublesome parts of the self ('where id is, there shall ego be'). At this point we see an important second distinction being made, which is implicit to all forms of psychological therapy not just that derived from the psychoanalytical tradition.

Freud was moving from a *description* of the mind to one in which the mind is *improved*. The daily life of the patient was then less constrained by their personal neurosis. Thus Freud was moving from a descriptive and interpretive form of investigation to a value-led one about what ought to be (see **axiology**). This is completely consistent with the overall intention of good medicine: identifying pathology as a first step to restoring health. The scientific aspiration of psychoanalysis was to document the unconscious, whereas the aspiration of fee-paying therapy, within that exercise, was to help the patient to change. At this point it is relevant to compare psychoanalysis with its later competitor, behaviour therapy, because it illuminates the durable relevance of the ontology of our inner lives when psychological therapists of any theoretical persuasion practice their trade.

Psychoanalysis versus behaviour therapy

Hans Eysenck was opposed in the first instance, within his professionalisation strategy for British clinical psychology, to this shift from describing psychopathology to treating it, because he said that therapy was value-led. He was correct in this assertion, nonetheless by 1958 and in a major U-turn he commended that psychologists *should* treat neurosis but only with behaviour therapy. Suddenly his earlier anti-therapy stricture had been abandoned and psychologists were given his blessing to indulge in value-led therapy. This contradicted his earlier positivist rhetoric that psychologists should *only* conduct experiments and provide psychometric testing. Which raises the matter of Eysenck's dubious mandate as a leader of a new form of psychological therapy.

Freud saw patients (lots of them) but Eysenck was a *research* psychologist and so practice-based knowledge-production featured quite differently for them. Indeed Eysenck's lack of experience and competence as a therapist meant that it had to be his clinical colleagues, such as Monte Shapiro, Harold Gwynne-Jones and Jack Rachman, who developed and promoted behaviour therapy in practice, within the Department of Psychology of the Institute of Psychiatry in South London.

That seemingly subtle point, easily lost in history, can be missed if we only attend to the published (and therefore very public-facing) self-appointed leadership role of Eysenck about the development of behaviour therapy after the late 1950s (Eysenck, 1960); a role he later shamelessly boasted, while admitting that he only ever treated one patient (Eysenck, 1997b). For example, despite that lack of clinical experience, he became the founding editor of what was to become a prestigious journal, *Behaviour Research and Therapy*. Eysenck was more politician than clinician, which is reflected in his skilful tactics about warding off the cultural legacy of psychoanalysis, noted at the outset above.

Thus if Freud could be accused, quite fairly, of opportunistically changing his mind, then much the same could be said of a key disdainful critic and new leader in clinical psychology (Eysenck, 1949; cf. Eysenck and Gwynne-Jones, 1958). Eysenck glimpsed a future professional regime in which psychosis would be treated medicinally by psychiatrists and neurosis treated by psychologists, but definitely not within the psychoanalytical tradition (Eysenck, 1975). This was about science being used rhetorically as part of a bid for professional legitimacy from clinical psychology. The aim was to displace medically dominated psychodynamic psychotherapy with behaviour therapy (Pilgrim and Treacher, 1991).

Eysenck and his South London colleagues, along with others in the USA and South Africa, began what is now dubbed 'first wave cognitive-behavioural therapy' (CBT), though this is a misnomer in my view. It was basically about *behaviour therapy* underpinned by Pavlovian principles and some concessions to North American learning theory. In this view, our reported distress and behavioural dysfunction were simply about our conditioning history, interacting with our variable susceptibility to the inherited personality characteristic of neurosis (see Chapter 4). Eysenck's adapted form of methodological behaviourism, blended with his personality theory, was a version of reductionism and just another epistemic fallacy within positivist psychology.

Behaviour therapy's insistence on working only with the surface behaviour of concern to patients, or those around them, permitted or connoted only a very a thin account of being human, with conditioning alone explaining our distress in life (an arrogant and reductionist version of *erklären*). Psychoanalysis, as well as existentialism and phenomenology, offered us instead richer and deeper versions of psychology; as a consequence because personal accounts are listened to credulously, nothing is barred in principle from respectful understanding and interpretation (*verstehen*). Behavioural psychology dismisses anything beyond presenting symptoms (distressed or dysfunctional behaviour) as being an irrelevant diversion and scientifically redundant. Methodological behaviourism was based on a naïve form of realism, which failed to attend properly to the full and complex ontology of our inner lives in its fluxing entirety. Ironically then, psychoanalysis, existentialism and phenomenology had a *greater* claim to objectivity than behaviourism because the object of their enquiry (inner life) was being addressed carefully and in detail.

In the 1960s, behaviour therapy started simply with the deconditioning of specific neurotic symptoms, but these represented only a small percentage of the range of complex problems presenting in practice to mental health professionals, which posed a problem for its credibility (Yates, 1970). Under the force of evidence of this limitation of success and applicability positivists were hoist by their own petard. Behaviour therapy (the clue is in the name, with its limited focus on *behaviour*) from pragmatic necessity now began to take *inner events* seriously and so they were let back into the fold of empiricist psychology. These were the *meanings* reported by patients about their presenting problems, disrupting a fundamental behaviourist assertion. Surely if behaviourism stood for anything, in its various guises, it supposedly stood for *behaviour* as the one and only *sine qua non* of human science.

That metaphysical axiom from behaviourism had now been betrayed by these 'second wave' CBT practitioners (Pilgrim, 2011). As a consequence, the oxymoron of 'Cognitive-Behavioural Therapy' emerged in our culture. By the turn of this century it had captured the imagination of mental health policy makers, still in the thrall of British empiricism (Layard et al., 2006). The latter report, led by an economist, noted that CBT was short and straightforward: it could 'cure' (sic) mental illness in just a few sessions and it was not 'backward looking', a snipe at psychoanalysis. These alleged advantages were aligned with the mass availability of therapy from the British National Health Service (NHS) and with a long-held British cultural wariness about in-depth psychological explorations.

During the 1970s, 'second wave' CBT emerged in this varied and highly weakened behaviourist vein (e.g. Mahoney, 1974). Today, in its 'third wave', CBT has become so open-textured that Eysenck's original scientism has been churned up and lost in a vortex of eclecticism. Although it marks a return to behaviourism from cognitivism in some ways, it also can be 'person centred'; a humanist not behaviourist ideology in the discipline. Even Buddhism is used as a source of therapeutic authority, though the modernist positivist pre-occupation with both diagnostic categories and evidence of therapeutic efficacy remains in the eclectic mix (e.g. Hayes, 2004). 'Third wave CBT' is so pluralistic now that it is difficult to define its core premises.

The legitimacy of psychoanalysis reconsidered in the light of the rise of behaviourism

The scientism of the behavioural tradition, begun after the Second World War, deflected mainstream psychology from considering properly the strengths and weaknesses of the older tradition of psychoanalysis. The displacement of psychoanalysis by behaviour therapy for many brought an end to any remaining significance of the old psychodynamic tradition. However, today a critical realist account is still relevant about the latter.

So, returning to Freud's account of the mind, he considered that the ego needed to survive unencumbered by anxiety and guilt. Thus in his wider theorising, drawn from a form of biographical psychology in the consulting room, Freud was assuming that his descriptions of reality (for example the structures of the id and ego, or the defence mechanisms) *were* the reality of the mind, rather than his preferred *knowledge* of the mind. This was to be the first of many examples of epistemic fallacy to be evident in the psychoanalytical tradition; but to be fair that tendency has been the case in *all* psychological theories, as I noted above in relation to behaviour therapy.

Because interpretation was an explicit and central part of psychoanalytical practice, then its practitioners were always discussing proposals, possibilities and hypotheses in their musings in both case discussions and actual conversations with patients. In other words they were indulging in experiments in epistemological relativism but with the therapist's power having the last word in the clinic (see Szasz's point on transference above).

Thus we see a contradiction at the heart of psychoanalysis. On the one hand, at times it was claiming to offer a description in general of how the mind worked (it was called a 'metapsychology') and offering covering laws. This then was a positivist assertion of ontology: a claim about how the mind actually is universally. On the other hand, at times it reserved the right to debate knowledge and to discard or prefer options, which was the inevitable task of any attempt at creating a legitimate hermeneutic science, with its emphasis on meanings in their *particular* contexts.

On the couch, a statement of a patient or their emotional reaction to their therapist *could mean this and not that.* However, by making that point, psychoanalysts wanted to debate other possibilities with their colleagues outside the consulting room, for example in case conferences or when reading papers at their scientific meetings. The option was left open that the very same reported statement or irrational conduct of the patient *could mean several* things, in deliberations between professional colleagues.

This then is a complex matter because psychoanalysts are dealing with meaning in a range of ways. There is the initial or raw meaning to the patient and then there is its meaning expressed response suggested in interpretation by their therapist (a transitive comparison of a statement and a meta-statement). There is also potentially the meaning of the patient's statement as an actual description of an aspect of their life in its concrete singularity (i.e. 'this really happened to me in my particular life'), which has an intransitive biographical referent. In Chapter 7 I noted this point made by Eide

(2012) when accounts from survivors of child sexual abuse were being depicted by paedophile advocacy groups as 'fictions'.

Personal accounts are in part memories giving testimony to particular events in our particular lives. In this sense some of the time psychoanalysts, like all psychological therapists whatever their model, are inevitably existential analysts (Sartre, 1998) and are dealing with accounts like a detective might deal with past crimes newly reported. In the client's personal account, there is a mixture of imperfect memory, shifting meaning attributions and allusions to events that actually happened.

Then there are all the meanings compared and contrasted *post hoc* in psychoanalytical case discussions. This even lead at times to psychoanalysts developing taxonomies of psychopathology overlapping with those from within the eugenic tradition of Kraepelin (Abraham, 1912/1953). This was another reflection of ambivalence from psychoanalysts: were they studying unique biographies and subjecting them to a hermeneutic exercise, one by one, or were they, like confident positivists, *generalising* about human functioning and then slotting individuals into the taxonomic categories used across Kraepelinian psychiatry?

It is little surprising then that the ambiguity embedded in hermeneutic explorations is a scenario of great fluidity, demanding a substantial tolerance of uncertainty from its psychological researchers and practitioners. It is also little surprising that the analyst intermittently may wish to bring certainty (or some semblance of it) into the proceedings. The taxonomies of Abraham is one example here; so too is the concept of transference. This was invented by Freud and gave therapists a sense of security as an expected pattern in intimacy; see my summary above about Szasz (1963) and his critique of the concept.

The problem was that the real enough *tendency* of us replaying our way of relating to those we are intimate with, from the past to the present, risked becoming a (covering) *law*. This shifted us from a legitimate expectation of *probability* (approved of by critical realism) to one of regular or *certain prediction* (a dubious positivist aspiration). For many psychoanalysts *everything* that was expressed from patients was transference, which was a risky position to adopt as Szasz (ibid.) was keen to emphasise. It might simply be wrong sometimes; the matter of fallibility in all human thought. The 'everything is transference' position was at odds with **epistemic humility** and it encouraged a regime of power with the professional not the client at the centre.

The epistemological fluidity in Freud's developing work drew particular critical attention from some psychoanalysts themselves (the example of transference challenged by Szasz was an example just given). However, what does it matter that theories are revised, after all this is commonplace in both natural and social science? In this case though the answer to that question entailed an accusation that Freud was an early clinical detective who was quite properly identifying the mental health impact of child sexual abuse. He abandoned that theory and, his critics argue, he thereby abandoned its victims.

After 1920 Freud's ideas bedded down for a while, but not for long. The first contention of historical significance was the standoff between Anna Freud and Melanie Klein. Although this reflected two approaches to child analysis, Klein's over-zealous focus on inherited aggression and her insistent approach to very early (pre-Oedipal) infancy strained against the Freudian orthodoxies of his three psychosexual phases. Anna Freud defended her father's canon against the Kleinian deviation but Klein always considered herself a loyalist as well.

After the Second World War, a compromise between the two was adopted by a non-aligned ('Independent') group of analysts, which went on to develop the British object-relations theory associated with Ronald Fairbairn, Donald Winnicott and Ronald Laing (Guntrip, 1977; Raynor, 1990). It also triggered the development of 'attachment theory' from John Bowlby, noted above and which I discussed in Chapter 9 (Ainsworth and Bowlby, 1991). In the USA 'ego psychology' developed within clinical psychoanalysis, aligned according to its critics with American individualism and adaptation to capitalist alienation (Hartmann, 1939/1958; cf. Fromm, 1970).

We can note then that the breadth of views within the fragmented psychoanalytical community placed varying forms of emphasis on different parts of our four planar social being. Freud 'the biologist of the mind' arguably focused primarily on our relationship with the natural world, a point emphasised then by Klein and hence her pleading that she was a loyalist not a dissenter in relation to the Freudian cause. The more environmentally orientated object-relations group focused on the plane of relationality. Bowlby hovered on the boundary between the two planes of the biological and relational. The more existentially orientated analysts like Laing and Lomas focused more on the plane of our unique personalities. I come back to the recurring question of the positioning of *any* version of psychology in relation to the four planar social being in the next and final chapter.

Discussion

We might offer an answer to the question at the beginning of this chapter, about the marginalisation of psychoanalysis, by referring to a few factors in the story of Freud and his legacy. His theory was driven by practice-based evidence, not evidence-based practice. This was out of sync with the norms expected within laboratory psychology, favoured by the positivist orthodoxy in the emerging discipline I discussed in Chapter 2.

Both the laboratory and the clinic as closed systems encourage the error of transduction. However, within the rhetoric of empiricist academic psychology, the first one is valorised, whereas the second is considered highly suspect, when offered in good faith by, for example, psychoanalysts. Also Freud's theory wobbled variably between positivism (particularly his hoped-for neuro-reductionism, derived from his early days as a neurologist) and more speculative forms of hermeneutics, which may have been confusing even for those *not* hostile to his cause.

His case was not helped by his dogmatic move from one version of theory to another, his tendency sometimes to reject those expressing views he disagreed with and his poor acknowledgement of the contribution of others, particularly female analysts. That dogmatism was shaped by Freud's understandable defensiveness in the face of vitriolic and foreboding anti-Semitism common in Europe in the first part of the 20th century. And then later the psychoanalytical tradition would be out of favour with the anti-subjectivism of behaviourists in the middle of the 20th century, even though 19th-century empiricists had been quite content to study inner life (see Chapter 6).

Psychoanalysis after the Second World War was scorned for being incorrigibly unscientific (from Eysenck) or queried less aggressively for being unfalsifiable (from Popper). However, falsifiability is not a trump card because it is not how science is able to proceed much of the time in practice; in truth more typically it relies on **retroduction**, case by case, than the hypothetico-deductive method. Accordingly, for critical realists, the latter cannot determine the legitimacy of academic reflections or forms of methodology in human science, especially when we are dealing with the hidden aspects of our inner realities, which are in constant flux. As for the meaning of 'science' (a systematic form of enquiry), then a psychoanalyst has as much right *as any other psychologist* to suggest ways of exploring the complexities of our inner realities.

Listening to accounts of people in their concrete singularity and interpreting their meanings is surely a good enough start in psychology as an exercise in retroduction. It may not produce an *exhaustive version* of human science, and may be open to healthy contestation (as my criticisms rehearsed above indicate), but it has every right to make an *illuminative contribution*. If psychoanalysts limit themselves to the latter and avoid the aspirations of the former (which Freud slipped into at times), then their contribution to human science is fully legitimate and deserves our full respect.

Moreover, as I argued earlier, but repeat here for emphasis, psychoanalysis has every right to claim a form of *objectivity* about inner life because it takes that reality seriously as its object of enquiry; that is the hallmark of objectivity, not the false promise of value-neutrality from positivism. Rejections from behaviourism of inner life, with its claim of enhanced objectivity, actually weakened its case by producing a crass, simplistic and disrespectful account of our humanity. Inner life is real, complex and powerful. It can be, and often is, causally efficacious. 'Second' and 'third' wave CBT *had* to concede this point eventually because the powers of inner reality, like the roots of a tree or the deep currents of an ocean, keep making themselves manifest.

Those powers might be denied, within a game of scientific rhetoric, but they cannot be *defied* for too long, as the collapse of behaviour therapy, as a shallow and simplistic form of putative scientific therapeutics, demonstrated. Moreover, like the seabed or outer space, inner life has vast areas of unobserved reality. Freud offered his version of exploring that fact, though this was by no means the first look at the unconscious. This reinforces the point that our interiority is ontologically durable and this logically necessitates our long-term interest in offering knowledge about its mysteries (Whyte, 1960).

Echoing Auden's point earlier, for all its faults psychoanalysis, as an epistemological venture with a particular preferred methodology (the 'talking cure' with its focus on the concept of transference), was broadly and appropriately aligned with the ontology of inner life. That ontology rendered psychoanalysis (it could have been something else approximating to) fit for purpose. In addition, as a profession it emerged in a particular social context. As Isaksen (2016) correctly points out, relevant conditions of possibility include *both* considerations of the content of disciplinary knowledge *and* the wider features of the world that might enable or disable its growth, at a time and place.

One condition of possibility we can consider, reflecting both of these, is the limited disciplinary character of psychology, as an immature but ambitious discipline in the early 20th century. As I noted in Chapters 2 and 6, psychology then, as now, was caught between defaulting methodologically to empiricism and positivism, in order to develop ambitiously an explanatory and potentially predictive science (the empirically detached method of *erklären*), or opting more cautiously for interpretive science instead (the empathically engaged method of *verstehen*). Psychoanalysis, both during and after Freud's lifetime, criss-crossed this divide between positivist attempts of detached certainty, with their expected covering laws about the human psyche in all circumstances, and speculative forms of hermeneutics about the situated-meanings of personal accounts and praxis (Luyten et al., 2006).

For those hostile to the Freudian cause, its occasional implausible claim to positivist certainties about the mind confirmed that psychoanalysis could not, and should not, be taken seriously by mainstream psychology. And this was not only about the scorn from behaviourism, within the new discipline of psychology. Contempt from behaviourists in the mid-20th century was preceded, much earlier, by a *medical* rejection in Anglo-Saxon circles (Turner, 1996). In the case of these 'anti-psychoanalysts', from within the profession of psychiatry at the turn of the century, it was a call to British 'stiff upper lip' stoicism and anti-German sentiments that shaped the rejection of psychoanalysis, rather than any coherent philosophical or scientific position. After the First World War there was a very temporary public interest in psychoanalysis, but this declined in favour of a desexualised version of depth psychology (Rapp, 1988).

Thus mainstream opposition to psychoanalysis in psychology and psychiatry reflected both philosophical and ideological objections, inflected by cultural antipathy (in the case just noted in Britain). Some of these objections were rooted in a wider Gentile middle-class culture, reflecting wider prejudices of their time and place about sex and Jews. An analogy here is the willingness of early empiricist psychology to prosecute a eugenic case against the poor and the alien, with the development of the psychology of individual differences, which I discussed in Chapter 4. This found extensive middle-class sympathy across the political spectrum.

Conclusion

We can only answer the question posed at the outset about the marginalisation of psychoanalysis in mainstream psychology if we adopt a historical analysis. This starts with the early threat it posed to the positivist orthodoxy of psychology as an aspiring scientific discipline. It then goes on to consider epistemological matters (such as practice-based evidence, not evidence-based practice, and Freud's ambivalence about medical positivism and the contrasting merits of hermeneutics), as well as ontological matters, which would refer to the details of *both* our inner *and* outer reality. Apart from this elephant in the room about the ontology of our interiority, we can also reflect critically on the particular context of the emergence of psychoanalysis: the ambiguous threat or promise of medical dominance in the early days of the new discipline of psychology; the role of patriarchy; and the anti-Semitism prevalent at the time in Europe.

The last of these shaped in which cultural context the debates about psychoanalysis were located. The expansive but doomed 'Aryan' war on both liberal democracy and communism by the Nazis, with anti-Semitism as its dogmatic and unrepentant driver, was then an important condition of possibility for later developments in psychoanalysis. Without it the Freudians and the Kleinians would not have had their lively debates in North London for the world to witness and evaluate. British empiricism had to give way in London for a while to an anomalous cultural period, when hosting debates about Continental hermeneutics. Without that war, the Frankfurt School would not have made its notable contribution, with psychoanalytically informed critical theory flourishing in the USA, before being partially restored, post-war, in Germany.

Although psychoanalysis was marginalised in mainstream psychology it retained a globally recognised cultural and intellectual relevance. Eysenck's attempt at a contemptuous deletion was only a very partial success *within* the discipline of psychology, where many adherents remained in its clinical wing or rejected methodological behaviourism in a range of other ways. An ironical historical footnote is that Eysenck left his native Austria in response to the rise of Nazism. He found the home of British empiricism a welcoming and secure base for his aggressive turn against continental hermeneutics. Without Eysenck and other émigrés, British empiricism would not have been rejuvenated so expertly. This point about cultural renewal in British intellectual life also applies to another relevant émigré, Karl Popper.

British empiricism, by its own logic, undermines philosophical debate; hence the Ward and Rivers citation in Chapter 2 being both powerful and self-negating. By triggering a narrow obsession with the facts and by deriding philosophical speculation, British empiricism depleted the capacity of native intellectual labour to be confidently reflective. Foreign intellectual labour was then imported to replenish that weak capacity, in this case the role of Eysenck and Popper were key but there were many other émigrés at the Institute of Psychiatry in South London after the Second World War that could be listed. They played their part in the spats with other émigrés north of the Thames, in the rapidly convened psychoanalytical community of middle-class Hampstead.

Thus the story of psychoanalysis is important to tell for a wide range of reasons, some disciplinary, some political, some cultural and some historical. Psychology students today should not be denied access to a proper appraisal of psychoanalysis, any more than they should remain ignorant of existentialism and phenomenology. The durable fact of our inner reality warrants this assertion. Our inner lives are real, part fluid and part stable, and they are always embedded in a complex open system as a function of our four planar social being. Accordingly, we should approach them with a mixture of caution and respect in a spirit of epistemic humility.

Psychologists should not be ashamed to explore inner reality imaginatively, including the use of insights from psychoanalysis and existentialism. If they abandon that exploration then sensitive poets, observant novelists, clever lyricists, wise yoga teachers, honest faith leaders, Zen masters and applied philosophers will be on hand to fill the gap. The risk then would be that their versions of *phronesis* about the bigger picture of human life might make a mockery of orthodox psychological expertise, with its pedestrian history of misleading positivism and unimaginative closed-system reasoning.

With that caution in mind, the wise lessons from psychanalysis, not just its (real enough) shortcomings, should be part of the curriculum for psychology students. And with that broader education, psychologists would be better prepared and placed to collaborate with other disciplines interested in building a genuinely human science. Academic psychology does not have a monopoly on understanding human experience and behaviour, despite its tendency towards disciplinary imperialism in this regard. This plea for interdisciplinary collaboration is a cue for my next and final chapter.

12

THE POSSIBILITY OF A CRITICAL REALIST HUMAN SCIENCE

Introduction

The scatter of case studies I have offered to illustrate the advantages of using the philosophy of critical realism reflect my mixed background in clinical psychology and (subsequently) mental health policy. It would be quite possible for another psychologist to apply the strictures of critical realism to a different list of topics if they wished, which I would more than welcome. That hope can be contrasted with the professional bid for legitimacy offered by Ward and Rivers in 1904, which I quoted in Chapter 2 and alluded to occasionally later. They were intent on rejecting the authority of philosophy in general, while (paradoxically) relying upon the sovereignty of positivism. Over a hundred years have passed and those schooled in psychology in the academy are faced now with the turbulent and contradictory legacy of positivism and postmodernism. So how does the disciplinary rhetoric of psychology look today?

As I finalise the draft for this chapter (June 2019), I receive this month's edition of *The Psychologist*, which tempts me into a short version of critical discourse analysis (see end of Chapter 3). Every month its first inner page tells the reader that it is 'the magazine of The British Psychological Society'. It aims 'to fulfil the main object of the Royal Charter … to promote the advancement and diffusion of a knowledge of psychology pure and applied'. The definite article of the title of the magazine suggests no requirement to define its national source (until 1988 it was known as the *Bulletin of the British Psychological Society*). Along with the full pomp of Royal approval, this could suggest a taken-for-granted confidence, borne of the colonial past of an ethnocentric island, just off mainland Europe. (In case post-colonial ethnocentricity is in doubt, at the time of writing we are witnessing the chaos triggered by half of the British population wanting to reject its European status: 'Brexit'.)

The eclectic mix of this particular edition of *The Psychologist* is typical. It includes a well-written piece on the emotional life of the 'England men's football team'; for

Australian and US readers, this refers to soccer. Others pose and answer questions: 'Why are life events troubling?', 'Can I sympathise with mothers who have hurt their children?', 'How does the weather and climate affect personality and behaviour?' and 'Where in the brain is creativity?'. In the last of these pieces Dietrich (2019) explores some of the risks of neuro-reductionism I addressed in Chapter 5.

The whole of page 14 of the edition is taken up with a promotional colour spread of three unsmiling adults, entitled 'We are Psychologists'. Given that *The Psychologist* is the in-house journal of the British Psychological Society, it seems to be telling the readers who they are, in case they need reminding. Maybe it is encouraging the use of the piece as propaganda to others, as a video link is provided. At the top of the page is a middle-aged white woman gazing wistfully into the distance. The images below her contain a young white man, head tilted down pensively, like Rodin's 'The Thinker', and a smartly dressed (neck tie faintly loosened) bespectacled middle-aged black man. He is clutching a mug of tea or coffee and looking straight into the camera; the mixed semiotics of this photograph alone could warrant a full page of interpretation.

More clarity is offered about this photo depiction in the crafted accompanying narrative. It begins '… We are Compassionate, Curious and Caring'. This is a two-to-one ratio of axiology to epistemology, which can be contrasted with the value-free naïve realism promoted by Ward and Rivers in 1904. And of course being 'curious' could take many forms, warranting an open mind about methodology. The narrative goes on to be more assured: 'Psychology is everywhere. We invented the tea break in factories, we changed the face of criminal investigation and we made advertising a whole lot more effective … sorry about that'. So if the discipline is 'everywhere', might this reflect shameless disciplinary imperialism?

Stereotypes are challenged as the narrative continues: 'No we can't read your mind, but we can help you to understand it better. Every day, psychologists are working to tackle stigma, to find answers, to learn more our behaviour as humans'. Bets are being hedged here about the metaphysics of the discipline. Your mind cannot be read (the unobservable is off limits) but 'it' can be understood 'better'. Ditto in relation to your 'behaviour' (note not your conduct or your actions). However, *human* behaviour is being distinguished, albeit vaguely, and so the role of agency is neither acknowledged nor denied.

The overall intended sense of the page is a Pollyanna depiction of a diversity of people, their topics of interest and their earnest and binding professional curiosity. The unapologetic sullying of disinterested science with value-loaded good intentions, seemingly or maybe deliberately, takes us a long distance, not just from Ward and Rivers, but also from Galton and Pearson. There is no confession in the narrative about the cacophony of meanings created by the clashing legacies of positivism and postmodernism, or of the fracturing displacement of behaviourism by versions of cognitivism and phenomenology.

The rhetorical focus is on people, with operationalised credentials in Psychology (capital 'P'), who inhabit a shared and reassuring disciplinary culture. Purportedly they know what they are doing when being 'Compassionate, Curious and Caring'. This might imply subtly that these attributes are missing from those who are *not*

Psychologists. But we now haves a serious problem about the coherence of the discipline. If being 'compassionate' and 'caring' might have offended the positivists of the early 20th century (remember that Hans Eysenck in 1949 insisted that psychologists should not even be therapists), it would also not suit the later anti-humanism of the postmodernists. Both of those philosophical movements would agree on the need to be 'curious' but disagree on its meaning in practice. The page promoting Psychology sets many hares running when read critically, rather than gullibly.

The disciplinary authority of contemporary psychology

Most disciplines are divided internally and from one another. Even those close by may struggle to grasp the concepts and methods of their neighbour. That struggle may be compounded at times by *competition for ownership*: 'interest work' exists in academia as much as in any market place or political arena. Disciplines and sub-disciplines, as well as leaders and disciples of preferred theories, vie for attention and legitimacy.

Sometimes the debates can get heated. Henry Kissinger once commented, I think a little unfairly, that 'University politics are vicious precisely because the stakes are so small.' Whether vicious or politely argumentative, academics are the way they are in part at least because of the sub-division of their working life into disciplinary silos. The pretence of tribal cohesion and socially approved competencies (for example in the promotion page just examined) is common in conservative accounts within the sociology of the professions (in the tradition of Durkheim). However, Weberian and Marxian accounts are more critical about the role of professionals in society and the self-interest and fights for dominance they pursue (Macdonald, 1995).

Moreover, in the case of psychology still existing, as it does, on the cusp of the *naturwissenschaften* and the *geisteswissenschaften*, its internal fractiousness is amplified by a lack of clarity about on which side to fall or to take a leap. Those with a claim to the human sciences are not always generous to one another and forays into disciplinary imperialism create their own dynamics. At the turn of the 20th century, the gradual separation of psychology from medicine on one side and philosophy on the other was an early confirmation of this point. Neither medicine nor philosophy were to give up their authority over human experience and conduct readily. Even today some of the topics claimed with confidence by psychology are still treated possessively by its older and more self-confident 'parents'. Philosophy has certainly not abandoned its claim to expertise about the human mind and medicine still has much to say about abnormal psychology. In the latter regard, we see this not only in psychiatry but in specialities like sexual medicine and psychosomatics.

Accordingly, and despite its best efforts, the discipline of psychology has not unilaterally colonised human science. Moreover, I think that applied psychologists, in spite of their lesser status in the eyes of their colleagues in the academy, tend to be more in tune with the limitations of their trade and are more accepting that others in their field of work with alternative disciplinary credentials can be wise. That shared wisdom (*phronesis*) arising from praxis, say in the fields of healthcare, education or the daily world of work, emerged because of addressing the contingencies of human life as an open system, in particular organisational contexts facing particular dilemmas. To my mind, practical challenges outside of the arenas of the laboratory and testing room have driven the survival and popularity of psychology, in particular in its forensic, educational, occupational and clinical applications.

Those recruiting for university psychology courses remain buoyed by their continuing popularity. I doubt that this reflects a love of statistics in the young or an avid curiosity about the detail of a model within cognitive science. Cultural scenarios from mass media representations of the calm and perceptive clinician or the shrewd forensic advisor to exciting criminal investigations are more likely to capture the imagination of the young candidate for a psychology course. The discipline might even offer the naïve applicant the prospect of 'understanding myself and others'. The outcome of that expectation I suspect will be highly variable.

Academic orthodoxy in psychology has been constituted by particular sorts of methods and theories, which have not encouraged our confidence in the discipline's respect for our humanity in its rich contextualised complexity. Western academic psychology over a relatively short period of time (only a little over a hundred years really) has valorised or fetishised methods in the closed system of the laboratory (experimentalism), reduced humanity to fixed putative universal traits (psychometrics) and over-valued brain functioning (reductive neuroscience). There have been counter-trends as well though, which I discussed in Chapter 3. This contention is little surprising, given the challenge of understanding what it is to be human.

Reflecting on developments during the past hundred years, I suggest that the orthodox centre of the discipline has been characterised by the following overlapping features.

1) Methodologism

An anxiety in the discipline about its scientific legitimacy has tilted psychology towards methodologism, albeit now with the hegemony of quantitative methods being softened, to some extent, by a concession to the role of qualitative methods. With regard to the first of these, the search for Humean constant conjunctions, verified using the earnest statistical methods traceable to Pearson and Spearman, has dominated the field.

This methodological focus has limited the discipline's theoretical ambitions and reflected a strong residual self-conscious reliance on forms of empiricism, which I return to in point (3) below. For example, qualitative methods can still be retained within an empiricist view of research. This allows those on the corridors of psychology departments holding quite different views about theory, and looking at very diverse topics, to enjoy a sense of disciplinary loyalty: methodologism becomes their shared comfort blanket. Some critiques of modern psychology orthodoxy have focused on this problem of methodologism and they can be read to support the summary point I am making here with the space I have (e.g. Toomela and Valsiner, 2010; Danzinger, 1985). To be clear here, critical realism is not unconcerned with methodology (not at all) but it does put it into perspective. I come back to methodological specificity and methodological pluralism and tolerance below.

Making a fetish of methods does not solve the problem of theoretical contestation nor can it substitute for proper metaphysical reflection. In particular it risks the delusion that methodological integrity is all that matters in science. A danger of the spurious separation of facts and values by positivism is that we ignore the need to judge science by axiological, not just methodological, criteria. For example, it is possible to pursue an evil form of science with great methodological precision and potentially even useful outcomes (to some party or other). Did Nazi medical science in the concentration camps yield useful data for the military? Do some forms of torture increase or decrease the veracity of accounts under interrogation and prevent terrorist acts? Does capital punishment reduce the homicide rate? The fact that we can pose these sorts of discomforting questions demonstrates that not only can truth not be reduced to procedure (the fetish of methodological precision) but also that such an obsession deflects us from needed critical reflexivity about the values operating in our work and the different meanings we bring to it. The cruel and degrading treatment of human beings in the name of science has to be appraised by criteria other than the methodological. Instead we need to understand *why we value certain things in life and not others*; this necessitates a wider form of intellectual and moral sensibility (Sayer, 2011).

Moreover, that lack of theoretical coherence is itself an inevitable outcome of the tendency to settle on a particular plane of our four plane social being or a preferred niche within it (see below). This has left psychology prone to the problem of reductionism, illuminated by the metaphor of the blind men and the elephant. It provides temporary and situated claims to certainty but these lack transferability to, and therefore credibility about, complex open systems. And even if methodologism is seemingly an escape from this conundrum about a lack of theoretical consensus in the discipline, methods may themselves be incommensurable. For example, some are deductive and others inductive, some descriptive and some interpretive, some are committed to a faith in Humean constant conjunctions and some are not. However, the agreed consensus is on method *of some sort* defining proper or legitimate psychology, thereby creating a boundary separating it from forms of psychological amateurism. This cues the next point.

2) Magpie eclecticism

In Chapter 2 I noted the historical point made by Richards (2010) that, at the turn of the 20th century, Psychology with a capital 'P' set itself against a long-standing and wide range of forms of psychologising about life. In marking itself off from both ancient philosophy and contemporary amateurism, it looked around for academic resources and they were easily found. The emerging discipline could readily co-opt the methods and theories of cognate disciplines, even if one of them (philosophy) has been dismissed as 'old hat' because it is speculative, not fact-based. By and large, these forms of adoption emerged first from the pretensions of positivism and then from the reaction to that dominant trend in the form of postmodernist psychology; the opposing trends that I examined in Chapters 2 and 3 respectively.

Early experimentalism, in the work of Wilhelm Wundt and Gustav Fechner, modelled itself on physics, thereby sacralising 'the laboratory'. The behavioural statistics developed by the eugenically inspired psychology of individual differences relied, and continues to rely, on the power of a branch of mathematics in order to legitimise and promote psychometrics. (Karl Pearson had been a Professor of Applied Mathematics for over 25 years before taking up the first Chair in Eugenics, endowed by Francis Galton, at University College London.) These positivistic preoccupations operating in the hallowed closed system of the psychological laboratory or in the consulting room of the psychometrician, detached from the complex and idiosyncratic life-world of the human subject under their expert scrutiny, encouraged the risk of transduction.

Also, methods deployed *outside* the psychological laboratory were not the sole possession of the discipline nor, by and large, were they invented by it. A particular favoured qualitative method in social psychology is ethnography, which was developed by early 20th-century anthropologists, and offered prior to that by historians and geographers. Another is ethnomethodology, which was developed by sociologists and culminated in conversational analysis and discursive psychology (Garfinkel, 1967). As I noted in Chapter 3, discourse analysis and deconstruction came from philosophy and linguistics (Foucault, 1984; Harris, 1951). As for theory, social phenomenology is derived from a meld of sociology (the work of Alfred Schutz) and philosophy (the work of Martin Heidegger, Edmund Husserl and Maurice Merleau-Ponty). A version of this favoured currently by qualitative psychological researchers is that of interpretive phenomenological analysis. Some practical case studies taught in social psychology are traceable to the social interactionist micro-sociology of the Chicago School. Both social phenomenology and symbolic interactionism were stimulated by the writings of the sociologist Max Weber.

When social psychology *has* developed theories that it can fairly call its own, then these have tended to default to individualism. For example, such a decontextualising tendency can be found in attribution theory (Heider, 1958), cognitive dissonance theory (Festinger, 1957) and the elaboration likelihood model (Petty and Cacioppo, 1986). The opening use of the definite article in Heider's work, *The Psychology of Interpersonal Relations*, typifies the aspiration of positivist psychology to offer empirical invariance. It also undermines epistemic humility and it positions relationality as the *only* plane to consider, when *all* four in our four planar social being are important ontologically (see below). Theories within social psychology may quite validly note some human tendencies some of the time, but as theories about the putative *fixity* of human functioning they are inherently absurd. How is it feasible to claim a single and definitive decontextualised account of the complexities of human relationality with a notion of '*the* psychology' of anything?

The overlapping epistemologies of the cognate disciplines examining human conduct, dilute any uni-disciplinary claim to authority and they ensure that any attempt at disciplinary imperialism has a hollow ring. Several disciplines, other than psychology, have developed an understanding of being human, which can be elaborated into a long list: anthropology, human geography, legal studies, sociology, behavioural economics, philosophy, sociolinguistics, medicine, social history, ecology, primatology, ethnomusicology, literary and cultural studies, political science, comparative theology and neuroscience.

Magpie eclecticism in psychology then has emerged as one strategic alternative to conceding the need for proper interdisciplinary collaboration and a genuine respect for the insights of others on this list. Psychology *nor any other individual discipline* can reasonably claim a monopoly role within human science, even if such bids for legitimacy are seductive for disciplinary leaders operating in academic silos. Moreover many of the other disciplines, like psychology, vary in how much they too have been disabled by the methodological strictures of positivism or postmodernism.

However, psychology may have stolen a march on the other disciplines in one respect by the way it has channelled its magpie eclecticism. This is about its individualistic focus, I noted above, which is highly attractive to a range of parties with and without power. Politicians gain from being seen to value individual rights and experience and by focusing on decontextualised individual agency. This is a dominant trope in politically conservative ideology and a way of making people responsible for their own challenges in life. In social policy discourse this is now called 'responsibilisation' (Liebenberg et al., 2015), a process that may be attractive to us all, to some degree. We all like to be taken seriously as individuals and enjoy being told that we are free to choose to have anything or be anything we want to be, despite the contingent and unequally distributed constraints on those expressed needs being fulfilled. The culture of narcissism linked in recent years to neo-liberalism is a wrap-around enhancement to these pre-existing tendencies, for both the powerful and the powerless.

3) The fear of the unobservable

The methods and theories preferred by psychologists in their immature modern discipline reflected their fear and avoidance of the unobservable. Quite soon that anxiety culminated in a desire within the discipline for behaviourism to define its legitimacy, which was a political Titanic because the ontology of inner life was a hardy perennial. It also led to a priggish contempt for psychoanalysis and, to a lesser extent, existentialism. I opted for several chapters in this book to elaborate this point about our mercurial and often hidden interiority, ending in my critical but ultimately sympathetic defence of forms of depth psychology. The desire for psychological science to stay on the firm ground at all times of the observable and positively present (the naïve realism I covered in Chapter 2), if adhered to earnestly, negates the relevance of the majority of reality. If we stay on the surface we will only ever achieve a superficial account. This point is as true for the hermeneutic aspiration of qualitative methods, as it is within the positivist tradition of verification via measurement. The former, not just the latter, can be superficially empiricist, bringing with it the same indifference to, or ignorance about, deep ontology.

Most of reality is absent not present and so the challenge of a truly human science is to respect that basic fact and work with it. Ridiculing or despising psychoanalysis or existentialism for their wooliness or uncertainties is not an answer to this point because the point remains. A disdain for the unobservable has left the door open for other approaches to conduct and experience, outside of the discipline of psychology, to have greater credibility. This tempers my point above about psychology stealing a march on them. I mentioned the *phronesis* of applied psychologists and the non-psychologists they work with in particular fields of daily life signalling this tendency. We can then add to it some of the shared wisdom of the organised religious traditions; I say this as a secularist and an agnostic, so I am no advocate of their given or inevitable authority (cf. Hartwig and Morgan, 2012). In addition there are the sophisticated insights of artists and writers, as well as investigative journalists. Even some less trivial forms of 'reality television' can sometimes give us direct insights in the complexities of daily life, even if we need dutifully concede the 'observer effect'.

For example, documentaries on police or health work expose complexities that would be difficult at times for academic researchers to begin to study, for both methodological resource reasons and ethical restrictions of access. The entrance of Ervin Goffman into the world of the psychiatric system as a wandering and causal ethnographer in the 1950s would not be possible today (cf. Goffman, 1961). Journalist go undercover and are lauded when they expose malpractice or wrongdoing but academic research from any discipline in a similar vein would typically be deemed ethically illegitimate. As a consequence 'official' psychology is left in the dark about much that exists in the flow of everyday life in a wide range of contexts. Its authority to understand ourselves in real-life scenarios can be readily usurped by the smart documentary maker.

Given these broad considerations about psychology lacking a mandate to monopolise intellectual authority in the field of human science, I now explore where it leaves us. Beyond this particular discipline, critical realists have already made the clear case for the recurring importance of interdisciplinarity if academics are to make a contribution to human survival and flourishing (Bhaskar et al., 2018). The latter offer us another 'holy trinity' to consider, beyond the starting point I summarised in Chapter 1 of ontological realism, epistemological relativism and judgemental relativism. That is, interdisciplinary work needs to be guided by: i) meta-theoretical unity; ii) methodological specificity; and iii) methodological pluralism and tolerance. The first of these implies the need to look for transdisciplinary forms of theorisation. The second implies a 'horses for courses' approach, i.e. what method is needed to answer this particular research question? The third follows from the first and second. Quantitative or qualitative methods may be appropriate separately or mixed, depending on the particular retrodictive challenge at hand in a field of research. These points will be explored more now in relation to human science.

Transdisciplinary implications

Ontological realism provides what seems like a fair starting point for the division and sub-division of intellectual labour. The work of the chemist or cytologist finds a ready home, when staying loyal to the object of their enquiry. The natural world does indeed contain chemicals and cells to be studied and that world in one form or other will be there beyond the Anthropocene. However, for now the latter exists even if precariously, so when we turn to human science then our view of ontology has to be elaborated as well.

Critical realism prompts us to accept reality as complex, laminated, largely absent and often unobservable, making our knowledge fallible and provisional but still the useful basis for judgemental rationality, case by case. Contextualised human complexity brings with it 'wicked problems' not amenable to formulaic solutions in advance but requiring a respect for case-by-case complexity in human life (Kunz and Rittel, 1970). That complexity in flux reflects the ontology of open systems and their inherent uncertainty, part obviousness (presence) and part mystery (absence). The closed-system logic of positivism offers no help to us (whatever it has done to sustain the disciplinary rhetoric of psychology). The scorn that positivism encouraged for the absent and the unobservable now needs to be reflected on in order to rebut it. Later I will focus on our four planar social being as a way forward but first I will offer some personal reflections on the unobservable, as the legitimacy of psychology has often been bound up with fetishising the positively present.

A re-look at the unobservable

In his later work Roy Bhaskar placed an increasing emphasis on absence and silence. As he put it, the positive is 'a tiny but important ripple on the surface of a sea of negativity' (Bhaskar, 1993: 5). Here Bhaskar is talking of the importance we place upon the *present* aspect of *ontology*, reconstruing Sartre's interest, as an existentialist, in understanding 'being in a plenitude of non-being'. Once we move towards understanding, not just accepting in principle, the complexity of reality, then we shift to *epistemology*. Naïve realists may not recognise that they have made the shift at all and then the **epistemic fallacy** follows, like night follows day.

As for postmodernists, they may disdain ontology but they need it in practice to do their work, when sticking repeatedly to the narrow epistemic concern with deconstructing texts. They protest that we only understand the world via the way we talk about and represent it and so reality has no independence from us. Ironically, in a mirror image of behaviourism, postmodernists render some explorations off-limits or futile or they negate our existence as unique individual agents (see Chapter 3). But it is positivism that has proved the biggest stumbling block in psychology to respecting the unobservable; at least postmodernists have a respect, in their unending discourses about discourses, about everything that is said and *not said*.

Positivism emphasises positivity: what is present and evident is real and true, rendering everything else untrustworthy and beneath the contempt of science. In doing so, this ensures that we enter a house of enquiry with a sign saying, 'Welcome To The Only True Path to Reality', and for emphasis in parenthesis, '(If You Can't See It, Then It Ain't Real)'. Bhaskar (see discussion above) does not reject the positive: it is 'important' but note it is only 'tiny'. Instead, positivism as a scientistic ideology renders the present sacred and the absent profane. This breeds a predictable arrogance in naïve realism, with humility in positivism being limited to a compliance with the (dubious) principle of verification. This is why Eysenck, with the smug confidence of a positivist, could describe psychoanalysis as being like 'reading sheep's entrails' (referring to a pre-scientific world of superstition).

As a humanist and an agnostic I mix in circles today in which the largely atheistic scientific community still at times breathes a superior sense of frustrated rationality in the face of the non-rational in human affairs, as if evidence produced by positivist science should, self-evidently, be an exclusive authority to solve all of our problems as a species. However, if in truth we know very little and if we honestly recognise the need for epistemic humility, then evidence about the surface of reality is important but it is still part of the 'tiny'. Moreover, the non-rational, not just the rational, are part of human reality so it behoves us to find ways to explore its messy complexity.

This point about tolerating complexity and needing in some way or other to deal with non-observable aspects of our experience, intentions and actions are of particular relevance for human scientists, as I quickly found out as a fledgling applied psychologist. When I moved from being a student of psychology to becoming a practitioner, it was like being hit by a truck. Virtually nothing I had learned prepared me for the real world in which people in distress or acting strangely, living complex lives and emerging from a wider range of past biographical contexts, put themselves before me for help. I had nothing much to offer them from my education except maybe the promise of a placebo effect from their faith in my notional credentials. My smile and willingness to listen was my only hope of surviving.

I knew very little and so I then had to find ways of thinking that turned a defeat into a victory. I found that in exploratory psychotherapeutic models from existentialism and psychoanalysis. Older hands I began to trust in supervision revealed a paradox to me, these traditions placed a positive value upon absence. Listen humbly. Do not speak authoritatively. Wait for a story to emerge. Do not decide in advance what is going on. Make sense and interpret tentatively. Share a view but let it be wrong without feeling insulted. Tolerate and clarify, but do not try to solve, uncertainty and confusion.

At some point I learned to name all of this as what the Romantic poet John Keats had called 'negative capability', that is 'when man is capable of being in uncertainties, mysteries, doubts, without any irritable reaching after fact and reason' (Keats, 1899: 277). A disdain for the unobserved and unobservable, encouraged by positivism in psychology, shuts out this wisdom. Expertise and confessed ignorance tend to fit poorly together. This is why therapists often seek comfort in the strictures of a preferred model of practice, with its offer of certainty in open systems. Uncertainty and professional authority are uneasy bedfellows but, as all applied psychologists know, a working compromise has to be found between them on a daily basis.

However, the 'tiny', but note 'important', relevance of positive evidence became helpful. This was not about *a priori* confidence from psychological findings guiding me about what to do and not do as a therapist. Rather it was about the confirmation that the models deployed and codified in textbooks by psychological therapists were of marginal relevance in practice. The quality of the relationship, not the slickness or coherence of the therapist's model or credentials, predicted outcomes. This created a clue that maybe relationality is intrinsically important to our sense of wellbeing (see later discussion on the four planar social being). It also confirmed that we have to mix fallibilism with the pragmatic need to make decisions in conditions of uncertainty.

The need for applied psychologists to tolerate uncertainty is not merely the affirmation of a disposition that characterises some of us more than others. This would make it only a useful idiosyncrasy that might be fetishised as an individual talent or reduced to a 'skill set' to be taught, that of patient and restrained empathy. More than that, it is *necessitated* by the ontology of human functioning, as part of an open system. When faced with ourselves, and even more so others, in truth most of the time we have no idea what is going on and what to make of it. Our ignorance of ourselves and others frequently outstrips clarity and insight.

Most of the time human beings simply think and act (quite successfully) and are not expected to understand and explain why. Hence ethnomethodology is intriguing and even amusing, when we challenge people to give an account of what they are doing and why. Personal accounts then can be offered but they are clunky and can be anxiety provoking or perplexing for the teller. Most of the time we only ask for personal accounts when 'things go wrong'. Ethnomethodologists and psychoanalysts reverse that traditional expectation by interrogating normally unreflective subjects in order to make sense of human life.

When and if we *do* secure a coherent personal account from ourselves or others, this provides only a very partial window into our social context; in my view ethnomethodologists are overly ambitious in their version of social science. We cannot understand human society by *simply* asking people about it, because they are largely oblivious to the complexities of the social structures that preceded their existence or situate it in the present (Archer, 2000). And if the psychoanalysts are correct, we can only offer a limited and 'defended' account of our lives. So whilst we should take personal accounts very seriously, they do not provide all of the answers when researching psychosocial complexity. Below I return to this from my experience as a psychologist working with a range of ordinary people and accounts of their lives.

That ontological picture of an open system in which the generative mechanisms of human functioning are often unobserved and not routinely reflected upon by social actors is our starting point for psychological enquiry. This means that anything the psychologist considers then converts into descriptions, interpretations and (even more riskily) explanations and so has to be provisional and partial. This warrants humility, which in turn has dialectically encouraged its opposite in psychology: believing that the constraints of the controlled psychological laboratory will provide us with certainties. This is a delusion because transduction fails us all: by controlling laboratory conditions we are *controlling out* the real world of our open system. Covering laws are wild goose chases then in human science. Positivism culminates in disciplinary arrogance and reductionism in psychology. It is a false prophet, as any applied psychologist who tells you the detailed truth about their working life and the emerging insights it furnishes will tell you.

When I worked as a clinical psychologist in the NHS in the north of England, I saw hundreds of patients from working-class and middle-class backgrounds with a range of presenting complaints, I had some capacity for problem solving with them. But that came from being open to experience and possessing some everyday knowledge, some of the time, of the lives they were living and had lived. My own life, with its mixture of early adversity and ordinariness had been replete with mistakes and prejudices but, despite or at times because of this baggage, somehow listening and responding to them seemed to help some of them some of the time. Sometimes the outcome was failure. Whether it was success or failure, any account of the outcome in my official reports and letters to colleagues was really an exercise in being smart after the event, clothing quite a lot of cluelessness with the semblance of coherence and certainty. Whether I was any good as a therapist remains an open question but what is in less doubt is that I got fairly smart at *post hoc* rhetoric.

This is precisely what we should expect in open human systems if we are applied psychologists. We join the fluxing lives of others very temporarily. We are one of a myriad causal influences in their lives, which might be a tipping point or an irrelevance. One arrogance of therapy is to talk of 'spontaneous remission' to account generically for change that happens without professional help. This is professional-centric and it disregards the ontology of open systems.

People may change for a wide range of reasons, which arise from the interplay of their own agency and the particular external contingencies of their lives. Their daily lives contain a shifting mix of benign influences, adversities and seemingly inconsequential events that may affect them, and they in turn respond to, attended by new and old forms of meanings and decision making. Sometimes people do not need therapy but a job or a new relationship. Sometimes they need to find a way of waking up to the fact that they are now an adult and no longer a child. The latter is a tough call for most of us, given the layers of dispositions, foibles and attachment styles we have inherited from childhood in our concrete singularity.

All of this points to a paradox, which I noted above: personal accounts should be taken seriously but *both* professional psychologists *and* those they research, or have as clients in applied settings, are also unaware, to varying degrees, about the context that was the source of their emergence. Whether we call this 'unconscious processes' or 'bad faith' or 'lack of awareness' is a debating (epistemic) point from moment to moment in our lives and in those of others. The answer does not lie either in rejecting personal accounts or in fetishising them but instead working seriously with the contradictions arising from us all being language-using social beings living in a mixed state of awareness and ignorance.

The insights I gleaned above, from my clinical experience, about ordinary people living in open systems and the need to tolerate uncertainty, emerged for a good while when I was completely ignorant of the strictures and illuminations of the philosophy of critical realism, as well as stumbling around in the dark much of the time, when trying to be an applied psychologist. I now elaborate on this point by turning from reflecting on my personal experience to reflecting on the implications of our four planar social being for human science as a basis for the development of transdisciplinary knowledge.

The utility of the concept of our four planar social being

We are part of the natural world and so human science would be unwise to ignore it. We exist in relation to others and so a human science without a handle on relationality will contain an enormous and distorting omission. We are thrown into a world of social structures, so experience and conduct minus an understanding of contingent social contexts will create a travesty of human science. We are persons in our unique concrete singularity and so a human science consisting only of discourses or reducing us to a few traits measured psychometrically will diminish our humanity.

Context is everything and covering laws are not feasible, though we can and should attempt to understand ourselves and our actions nonetheless. We might identify tendencies, demi-regularities or patterns that connect through time. For example, being poor or being abused in childhood tends to indicate the possibility of poor mental health and we might be curious about why people with friends seem to enjoy life more than those without and why winning the lottery is no guarantee of happiness. We can do all this while asking legitimate questions about concrete singularities: why is this particular person conducting themselves in this particular way at this time in their particular life in their particular social context past, present and future? Case formulation in psychology can be genuinely helpful to people and it does not require any belief in the rhetoric of positivist science. It also treats people as people and not merely as if they are a discourse or a text.

The co-existence of the four planes and the relationships within and between them makes human science challenging. However, it also clarifies our object of enquiry and this provides us with the basis for form of objectivity that differs radically from the specious claim to value-neutrality from positivism. Now objectivity means being true to our object of enquiry. By starting with ontology, critical realism encourages us to respect a range of foci for our curiosity about the world. Psychology is no different in this respect: our conduct as human agents and our interiority are its ontological focus. The form objectivity this implies is to find ways of taking them seriously and doing justice to their complexity.

There are broadly two ways to proceed with this considerable challenge. The first is to imagine grand theoretical schemes that are truly holistic and the second is to work collaboratively towards the development of transdisciplinary knowledge. On the first count some efforts have been made and I would include here Gregory Bateson's *Steps to an Ecology of Mind* (Bateson, 1972; Dalton, 2014) and the development of the concept of *autopoiesis* by Maturana and Varela (1980). A good recent summary of these arguments has been made in Jeremy Lent's *The Patterning Instinct* (Lent, 2017). Before these developments, Kurt Lewin in his field theory offered his version of holism and systemic reasoning (Lewin, 1951). Some versions of psychoanalysis have had similar ambitions but only its mergence with sociological currents from first Marx and later Weber and Parsons, in the work of the Frankfurt School, gave it a credibility beyond Freud's first attempt to offer a 'metapsychology'.

If grand theorising has its limitations as well as possibilities about an imagined future with a holistic form of human science, then the incremental alternative is the development of transdisciplinary knowledge in communities of scholars in constant respectful dialogue. We can think of steps towards this that begin with the pragmatics of multidisciplinary cooperation that morphs then into authentic interdisciplinary mutual understanding during the pursuit of shared goals and this then being the key to open the door into transdisciplinarity. This process is easier to envisage in principle than to put into practice for a number of reasons.

There are many situations in which multidisciplinary working could be a starting point for our optimistic journey. A caution though is that these are rarely flat power hierarchies with equal credence being given to participants. Healthcare is a good example where several disciplines have to work together on specific tasks of patient care. Sociologists have noted that they are characterised by medical dominance. That is, medical knowledge embodied in the leading physician predominates in any discussion and they have the last word. Ultimately the master-slave dynamic pervades decision making, though on pragmatic grounds this may not always matter for clinical outcomes. In the example of the perpetuation of a psychiatric positivism (see Chapter 10), this leaves critique aside during the perpetuation of a diagnose-and-treat approach to mental health problems. It obscures criticality about our understanding people who are distressed, troubling or unintelligible in society.

If you are a psychologist you may consider that we need to exercise that criticality (or you may opt to have blind faith in neo-Kraepelinian psychiatry). But the point is that to exercise that choice you need to explore matters beyond mere compliance with psychiatric positivism in the academy and the clinic, taking into account the complexity of our lives signalled by our four plane social being. A lack of criticality then creates a misleading feedback loop into the psychology curriculum in the academy, with textbooks being produced by *psychologists* aimed at *psychology* students, which is basically an uncritical regurgitation of psychiatric theory and practice; a sort of 'DSM-lite' version of reality (e.g. Comer, 2012; Carr, 2001).

In contexts in which medical dominance is less clear cut, such as health services research, there we also find multidisciplinary team work, including many health psychologists. Now the risk is not uni-disciplinary knowledge distortion (as is the case with abnormal psychology) but the challenge of communication between those socialised in separate disciplinary silos and their preferred theories and methods. As with the first vulnerability I noted about psychology above, we find a common default to methodologism to solve this problem (Gibbons et al., 1994). This allows those from different backgrounds to develop a commitment to methods required to answer a specific research question, about say the functioning of a part of the healthcare system or the effectiveness of an innovation.

The link between multidisciplinary research and methodologism is now a common feature of applied research, ensuring task completion and a process of cooperation towards a common goal. This now is not about the master-slave dynamic (cf. the example above about abnormal psychology) but pragmatism. The outcome may still be one of limited criticality and the philosophical assumption of empiricism may be present, but this scenario is not particularly reflected on by anyone in the team. Methodologism absents critical reflection about ontology and epistemology and might also divert researcher attention from considering values: why am I pursuing this particular goal and not another one and how does it contribute to human welfare and flourishing? Methodological capability can then become its very own self-contained *raison d'être*, rewarded intermittently by research grants.

These two examples demonstrate that multidisciplinary working is a necessary but not a sufficient condition to proceed towards transdisciplinarity. The vehicle for the journey, as it were, can stall easily and for good at this first stage. In order to move on, the practitioners or researchers involved need to have a larger horizon about their collaborative ambitions. This means some shared notion of holism and complexity and the value system they own. It is not surprising then that true interdisciplinary projects have been guided often by general systems theory for two reasons. First, it is open-textured enough in its assumptions to apply across all disciplinary boundaries. Second, it highlights a key distinction: the difference between closed (or isolated) systems and open systems. We can see the alignment of these features with critical realism, which I return to below.

The possible role of psychologists in a transdisciplinary future

In light of all the above discussion, I turn now to an imagined future. How might psychologists make a legitimate contribution to a transdisciplinary field of human science and what risks attend that process? We can answer that question by placing risks before opportunities or vice versa but I will rehearse risks first as advanced forms of caution.

1) *The risk of disciplinary imperialism* is present in the wide field of human science and is not restricted to psychology particularly, though its name suggests an entitlement to superiority in the midst of collaborators and competitors. In truth no discipline has all the answers and no claim to pre-eminence. Above I listed not just academic competitors but also non-academics such as writers, artists and faith leaders; all warrant a fair hearing.

2) *The risks of both positivism and postmodernism* still affect the discipline. In a spirit of epistemic humility and reflexive criticality, all psychologists could take stock of the particular risks either of these currents has posed for them in their research or practice. Statistically verified knowledge is not only questionable (because of the counterexamples that can be demonstrated if we rely only on deductions in scientific inference) but so is the inductive faith of qualitative methods in the idealist tradition. Transduction is the misleading outcome of relying on attempts to generalise from the laboratory to open system; all science is prone to this error but psychology runs the greatest risk because of its disciplinary insecurity prompting a firm commitment to the alleged advantages of experimentalism and its findings. As for discourse analysis, on its own (rather than its critical version in the context of other pertinent methods) it produces its own blinkers of understanding.

3) *The risk of planar and niche preferences* comes from the challenge of dealing with complexity and entails retreating into a limited and blinkered view of what is important. Theories and models developed in psychology which are too focussed and have no holistic plausibility will always be suspect. (I gave examples above

from social psychology.) Any theory or knowledge claim which offers itself as a covering law about human functioning is particularly suspect.

4) *Gullibility about positivist claims in cognate disciplines* is an ongoing risk in the arenas of applied research. The most obvious example is the uncritical acceptance of psychiatric knowledge by psychology in its teaching curriculum and research projects. To be clear here, gullibility does not reflect the lack of intelligence in those schooled in psychology (not at all) but at times it does reflect a naïve faith in positivism and the loss of reflective competence in its wake, as a consequence of rejecting philosophy and its authority. Critical realism is one way we can recapture the utility of philosophy and be clearer about what we are thinking and doing. The tramlines of empiricism and the incommensurable theoretical positions within the discipline created the conditions of possibility for the shared comfort blanket of methodologism. This outcome disabled psychologists from conducting pre-empirical and non-empirical research with confidence as that requires a philosophical framework for reflection (Smedslund, 2016).

If we turn from risks to opportunities, then here are some cautious suggestions (because the risks above are co-present):

1) *Psychology does and can make further particular contributions to the first plane (our relationship to the natural world).* This point is evident, for example, in relation to neuropsychology, ecological psychology, evolutionary psychology and primatology. The caveat here is that psychology should avoid the seductions of reductive neuroscience and the eugenic pull of biogenetic arguments. It should also recognise that this is only one plane amongst four (the general risk of reductionism).

2) *Psychology does and can make further contributions to the second plane (relationality).* This point is evident in relation to social psychology. The caveat here is that social psychology should avoid positivist pretensions such as '*the* psychology of interpersonal relationships' by being mindful of nearby sociological advice about the contingencies of social context. The lessons of relationality from fields such as health psychology (the health benefits of social networks) and psychological therapy (the role of trusting benign relationships to facilitate personal change) can be built upon. As with the other planes, the general risk of reductionism needs to be borne in mind at all times. For example, mantras of the type, 'It is all about positive relationships/good communication/empathy between people …', found at times in the world of human relations departments of organisations and some forms of liberal political programmes, are reductionist. They fail to acknowledge the role of the other three planes in our lives.

3) *Psychology eventually might make contributions to the third plane (addressing the role of social structures).* For reasons noted earlier this is probably the weakest feature of modern psychology, in the vein of positivism. The preoccupation with separating facts and values has led to psychology avoiding societal matters because this might be 'too political'. As I noted earlier, objectivity is a legitimate goal (being true and honest about our object of enquiry) but neutrality is a wild goose chase in human science. It is only when we turn to anti-positivist versions of psychology, such as the Frankfurt School, that such a sophisticated shift has been made deliberately and with good cause. An implication of this point is that psychology needs to reset its

relationship with society and listen to sociologists and political scientists about topics such as social inequalities, oppression and alienation. Human science cannot be politically neutral because human life is shaped by power relationships at all times and so that ontology needs to be part of our investigations. As for post-modern forms of psychology, they are *seemingly* social in orientation (because, as in critical realism, they consider that context is a perennial watchword), however the *post* in poststructuralism matters. It risks ditching the ontology of direct social causation, which continues to be relevant ontologically beyond considerations of texts and discourses. However, a collapse into sociological reductionism is not an answer for psychology, because the other three planes need to be borne in mind, not just this one of social structure. For example, to their detriment sociologists have been particularly suspicious of biology (cf. Benton, 1991) and routinely scorned the individualism of psychology. Some critical realist sociologists have avoided that reductionism by exploring relationality when discussing social structure (Donati and Archer, 2015). This latter is a very useful guide to the boundary work between psychology and sociology.

4) *Psychology does and can make contributions to the fourth plane (individual personality).* This plane seems the most obvious home and 'best bet' for psychology, given its history of concern for understanding individuals. However, as psychology students know when being asked to compare and contrast personality theories, the trait approach of positivism (the consensus on the putative 'Big Five') differs from the postmodern take on situated identities and both differ from accounts offered in the variegated traditions of depth psychology. How do we describe personality and can it be readily measured psychometrically? Does the latter approach do justice to our idiosyncratic ways of being in the world in a range of contexts? Also, long standing debates have remained since antiquity about 'temperament' and its assumed genetic roots, and their possible interaction with family and school life or other sources of primary socialisation. (The commitment to the importance of inherited temperament has united psychologists as diverse as Carl Jung and Hans Eysenck.) As with the repeated point above, these questions about our concrete singularity, our continuous sense of self and the attributions others regularly make about us as unique people need to be put in the context of the other three planes of ontology. Any discussion of personality in isolation from those other planes will lead to a partial and reductionist account. Moreover, the spread of competing approaches to the study of personality are limited to the professional gaze. This raises a question: which of these offers most respect to the experience of the people being studied? My view is that the latter can only be found in versions of depth psychology and existentialism.

Business as usual or a change in the curriculum?

The lists above suggest that 'business as usual' for academic psychology is problematic. The points of illumination I have offered in this book, from the philosophy of critical realism, invite the understatement that the discipline needs a little rehabilitation. In particular, its graduates should be able to rehearse arguments in their field of work about ontology, epistemology and axiology. Even if their conclusions do not concur with critical realism, they ought to be able to articulate why that is the case.

As I noted in the introduction of this book, from teaching both undergraduate and postgraduate psychologists in Britain, I have learnt that they are genuinely interested in these sources of critical reflection but usually they have not been provided with the skills to do the job. Moreover, the open-mindedness of neophyte college students, about basic assumptions in relation to their own philosophical stance and that implicit in psychological theories can be shut down pre-emptively when and if they are merely force-fed fact after fact about cognitive science or neuroscience. An illuminative dialogue at that stage to encourage the 'explication of presuppositions' is replaced with an authoritative monologue (a form of master-slave relationship).

I have noted two exceptions to this trend. First, some students have been captivated by a more recent postmodern orthodoxy (usually from studying social psychology), which then means they are seeking confirmation that 'everything is socially constructed' and that deconstruction is the only methodological game in town. Second, for some idiosyncratic extra-curricular reason, a student may have learned to be philosophical or critical or both and so resist with an admixture of confidence and anger the master-slave dynamic.

If most psychology students are not *au fait* with basic philosophical concepts, nor are they necessarily familiar with the origins of assumptions in their own discipline, then change is needed. A basic understanding of the rationales of ontology, epistemology and axiology seems to be a minimum requirement if students are to put claims from their discipline to the test. One useful exercise might be for them to rehearse the competing advantages and disadvantages of deduction, induction and retroduction. Another might be to discuss the feasibility of separating facts and values. Another might be to interrogate the assumption that 'everything is socially constructed'. Another might be for them to explore the history of ideas in the discipline in a dialogical manner with their elders in the academy.

This is not about 'selling' one position about these historical and philosophical matters but simply being aware of their analytical advantages and the broad debates within them, as an ongoing basis for reflecting critically on psychological theory and practice. Returning to philosophy may seem retrograde and irrelevant, a conclusion that would sadly signal the success of the positivist zeal of Ward and Rivers I rehearsed in Chapter 2.

Today we are dealing with a reckoning about that mixed legacy. After the Second World War and the global shock created by the Holocaust, not only did psychology begin to enter a legitimation crisis (as I noted in Chapter 2) but philosophy itself became important again as an under-labourer for intellectual life (see my conclusion of Chapter 1). Not only Karl Popper but other post-positivists (such as Thomas Kuhn) began to make their case, Roy Bhaskar then joined that post-positivist philosophical trend in the 1970s, when he developed critical realism.

Moreover, axiology not just epistemology and ontology was in need of a re-think. For example, Hans Jonas began to defend a form of humanism rooted in our biological nature, which was neither reductionist nor anthropocentric. Today this speaks to the challenge of the threat to and from the Anthropocene, which I pick up again below (Jonas, 1984). His work has clear relevance today in defending scientific humanism in psychology against the challenges of both positivism and postmodernism (Brinkman, 2019). All of this turbulence in the field of post-positivist philosophy since the Second World War warrants our consideration as students and researchers in psychology.

Another change in the curriculum that may be helpful is the teaching of general systems theory and its derivatives. The risk of reductionism I mentioned of resting too readily in any enquiry upon a single plane prompts us to consider the advantages of thinking holistically, so that *all* of the four planes are attended to concurrently in the psychological formulation of a research question, the analysis of research findings or the exploration of a rich case study. Judgemental rationality can be applied case by case, within psychology, to the salience of one or more planes *and the relationship between them.*

For example, whereas the immediate cause of a psychological phenomenon (say disorientation in time and space in those with vascular dementia) may be in plane 1 (our relationship to the natural world, which includes our neurological functioning), the consequences will be in plane 2 (relationality – the person and their family will adapt to the condition in a range of ways) and in plane 4 (alterations in personality and personal competence may prompt others to reconstrue the person they knew in a pre-morbid state). Moreover, plane 3 (social structure) may have inflected the probability of the patient's signs and symptoms, because poor vascular health is more common in the poor than in the rich. This single example of a patient with vascular dementia demonstrates that all four planes can be reflected upon when we consider any psychological phenomenon.

General systems theory (GST) (von Bertalanffy, 1968; Weiss, 1969) created the foundations for holistic reasoning in the works of Bateson (1972) and Maturana and Varela (1980), as I noted above. In addition, a number of systems theory-informed developments, such as ecological psychology (Barker, 1968), cybernetics (Weiner, 1948; Ashby, 1964), communication theory (Wilden, 1972) and complexity theory (Walby, 2007) are aligned with a critical realist view of the world. That is, they consider open biological systems in flux, the emergence of new features within them, the importance of context to make that emergence intelligible and the interactive relationship between causes and meanings, given the species-specific role of human language and agency.

GST was also incorporated into the later developments of the Frankfurt School and absorbed favourably by critical realists (Habermas, 1981; Offe, 1984). The development of Margaret Archer's morphogenetic approach within critical realist sociology (Archer, 1995) was predicated in large part upon the systems theory influence of Lockwood (1964) and critical realist approaches to management studies are indebted to GST (Mingers, 2011). Also the prospect of using the biopsychosocial approach to human science, within critical realist writing, can be traced in part to GST (Bhaskar et al., 2018; Pilgrim, 2015b). All of these versions of anti-reductionist systems theory-informed work allow us to explore patterns that connect through time, without falling into the traps of relying upon dubious and contestable Humean constant conjunctions in our statistical methods, failing to grasp the problem of transduction when considering open systems, or of embarking upon the futile search for lawful predictability in human affairs.

Conclusion

This closing chapter is an appeal then for the development of transdisciplinary forms of knowledge about human thought and action in contingent contexts. Psychologists could make a genuine contribution to that project, while avoiding any pretension to disciplinary pre-eminence in the broad field of human science. However, in order to succeed a reckoning with the 20th-century legacy of positivism and postmodernism is required.

Roy Bhaskar noted that philosophy should be about seriousness and not trivial matters. As the current century proceeds, a dwindling number of us, sooner rather than later, may bear witness to the terminal impact of the Anthropocene. Given the current existential threat to our species from ecocide and the remaining chance of nuclear annihilation, which are conditions of our own making, Bhaskar's point about seriousness has a wider pertinence. For psychology, as other disciplines, the overarching question relates to what contribution it makes not only to human flourishing but now to its very survival. Critical realism provides a holistic philosophical framework to explore some answers.

BIBLIOGRAPHY

Abraham, K. (1912/1953) Notes on the psychoanalytical investigation and treatment of manic-depressive insanity and allied conditions. In *Karl Abraham: Selected Papers On Psychoanalysis*. New York: Basic Books.

Adler, A. (1912) *The Neurotic Constitution*. London: Kegan, Paul, Trench, Trubner & Co.

Adorno, T.W. (1973) *Negative Dialectics*. New York: Continuum.

Adorno, T.W. (1982) Freudian theory and the pattern of fascist propaganda. In A. Arato and G. Eike (eds) *The Essential Frankfurt School Reader*. New York: Continuum.

Ainsworth, M.D. and Bowlby, J. (1991) An ethological approach to personality development. *American Psychologist*, 46, 4, 333–341.

Allport, G.W. and Odbert, H.S. (1936) Trait-names: a psycho-lexical study. *Psychological Monographs*, 47, 1, i–171.

American Psychiatric Association (APA) (2013) *Diagnostic and Statistical Manual of Mental Disorders* (5th ed.). Washington, DC: APA.

American Psychological Association (2005) *Report of the American Psychological Association Presidential Task Force on Psychological Ethics and National Security*. Washington, DC: American Psychological Association.

American Psychological Association (2014) Incarceration nation. *Monitor on Psychology*, 45, 9, 56.

Amnesty International (2011) *The State of the World's Human Rights Report*. London: Amnesty International.

Anderson, B. (1991) *Imagined Communities*. London: Verso.

Anderson, P. (1968) Components of the national culture. *New Left Review*, 1, 50, 3–57.

Anderson, P. (1983) *In the Tracks of Historical Materialism*. London: Verso.

Antaki, C. (1981) (ed.) *The Psychology of Ordinary Explanations of Social Behaviour*. London: Academic Press.

Archer, M. (1995) *Realist Social Theory: the Morphogenetic Approach*. Cambridge: Cambridge University Press.

Archer, M. (2000) *Being Human: The Problem of Agency*. Cambridge: Cambridge University Press.

Arendt, H. (1963) *Eichmann in Jerusalem: A Report on the Banality of Evil*. New York: Viking.

Ashby, R.W. (1964) *Introduction to Cybernetics*. London: Routledge Kegan & Paul.

Auden, W.H. (1940) 'In Memory of Sigmund Freud'. In *Another Time*. New York: Random House.

Audini, B. and Lelliott, P. (2002) Age, gender and ethnicity of those detained under Part II of the Mental Health Act 1983. *British Journal of Psychiatry*, 180, 222–226.

Babiak, P. and Hare, R.D. (2007) *Snakes in Suits: When Psychopaths go to Work*. New York: HarperCollins.

Bale, J.M. (2007) Political paranoia v. political realism: on distinguishing between bogus conspiracy theories and genuine conspiratorial politics. *Patterns of Prejudice*, 41, 45–60.

Bannister, D. (1966) Psychology as an exercise in paradox. *Bulletin of the British Psychological Society*, 19, 63, 21–26.

Bannister, D. (1968) The myth of physiological psychology. *Bulletin of the British Psychological Society*, 21, 229–231.

Barber, B. (2007) *Consumed: How Markets Corrupt Children, Infantilize Adults, and Swallow Citizens Whole*. New York: Norton.

Barker, P. (1968) *Ecological Psychology: Concepts and Methods for Studying the Environment of Human Behavior*. Stanford, CA: Stanford University Press.

Barnes, F. (1960) Statement of Frank Barnes, President, NAACP, Southern California Area Conference Hearings Before the United States Commission on Civil Rights. Washington, DC: Government Printing Office.

Baron-Cohen, S. (2003) *The Essential Difference: The Truth About the Male and Female Brain*. New York: Basic Books.

Barr, B., Higgerson, J. and Whitehead, M. (2017) Investigating the impact of the English health inequalities strategy: time trend analysis. *British Medical Journal*, 358, 3310.

Barton, H. (1976) Paedophile politics. *Kalos, on Greek Love*, 1, 1.

Bateson, G. (1972) *Steps to an Ecology of Mind*. New York: Chandler.

Bauer, M.W. and Gaskell, G. (1999) Towards a paradigm for research on social representations. *Journal for the Theory of Social Behaviour*, 29, 2, 163–186.

Bayer, R. and Spitzer, R.L. (1985) Neurosis, psychodynamics and DSM-III: a history of the controversy. *Archives of General Psychiatry*, 42, 187–196.

Bean, P. (1986) *Mental Disorder and Legal Control*. Cambridge: Cambridge University Press.

Beck, R. (2015) *We Believe The Children: A Moral Panic in the 1980s*. New York: Public Affairs.

Becker, G.S. (1976) *The Economic Approach to Human Behavior*. Chicago, IL: University of Chicago Press.

Beckett, R., Beech, A., Fisher, D. and Fordham, A.S. (1994) *Community-Based Treatment for Sex Offenders: An Evaluation of Seven Treatment Programmes*. London: Home Office.

Beiner, R. (2018) *Dangerous Minds: Nietzsche, Heidegger, and the Return of the Far Right*. Philadelphia, PA: University of Pennsylvania Press.

Bem, D.J. (1967) Self-perception: an alternative interpretation of cognitive dissonance phenomena. *Psychological Review*, 74, 183–200.

Benn Michaels, W. (2006) *The Trouble with Diversity: How We Learned to Love Identity and Ignore In Equality*. New York: Holt.

Bentall, R. (2010) *Doctoring The Mind*. London: Penguin.

Benton, T. (1991) Biology and social science: why the return of the repressed should be given a (cautious) welcome. *Sociology*, 25, 1, 1–29.

Berger, P. and Luckmann, T. (1967) *The Social Construction of Reality A Treatise in the Sociology of Knowledge*. Garden City, NY: Doubleday.

Bergmann, G. (1957) *Philosophy of science*. Madison, WI: University of Wisconsin Press.

Berrios, G.E. (1985) Obsessional disorders during the nineteenth century: terminological and classificatory issues. In W.F. Bynum, R. Porter and M. Shepherd (eds) *The Anatomy of Madness, Vol. 1*. London: Tavistock Publications.

Bhaskar, R. (1975/1997) *A Realist Theory of Science*. London: Verso.

Bhaskar, R. (1986) *Scientific Realism and Human Emancipation*. London: Verso.

Bhaskar, R. (1993) *Dialectic: The Pulse of Freedom*. London: Verso.

Bhaskar, R. (1997) On the ontological status of ideas. *Journal for the Theory of Social Behaviour*, 27, 2/3, 135–137.

Bhaskar, R. (2000) *East To West: An Odyssey of the Soul*. London: Routledge.

Bhaskar, R. (2008) *Dialectic: The Pulse of Freedom*. London: Routledge.

Bhaskar, R. (2016) *Enlightened Common Sense: The Philosophy of Critical Realism*. London: Routledge.

Bhaskar, R., Danermark, B. and Price, L. (2018) *Interdisciplinarity and Wellbeing: A Critical Realist General Theory of Interdisciplinarity*. London: Routledge.

Black, D.W. (2013) *Bad Boys, Bad Men: Confronting Anti-Social Behavior*. New York: Oxford University Press.

Blackburn, R. (1988) On moral judgements and personality disorders: The myth of psychopathic disorder re-visited. *British Journal of Psychiatry*, 153, 505–512.

Bleuler, E. (1911/1950) *Dementia Praecox or the Group of Schizophrenias* (trans. J. Zinkin). New York: International Universities Press.

Bloch, S. and Reddaway, P. (1977) *Russia's Political Hospitals: The Abuse of Psychiatry in the Soviet Union*. London: Viktor Gollanz.

Board, B.J. and Fritzon, K. (2005) Disordered personalities at work. *Psychology, Crime and Law*, 11, 1, 17–32.

Boddy, R.P., Ladysjewsky, R. and Galvin, P.L. (2010) Leaders without ethics in global business: Corporate psychopaths. *Journal of Public Affairs*, 10, 1, 131–138.

Bohacek, J. and Mansuy, I.M. (2015) Molecular insights into transgenerational non-genetic inheritance of acquired behaviours. *National Review of Genetics*, 1, 11, 641–652.

Borch-Jacobsen, M. and Shamdasani, S. (2008) Interprefactions: Freud's legendary science. *History of the Human Sciences*, 21, 3, 1–25.

Bourdieu, P. (1984) *Distinction: A Social Critique of the Judgment of Taste*. London: Routledge.

Bowlby, J. (1957) *Attachment and Loss* (3 volumes). New York: Basic Books.

Bowring, B. (2008) *The Degradation of the International Legal Order? The Rehabilitation of Law and the Possibility of Politics*. Abingdon, UK: Routledge.

Bridgman, W.P. (1938) Operational analysis. *Philosophy of Science*, 5: 114–131.

Brinkman, S. (2019) Retrieving humanism in the posthuman condition. Paper presented at the Joint Annual Conference of the QMiP and HPP Sections of the British Psychological Society, Cardiff, UK.

Brizendine, L. (2006) *The Female Brain*. New York: Morgan Road.

Broad, C.D. (1925) *The Mind and Its Place in Nature*. London: Routledge & Kegan Paul.

Brody, B. (1970) Freud's case-load. *Psychotherapy Theory Research & Practice*, 7, 1, 8–12.

Brooks-Gordon, B. (2010) Sexually harmful adults. In G.J. Towl and D.A. Crighton (eds) *Forensic Psychology*. Chichester, UK: Wiley.

Bud, R. and Bunge, M. (2010) Should psychoanalysis be in the Science Museum? *New Scientist*, 29 September, 20–21.

Burnett, A. and Peel, M. (2001) Asylum seekers and refugees in Britain: the health of survivors of torture and organised violence. *British Medical Journal*, 322, 606–609.

Burt, C.L. (1909) Experimental tests of general intelligence. *British Journal of Psychology*, III, 94–107.

Burt, C.L. (1912) The inheritance of mental characters. *Eugenic Review*, IV, 1–33.

Burt, C.L. (1946) Intelligence and fertility. *Eugenics Society Occasional Papers*, Number 2.

Cacciola, J.S., Rutherford, M.J., Alterman, A.I., McKay, J.R. and Mulvaney, F.D. (1998) Long-term test-retest reliability of personality disorder diagnoses in opiate dependent patients. *Journal of Personality Disorders*, 12, 4, 32–37.

Callinicos, A. (1991) *Against Postmodernism: A Marxist Critique*. Bristol, UK: Polity.

Carpenter, M., Nagell, K., Tomasello, M. (1998) Social cognition, joint attention, and communicative competence from 9 to 15 months of age. *Monographs of the Society for Research in Child Development*, 63, 4, 1–143.

Carr, A. (2001) *Abnormal Psychology*. London: Routledge.

Caruso, C. (2017) Psychiatrists debate weighing in on Trump's mental health. *Scientific American*, 15 February.

Cattell, R.B. (1943) The description of personality: basic traits resolved into clusters. *Journal of Abnormal and Social Psychology*, 38, 4, 476–506.

Ceballos, G., Ehrlich, P.R. and Dirzo, R. (2017) Biological annihilation via the ongoing sixth mass extinction signalled by vertebrate population losses and declines. *Proceedings of the National Academy of Sciences*, 11, 3, E6089–6090.

Chaiklin, S. (1992) From theory to practice and back again: what does postmodern philosophy contribute to psychological science? In S. Kvale (ed.) *Psychology and Postmodernism*. London: Sage.

Cheit, R. (2014) *The Witch-Hunt Narrative: Politics, Psychology and the Sexual Abuse of Children*. Oxford: Oxford University Press.

Children's Commissioner's Report (2016) *Barnahus: Improving The Response to Child Sex Abuse in England*. London: UK Children's Commissioner's Office.

Chomsky, N. (1959) Reviews: Verbal Behavior by B.F. Skinner. *Language*, 35, 1, 26–58.

Ciompi, L. (1984) Is there really a schizophrenia? The long-term course of psychotic phenomena. *British Journal of Psychiatry*, 145, 636–640.

Clapton, G., Cree, V.E. and Smith, M. (2012) Moral panics and social work: towards a sceptical view of UK child protection. *Critical Social Policy*, 33, 2, 197–217.

Clark, D.M., Ehlers, A. and McManus, F. (2003) Cognitive therapy versus fluoxetine in generalized social phobia: a randomized placebo-controlled trial. *Journal of Consulting and Clinical Psychology*, 71, 1058–1067.

Clark, M. (2015) Co-production in mental health care. *Mental Health Review Journal*, 20, 4, 213–219.

Clarke, G. (2008) The internal conversation: a personal relations theory perspective. *Journal of Critical Realism*, 7, 1, 57–82.

Clayton, P. and Davies, P. (eds) (2006) *The Re-Emergence of Emergence*. Oxford: Oxford University Press.

Cleckley, H. (1941) *The Mask of Sanity*. St Louis, MO: C.V. Mosby.

Cohen, J. (1994) The world is round (p <.05). *American Psychologist*, 49, 997–1003.

Cohen, S. (1972) *Folk Devils and Moral Panics* (1st edition). London: MacGibbon and Kee.

Cohen, S. (2001) *States of Denial: Knowing About Atrocities and Suffering*. Cambridge: Polity.

Cohen, S. (2002) *Folk Devils and Moral Panics* (3rd edition). London: Routledge.

Cohen, S. and Scull, A. (eds) (1983) *Social Control and the State: Historical and Comparative Essays*. Oxford: Basil Blackwell.

Collier, A. (1977) *R.D. Laing: The Philosophy and Politics of Psychotherapy*. New York: Pantheon.

Collier, A. (1991) Explanation and emancipation. In M. Archer, R. Bhaskar, A. Collier, T. Lawson and A. Norrie (eds) *Critical Realism: Essential Readings*. London: Routledge.

Comer, R.J. (2012) *Abnormal Psychology: International Edition*. Basingstoke, UK: Palgrave Macmillan.

Connolly, D.A. and Read, J.D. (2006) Delayed prosecutions of historic child sexual abuse: analyses of 2064 Canadian criminal complaints. *Law and Human Behavior*, 30, 4, 409–434.

Conrad, E.C. and De Vries, R. (2011) Field of dreams: a social history of neuroethics. In M. Pickersgill and I. van Keulen (eds) *Sociological Reflections on the Neurosciences*. Bingley, UK: Emerald.

Constantine, L. and Martinson, F.M. (1981) *Children and Sex: New Findings, New Perspectives*. Boston, MA: Little, Brown and Company.

Coulter, J. (1973) *Approaches to Insanity*. New York: Wiley.

Council of Europe (2007) Council of Europe Convention on the Protection of Children Against Sexual Exploitation and Sexual Abuse, 12 July, *CETS*, No. 201. http://www.refworld.org/docid/4d19a904615b.html [22 October 2015].

Craib, I. (1997) Social constructionism as a social psychosis. *Sociology*, 31, 1, 1–15.

Cromby, J. (2015) *Feeling Bodies: Embodying Psychology*. London: Palgrave.

Cromby, J. and Nightingale, D.J. (1999) What's wrong with social constructionism? In D.J. Nightingale and J. Cromby (eds) *Social Constructionist Psychology: A Critical Analysis of Theory and Practice*. Buckingham, UK: Open University Press.

Crossley, N. (2006) *Contesting Psychiatry: Social Movements in Mental Health*. Abingdon, UK: Routledge.

Cryan, J.F. and Dinan, T.G. (2012) Mind-altering microorganisms: the impact of the gut microbiota on brain and behaviour. *Nature Reviews Neuroscience*, 13, 701–712.

Cutajar, M.C., Mullen, P.E., Ogloff, J.R.P., Thomas, S.D., Wells, D.L. and Spataro, J. (2010) Psychopathology in a large cohort of sexually abused children followed up to 43 years. *Child Abuse & Neglect*, 34, 11, 813–822.

Dalton, C. (2014) Beyond description to pattern: the contribution of Batesonian epistemology to critical realist research. *Journal of Critical Realism*, 13, 2, 163–182.

Danzinger, K. (1985) The methodological imperative in psychology. *Philosophy of the Social Sciences*, 15, 1, 1–13.

Dawson, J., Bannerman, B.A. and Lalumière, M.L. (2014) Paraphilic interests: an examination of sex differences in a nonclinical sample. *Sexual Abuse: A Journal of Research and Treatment*, 28, 1, 20–45.

De Groot, M., Golden, S.H. and Wagner, J. (2016) Psychological conditions in adults with diabetes. *American Psychologist*, 71, 552.

Deleuze, G. (1994) *Difference and Repetition* (trans. P. Patton). New York: Columbia University Press.

Del Gaizo, A.L., Elhai, J.D. and Weaver, T. (2011) Posttraumatic stress disorder, poor physical health and substance use behaviors in a national trauma-exposed sample. *Psychiatry Research*, 188, 3, 390–393.

Dennett, D. (1984) *Elbow Room*. Cambridge, MA: MIT Press.

Derrida, J. (1982) The ends of man. In *Margins of Philosophy* (trans. A. Bass). Chicago, IL: University of Chicago Press.

Dews, P. (1989) The return of the subject in the late Foucault. *Radical Philosophy*, 51, 37–41.

Dicker, G. (2011) *Berkeley's Idealism. A Critical Examination*. Cambridge: Cambridge University Press.

Dickman, S.L., Himmelstein, D.U. and Woolhander, S. (2017) Equity and equality in health: inequality and the health-care system in the USA. *Lancet*, 389, 10077, 1431–1441.

Dietrich, A. (2019) The Rocky Horror Pixel Show. *The Psychologist*, 32, 30–35.

Donati, P. (2016) The 'relational subject' according to a critical realist relational sociology. *Journal of Critical Realism*, 15, 4, 352–375.

Donati, P. and Archer, M. (2015) *The Relational Subject*. Cambridge: Cambridge University Press.

Double, D. (2007) Adolf Meyer's psychobiology and the challenge for biomedicine. *Philosophy, Psychiatry & Psychology*, 14, 4, 331–339.

Edley, N. (2001) Unravelling social constructionism. *Theory & Psychology*, 11, 3, 433–441.

Eichenbaum, L. and Orbach, S. (1982) *Outside In … Inside Out: Women's Psychology: A Feminist Psychoanalytic Approach*. London: Pelican.

Eide, A.K. (2012) Life stories: beyond construction. *Journal of Critical Realism*, 11, 2, 139–162.

Eisenberg, L. (2006) The social construction of the brain. *American Journal of Psychiatry*, 163, 4, 750–756.

Elder-Vass, D. (2012) The Reality of Social Construction. Cambridge: Cambridge University Press.

Eliot, T.S. (1932) *Sweeney Agonistes*. London: Faber and Faber.

Engel, G.L. (1980) The clinical application of the biopsychosocial model. *American Journal of Psychiatry*, 137, 535–544.

Engels, F. (1902) *The Origin of the Family, Private Property and the State* (trans. E. Untermann). Chicago, IL: Charles H. Kerr & Co.

Erickson, K., Hillman C. and Kramer, A. (2015) Physical activity, brain, and cognition. *Current Opinion in Behavioral Sciences*, 4, 27–32.

Eysenck, H.J. (1947) *Dimensions of Personality*. London: Routledge and Keegan Paul.

Eysenck, H.J. (1949) Training in clinical psychology: an English point of view. *American Psychologist*, 4, 174–176.

Eysenck, H.J. (1960) *Behaviour Therapy and the Neuroses*. London: Pergamon.

Eysenck, H.J. (1975) *The Future of Psychiatry*. London: Methuen.

Eysenck, H.J. (1985) *Decline and Fall of the Freudian Empire*. London: Penguin.

Eysenck, H.J. (1997a) Personality and experimental psychology: The unification of psychology and the possibility of a paradigm. *Journal of Personality and Social Psychology*, 73, 1224–1237.

Eysenck, H.J. (1997b) *Rebel With A Cause*. London: Transaction.

Eysenck, H.J. and Eysenck, S.B.G. (1976) *Psychoticism as a Dimension of Personality*. London: Hodder and Stoughton.

Eysenck, H.J. and Gwynne-Jones, H. (1958) The psychiatric treatment of neurosis. Paper presented to the Royal Medico-Psychological Association, London.

Fahnestock, J. (1998) Accommodating science: the rhetorical life of scientific facts. *Written Communication*, 3, 3, 275–296.

Fairbairn, W.R.D. (1952) *Psychoanalytical Studies of the Personality*. London: Hogarth.

Ferguson, H. (2007) Abused and looked after children as moral dirt. *Journal of Social Policy*, 36, 1, 123–139.

Festinger, L. (1957) *A Theory of Cognitive Dissonance*. Stanford, CA: Stanford University Press.

Filipas, H.H. and Ullman, S.E. (2001) Social reactions to sexual assault victims from various support sources. *Violence and Victims*, 16, 6, 673–692.

Fine, C. (2008) Will working mothers' brains explode? The popular new genre of neurosexism. *Neuroethics*, 1, 1, 69–72.

Finkelhor, D., Hammer, H. and Sedlak, A.J. (2008) *Sexually Assaulted Children: National Estimates and Characteristics*. Washington, DC: US Department of Justice.

Fisher, R.A. (1918) The correlation between relatives on the supposition of Mendelian inheritance. *Transactions of the Royal Society Edinburgh*, LII, 399–433.

Fisher, R.A. (1930) *The Genetical Theory of Natural Selection*. Oxford: Clarendon Press.

Fiske, A.P. (1992) The four elementary forms of sociality: framework for a unified theory of social relations. *Psychological Review*, 99, 689–723.

Fitzgerald, D., Rose, N. and Singh, I. (2016) Revitalizing sociology: urban life and mental illness between history and the present. *British Journal of Sociology*, 67, 1, 138–160.

Fitzgerald, J. (2006) The attrition of sexual offences from the New South Wales criminal justice system. *Crime and Justice Bulletin: Contemporary Issues in Crime and Justice*, Number 92. Sydney, Australia: NSW Bureau of Crime Statistics and Research.

Flatschart, E. (2016) Critical realist discourse analysis: a necessary alternative to post-Marxist discourse theory. *Journal of Critical Realism*, 15, 1, 21–52.

Flatschart, E. (2017) Feminist standpoints and critical realism: the contested materiality of difference in intersectionality and the new materialism. *Journal of Critical Realism*, 16, 3, 284–302.

Foucault, M. (1965) *Madness and Civilisation*. New York: Pantheon.

Foucault, M. (1984) What is Enlightenment? (trans. C. Porter). In P. Rabinow (ed.) *The Foucault Reader* (pp. 31–50). New York: Pantheon.

Fox, D. and Prilleltensky, I. (eds) (1997) *Critical Psychology An Introduction*. London: Sage.

Frankl, V. (1988) *The Will To Meaning*. New York: Meridian.

Fraser, M. (1981) The Child. In B. Taylor (ed.) *Perspectives on Paedophilia*. London: Batsford Academic and Educational.

Freud, S. (1895) Über die Berechtigung, von der Neurasthenie einen bestimmten Symptomenkomplex als "Angst-Neurose' abzutrennen. *Neurol. Zbl.*, XIV, 50–66.

Freud, S. (1905/1962) *Three Essays on the Theory of Sexuality* (trans. J. Strachey). New York: Basic Books.

Freud, S. (1912) Zur Dynamik Der Übertragung. *Zbl. Psychoan.*, 2, 4, 167–173.

Freud, S. (1920/1922) *Beyond the Pleasure Principle* (trans. C.J.M. Hubback). London/Vienna: International Psychoanalytical Association.

Freud, S. (1926) *Die Frage der Laienanalyse. Unterredungen mit einem Unparteiischen*. Leipzig/Vienna/Zurich: Internationaler Psychoanalytischer Verlag.

Freud, S. (1935) *The Ego and the Mechanisms of Defence*. London: Karnac.

Friedman, M. (1962) *Capitalism and Freedom*. Chicago, IL: University of Chicago Press.

Fromm, E. (1941) *Escape from Freedom* (in the UK published as The Fear of Freedom). New York: Farrar and Rinehart.

Fromm, E. (1963) Disobedience as a psychological and moral problem. In C. Urquhart (ed.) *A Matter of Life*. London: Jonathan Cape.

Fromm, E. (1964) *The Heart of Man: Its Genius for Good and Evil*. New York: Harper & Row.

Fromm, E. (1966) *The Sane Society*. London: Routledge.

Fromm, E. (1970) *The Crisis of Psychoanalysis*. Greenwich, UK: Fawcett.

Fromm, E. (1973) *The Anatomy of Human Destructiveness*. New York: Holt Reinhart.

Fromm, E. (2010) *On Disobedience: Why Freedom Means Saying 'No' To Power*. London: Harper Perennial Modern Thought.

Frosh, S. (2005) *Hate and the 'Jewish Science': Anti-Semitism, Nazism and Psychoanalysis*. Basingstoke, UK: Palgrave.

Furedi, F. (2013) *Moral Crusades in an Age of Mistrust: The Jimmy Savile Scandal*. Basingstoke, UK: Palgrave.

Furedi, F. (2015) The moral crusade against paedophilia. In V.E. Cree, G. Clapton and M. Smith (eds) *Moral Panics in Theory and Practice*. Bristol, UK: Policy Press.

Galea, S., Uddin, M. and Koenen, K. (2011) The urban environment and mental disorders: epigenetic links. *Epigenetics*, 6, 4, 400–404.

Galton, F. (1869) *Hereditary Genius*. London: Macmillan.

Galton, F. (1881) *Natural Inheritance*. London: Macmillan.

Galton, F. (1884) Measurement of character. *Fortnightly Review*, 36, 179–185.

Garfinkel, H. (1967) *Studies in Ethnomethodology*. Englewood Cliffs, NJ: Prentice Hall.

Gay, P. (1988) *Freud: A Life for Our Time*. London: Dent.

Geertz, C. (1984) A colloquy of cultural theorists. In R.A. Schweder and R.A. LeVine (eds) *Culture Theory: Essays on Mind, Self and Emotion*. Cambridge: Cambridge University Press.

Gergen, K. (1992a) Toward a postmodern psychology. In S. Kvale (ed.) *Psychology and Postmodernism*. London: Sage.
Gergen, K. (1992b) The decline and fall of personality. *Psychology Today*, 25, 6, 58–63.
Gergen, K. (2009) *Relational Being*. New York: Oxford University Press.
Gibbons, A. (2014) Shedding light on skin color. *Science*, 3046, 5312, 9034–9036.
Gibbons, M., Limoges, C., Nowotny, H., Schwartzman, S., Scott, P. and Trow, M. (1994) *The New Production of Knowledge: The Dynamics of Science and Research in Contemporary Societies*. London: Sage.
Gibson, S. (2019) *Arguing, Obeying and Defying: A Rhetorical Perspective on Stanley Milgram's Obedience Experiments*. Cambridge: Cambridge University Press.
Gillespie, A., Murphy, J. and Place, M. (2010) *Adaptation and Identity in Informal Care Relationships which have been disrupted by Aphasia*. London: ESRC.
Goffman, E. (1959) *The Presentation of Self in Everyday Life*. New York: Doubleday Anchor.
Goffman, E. (1961) *Asylums*. New York: Doubleday Anchor.
Goode, E. and Ben-Yehuda, N. (1994) Moral panics: culture, politics and social construction. *Annual Review of Sociology*, 20, 149–171.
Goode, S. (2011) *Paedophiles in Society: Reflecting on Sexuality, Abuse and Hope*. Basingstoke, UK: Palgrave.
Gray, G. and Zielinski, A. (2000) Psychology and US psychologists in torture and war in the Middle East. *Torture*, 16, 2, 128–133.
Greer, C. and McLaughlin, E. (2015) Denial of child sexual abuse. In D. Whyte (ed.) *How Corrupt Is Britain?* London: Pluto Press.
Guntrip, H. (1977) *Schizoid Phenomena, Object Relations and the Self*. London: Hogarth Press.
Habermas, J. (1981) *Theory of Communicative Action*. Boston, MA: Beacon Press.
Hallam, A.M. (1925) The threshold of practical psychology. *Practical Psychologist*, 1, 1, 1.
Hanson, R.K. and Morton-Bourgon, K.E. (2005) The characteristics of persistent sexual offenders: a meta-analysis of recidivism studies. *Journal of Consulting and Clinical Psychology*, 73, 6, 1154–1163.
Hardy, N. (2019) Integrating Archer and Foucault. *Journal of Critical Realism*, 18, 1, 1–17.
Hare, R.D. and Neumann, C.S. (2008) Psychopathy as a clinical and empirical construct. *Annual Review of Clinical Psychology*, 4, 217–246.
Harper, D. (2007) The complicity of psychology in the security state. In R. Roberts (ed.) *Just War, Iraq and Psychology*. Ross-on-Wye, UK: PCCS.
Harris, Z. (1951) *Methods in Structural Linguistics*. Chicago, UK: University of Chicago.
Hartmann, H. (1939/1958) *Ego Psychology and the Problem of Adaptation* (trans. D. Rapaport). New York: International Universities Press.
Hartwig, M. (2007) *Dictionary of Critical Realism*. London: Routledge.
Hartwig, M. and Morgan, J. (eds) (2012) *Critical Realism and Spirituality*. London: Routledge.
Hayek, F.A. (1944) *The Road To Serfdom*. London: Routledge.
Hayes, S.C. (2004) Acceptance and commitment therapy and the new behavior therapies: mindfulness, acceptance and relationship. In S.C. Hayes, V.M. Follette and M.M. Linehan (eds) *Mindfulness and Acceptance: Expanding the Cognitive-Behavioral Tradition*. London: Guilford Publications.
Healy, D. (2004) Psychopathology at the interface between the market and the new biology. In D. Rees and S. Rose (eds) *The New Brain Sciences: Perils and Prospects*. Cambridge: Cambridge University Press.
Hearnshaw, L.S. (1964) *A Short History of British Psychology*. London: Methuen.
Heider, F. (1958) *The Psychology of Interpersonal Relations*. New York: Wiley.
Henderson, D.K. (1939) *Psychopathic States*. London: Chapman and Hall.

Hibberd, F. (2001) Gergen's social constructionism, logical positivism and the continuity of error: Part 2: Meaning-as-use. *Theory & Psychology*, 11, 3, 323–326.

Hillberg, T., Hamilton-Giachritsis, C. and Dixon, L. (2011) Review of meta-analyses on the association between child sexual abuse and adult mental health difficulties: a systematic approach. *Trauma Violence & Abuse*, 12, 1, 38–49.

Hobaiter, C. and Byrne, R.W. (2014) The meanings of chimpanzee gestures. *Current Biology*, 24, 14, 1596–1600.

Hobman, J.B. (1945) *David Eder: Memoirs of a Modern Pioneer*. London: Gollancz.

Hochschild, A.R. (2016) *Strangers in their Own Land: Anger and Mourning on the American Right*. New York: New Press.

Hook, D. (2001) Discourse, knowledge, materiality, history: Foucault and discourse analysis. *Theory and Psychology*, 11, 4, 521–527.

Horkheimer, M. and Adorno, T.W. (1969) *Dialectic of Enlightenment*. New York: Continuum.

Howard, G.S. (1986) *Dare We Develop a Human Science?*Notre Dame, IN: Academic Publications.

Hughes, B.M. (2018) *Psychology in Crisis*. London: Macmillan.

Human Brain Project – Preparatory Study (HBP-PS) Consortium (2012) *The Human Brain Project: A Report to the European Commission*. Lausanne, Switzerland: The HBP-PS Consortium.

Hume, D. (1854) *Philosophical Works of David Hume*. Boston, MA: Little, Brown & Co.

Hunter, R. and Macalpine, I. (1974) *Psychiatry for the Poor*. London: Dawsons.

Iacoboni, M. (2008) *Mirroring People: The Science of Empathy and How We Connect With Others*. New York: Picador.

Independent Asylum Commission (2008) *Fit For Purpose Yet?* London: Independent Asylum Commission.

Isaksen, K.R. (2016) Reclaiming rational theory choice as central: a critique of methodological applications of critical realism. *Journal of Critical Realism*, 15, 3, 245–262.

Jakobsen, T.G. (2017) Environmental ethics: anthropocentrism and non-anthropocentrism revised in the light of critical realism. *Journal of Critical Realism*, 16, 2, 184–199.

James, P. and Goetze, D. (2001) *Evolutionary Theory and Ethnic Conflict*. New York: Greenwood.

Jeffries, S. (2016) *Grand Hotel Abyss: The Lives of the Frankfurt School*. London: Verso.

Jenkins, A.H. (2001) Individuality in cultural context: the case for psychological agency. *Theory & Psychology*, 11, 3, 347–362.

Jenkins, P. (2004) *Moral Panic: Changing Concepts of the Child Molester in Modern America*. New Haven, CT: Yale University Press.

Johnson, J.M. and Littlefield, M.M. (2011) Lost and found in translation: popular neuroscience in the emerging neurodisciplines. In M. Pickersgill and I. van Keulen (eds) *Sociological Reflections on the Neurosciences*. Bingley, UK: Emerald.

Johnstone, L. and Boyle, M. with Cromby, J., Dillon, J., Harper, D., Kinderman, P., Longden, E., Pilgrim, D. & Read, J. (2018) *The Power Threat Meaning Framework: Towards the Identification of Patterns in Emotional Distress, Unusual Experiences and Troubled or Troubling Behaviour*. Leicester, UK: British Psychological Society.

Jonas, H. (1984) *The Imperative of Responsibility. In Search of Ethics for the Technological Age*. Chicago, UK: Chicago University Press.

Jonas, S., Bebbington, S., McManus, S., Meltzer, H., Jenkins, R., Kuipers, E., Cooper, C., King, M. and Brugha, T. (2011) Sexual abuse and psychiatric disorder in England: Results from the 2007 Adult Psychiatric Morbidity Survey. *Psychological Medicine*, 41, 4, 709–719.

Jones, D. and Elcock, J. (2001) *Histories and Theories of Psychology*. London: Arnold.

Jones, E. (1927) Discussion: lay analysis. *International Journal of Psychoanalysis*, 8, 174–175.

Jones, E. (1957) *Sigmund Freud: Life and Work. Vol. 3: The Last Phase 1919–1939*. London: Hogarth Press.

Jones, E.G. and Mendell, L.M. (1999) Assessing the 'decade of the brain'. *Science*, 284, 5415, 739.

Joseph, J. (2005) The 1942 'euthanasia' debate in the American Journal of Psychiatry. *History of Psychiatry*, 16, 2, 171–179.

Joseph, J. (2007) Philosophy in international relations: a scientific realist approach. *Millennium: Journal of International Studies*, 35, 2, 354–359.

Kagan, J. (2016) *On Being Human: Why Mind Matters*. New Haven, CT: Yale University Press.

Kagan, J. (2018) Personal correspondence with the author.

Kandel, E.R. (2018) *The Disordered Mind: What Unusual Brains Tell Us About Ourselves*. New York: Farrar, Straus and Giroux.

Kasanin, J. (1933) The acute schizoaffective psychoses. *American Journal of Psychiatry*, 90, 97–126.

Keats, J. (1899) *The Complete Poetical Works and Letters of John Keats*. Cambridge: Houghton, Mifflin and Company.

Kelly, G. (1955) *The Psychology of Personal Constructs*. New York: Norton.

Kelsen, H. (2002) *Pure Theory of Law Clark*. New Jersey: Law Book Exchange.

Kendall-Tackett, K.A. (2002) The health effects of childhood abuse: four pathways by which abuse can influence health. *Child Abuse & Neglect*, 26, 6–7, 715–729.

Kendell, R.E. (2002) The distinction between personality disorder and mental illness. *British Journal of Psychiatry*, 180, 110–115.

Kernberg, O.F. (1975) *Borderline Conditions and Pathological Narcissism*. New York: Aronson.

Kernberg, O.F. (1984) *Severe Personality Disorders: Psychotherapeutic Strategies*. New Haven, CT: Yale University Press.

Kitzinger, J. (2004) *Framing Abuse: Media Influence and Public Understanding of Sexual Violence Against Children*. London: Pluto Press.

Klages, L. (1929) *The Science of Character*. London: George Allen & Unwin.

Korzybski, A. (1933) *Science and Sanity. An Introduction to Non-Aristotelian Systems and General Semantics*. Lancaster, PA and New York: The International Non-Aristotelian Library Publishing Co.

Kraepelin, E. (1883) *Compendium der psychiatrie*. Leipzig: Abel.

Kran, A. (2010) Comparing causality in Freudian reasoning and critical realism. *Journal of Critical Realism*, 9, 1, 5–32.

Krizman, D. (ed.) (1990) *Politics, Philosophy, Culture – Interviews and Other Writings 1977–1984*. London: Routledge. https://www.theguardian.com/world/2001/feb/24/jonhenley [accessed 10 February 2019].

Kunz, W. and Rittel, H. (1970) Issues as Elements of Information Systems. Working Paper 131, Institute of Urban and Regional Development, California: University of California at Berkeley.

Laclau, E. and Mouffe, C. (1985) *Hegemony and Socialist Strategy: Toward A Radical Democratic Politics*. London: Verso.

Laing, R.D. (1960) *The Divided Self: An Existential Study in Sanity and Madness*. London: Tavistock Publications.

Laing, R.D., Phillipson, H. and Lee, A.R. (1966) *Interpersonal Perception: A Theory and a Method of Research*. London: Tavistock Publications.

Lakoff, A. (2005) *Pharmaceutical Reason: Knowledge and Values in Global Psychiatry*. Cambridge: Cambridge University Press.

Landecker, H. and Panofsky, A. (2013) From social structure to gene regulation, and back: a critical introduction to environmental epigenetics for sociology. *Annual Review of Sociology*, 39, 1, 333–357.

Lane, C. (2008) *Shyness: How Normal Behavior Became a Sickness*. New Haven, CT: Yale University Press.

Lasch, C. (1978) *The Culture of Narcissism*. New York: Norton.

Lash, S. (1990) *Sociology of Postmodernism*. London: Routledge.

Layard, R., Clark, D., Bell, S., Knapp, M., Meacher, B., Priebe, S., Turnberg, L., Thornicroft, G. and Wright, B. (2006) *The Depression Report; A New Deal for Depression and Anxiety Disorders*. London: The Centre for Economic Performance's Mental Health Policy Group, LSE.

Lederbogen, F., Kirsch, P., Haddad, L., Streit, F., Tost, H., Schuch, P., Wüst, S., Pruessner, J.C., Rietschel, M., et al. (2011) City living and urban upbringing affect neural social stress processing in humans. *Nature*, 474, 7352, 498–501.

Lemert, C.C. (1979) *Sociology and the Twilight of Man*. Carbondale, IL: Southern Illinois University Press.

Lent, J. (2017) *The Patterning Instinct: A Cultural History of Humanity's Search for Meaning*. New York: Prometheus Books.

Lerner, G. (1986) *The Creation of Patriarchy*. New York: Oxford University Press.

Lewin, K. (1951) *Field Theory in Social Science*. New York: Harper.

Leyens, J.Ph., Paladino, M.P., Rodriguez, R.T., Vaes, J., Demoulin, S., Rodriguez, A.P. and Gaunt, R. (2000) The emotional side of prejudice: The attribution of secondary emotions to ingroups and outgroups. *Personality and Social Psychology Review*, 4, 2, 186–197.

Liebenberg, L., Ungar, M. and Ikeda, J. (2015) Neo-liberalism and responsibilisation in the discourse of social service workers. *The British Journal of Social Work*, 45, 3, 1006–1021. https://doi.org/10.1093/bjsw/bct172

Liebrucks, A. (2001) The concept of social construction, *Theory & Psychology*, 11, 3, 363–391.

Lockhart, L.L., Saunders, B.E. and Cleveland, P. (1989) Adult male sexual offenders: An overview of treatment techniques. In J.S. Wodarski and D.L. Whitaker (eds) *Treatment of Sex Offenders in Social Work and Mental Health Settings* (pp. 1–32). New York: Haworth Press.

Lockwood, D. (1964) Social integration and system integration. In G. Zollschan and W. Hirsch (eds) *Explorations in Social Change* (pp. 244–257). Boston, MA: Houghton Mifflin.

Lomas, P. (1994) *True and False Experience: The Human Element in Psychotherapy*. New York: Transactional Books.

Low, B. (1920) *Psychoanalysis: A Brief Account of the Freudian Theory*. London/Vienna: International Psychoanalytical Association.

Lukács, G. (1968) *History and Class Consciousness*. Cambridge, MA: MIT Press.

Luyten, P., Blatt, S.J. and Corveleyn, J. (2006) Minding the gap between positivism and hermeneutics in psychoanalytic research. *Journal of American Psychoanalytical Association*, 54, 2, 571–610.

Lyotard, J.-F. (1979) *La condition postmoderne: rapport sur le savoir*. Paris: Minuit.

Macdonald, K. (1995) *The Sociology of the Professions*. London: Sage.

Mackay, N. and Petocz, A. (2011) *Realism and Psychology: Collected Essays*. Boston, MA: Brill.

MacMurray, J. (1957) *The Self as Agent*. London: Faber & Faber.

Mahoney, M.J. (1974) *Cognition and Behaviour Modification*. Cambridge, MA: Ballinger.

Makari, G. (2010) *Revolution in Mind: The Creation of Psychoanalysis*. London: Duckworth Overlook.

Marcuse, H. (1964) *One Dimensional Man: Studies in the Ideology of Advanced Industrial Society*. Boston, MA: Beacon Press.

Marshall, B.J. and Warren, J.R. (1984) Unidentified curved bacilli in the stomach of patients with gastritis and peptic ulceration. *Lancet*, 1, 8390, 1311–1315.

Maslow, A. (1968) *Toward A Psychology of Being*. New York: Simon & Schuster.

Masson, J. (1985) *The Assault on Truth: Freud's Abandonment of the Seduction Theory*. London: Penguin.
Maturana, H. and Varela, F. (1980) *Autopoiesis and Cognition: The Realization of the Living*. Boston, MA: Reidel.
May, R. (1969) *Love and Will*. New York: Norton.
Maze, J.R. (2001) Social constructionism, deconstructionism and some requirements of discourse. *Theory & Psychology*, 11, 3, 393–417.
Medlock, G. (2017) Seeking consensual understanding of personal meaning: reflections on the meaning summit at first congress on the construction of personal meaning. *Journal of Constructivist Psychology*, 30, 1, 1–13.
The Mental Health Act Commission (MHAC) (2009) *Coercion and consent: monitoring the Mental Health Act 2007–2009 (Thirteenth Biennial Report)*. London: Stationery Office.
Meyer, J.E. (1988) The fate of the mentally ill in Germany during the Third Reich. *Psychological Medicine*, 18, 575–581.
Mihailides, S., Devilly, G.J. and Ward, T. (2004) Implicit cognitive distortions and sexual offending. *Sexual Abuse: A Journal of Research and Treatment*, 16, 333–350.
Milgram, S. (1974) *Obedience to Authority: An Experimental View*. New York: Harper & Row.
Miller, A. (1984) *Thou Shalt Not Be Aware: Society's Betrayal of the Child*. New York: Farrar, Strauss and Giroux.
Mingers, J. (2011) The contribution of systemic thought to critical realism. *Journal of Critical Realism*, 10, 3, 303–330.
Moncrieff, J. (2008) *The Myth of the Chemical Cure*. Basingstoke, UK: Palgrave.
Mooney, M.A. (2016) Human agency and mental illness. *Journal of Critical Realism*, 15, 4, 376–390.
Moore, J. (1985) Some historical and conceptual relations among logical positivism, operationism, and behaviorism. *Behavioral Anaysis*, 8, 1, 53–63.
Morris, D. (1967) *The Naked Ape: A Zoologist's Study of the Human Animal*. London: Jonathan Cape.
Moscovici, S. (1963) Attitudes and opinions. *Annual Review of Psychology*, 14, 231–260.
Moscovici, S. (2008) *Psychoanalysis: Its Image, Its Public*. Bristol, UK: Polity Press.
Nadesan, M.H. (2005) *Constructing Autism: Unravelling the 'Truth' and Understanding the Social*. New York: Routledge.
Neimeyer, R.A. (1985) *The Development of Personal Construct Psychology*. Lincoln: University of Nebraska Press.
Norrie, A. (2010) *Dialectic and Difference: Dialectical Critical Realism and the Grounds of Justice*. London: Routledge.
Norris, C. (1990) *What's Wrong With Postmodernism?* Baltimore, MD: John Hopkins.
O'Carroll, T. (1980) *Paedophilia: The Radical Cause*. London: Owen.
O'Mahoney, J. (2011) Critical realism and the self. *Journal of Critical Realism*, 10, 1, 122–129.
Offe, C. (1984) *Contradictions of the Welfare State*. Boston, MA: MIT Press.
Parker, I. (1997) Discursive psychology. In D. Fox and I. Prilleltensky (eds) *Critical Psychology An Introduction*. London: Sage.
Partridge, G.E. (1910) *An Outline of Individual Study*. New York: Sturgis & Walton.
Pataki, T. (2014) *Wish-fulfilment in Philosophy and Psychoanalysis: The Tyranny of Desire*. London: Routledge.
Patel, N. (2012) The psychologization of torture. In M. Rapley, J. Moncrieff and J. Dillon (eds) *De-Medicalising Misery: Psychiatry, Psychology and the Human Condition* (pp. 239–255). London: Palgrave Macmillan.

Patel, N. and Granville-Chapman, C. (2010) *Health Assessments with Survivors of Torture: Good Practice Clinical Guidelines*. London: Medical Foundation for the Care of Victims of Torture/Department of Health.

Patel, N. and Mahtani, M. (2004) A psychological approach to rape as torture. In M. Peel (ed.) *Rape as Torture*. London: Medical Foundation Publications.

Patel, N. and Pilgrim, D. (2018) Psychologists and torture: critical realism as a resource for analysis and training. *Journal of Critical Realism*, 17, 2, 176–191.

Pearce, J.M. and Charman, A. (2011) A social psychological approach to understanding moral panic. *Crime, Media, Culture*, 7, 3, 293–311.

Pearson, K. (1904) On the inheritance of mental and moral characteristics in man. *Biometrika*, IV, 265–303.

Pearson, K. (1905) *National Life from the Standpoint of Science*. Newcastle, UK: A&C Publications.

Pereda, N., Guilera, G., Forns, M. and Gomez-Benito, J. (2009) The prevalence of child sexual abuse in community and student samples: a meta-analysis. *Clinical Psychology Review*, 29, 4, 328–338.

Perkins, M.L. (1926) The teaching of ideals and the development of the traits of character and personality. *Proceedings of the Oklahoma Academy of Sciences*, 6, 2, 344–347.

Petty, R. and Cacioppo, J.T. (1986) The elaboration likelihood model of persuasion. *Advances in Experimental Social Psychology*, 19, 1, 126.

Phillips, T. (2018) *A Brief History of How We F***ed It All Up*. London: Wildfire.

Pigden, C. (2007) Conspiracy theories and the conventional wisdom. *Episteme: A Journal of Social Epistemology*, 4, 2, 219–232.

Pilgrim, D. (2007) The survival of psychiatric diagnosis. *Social Science & Medicine*, 65, 3, 536–544.

Pilgrim, D. (2008) The eugenic legacy in psychology and psychiatry. *International Journal of Social Psychiatry*, 54, 3, 272–284.

Pilgrim, D. (2011) The hegemony of cognitive behavioural therapy in modern mental health policy. *Health Sociology Review*, 20, 2, 120–132.

Pilgrim, D. (2013) The failure of diagnostic psychiatry and the prospects of scientific progress offered by critical realism. *Journal of Critical Realism*, 12, 3, 336–358.

Pilgrim, D. (2015a) *Understanding Mental Health: A Critical Realist Exploration*. London: Routledge.

Pilgrim, D. (2015b) The biopsychosocial model in health research: its strength and limitations for critical realists. *Journal of Critical Realism*, 14, 2, 164–180.

Pilgrim, D. (2017a) Critical realism, psychology and the legacies of psychoanalysis. *Journal of Critical Realism*, 16, 5, 468–482.

Pilgrim, D. (2017b) Incorrigible conduct and incorrigible diagnoses: the case of personality disorder. *Journal of Social Theory & Health*, 15, 4, 388–406.

Pilgrim, D. (2017c) The perils of strong social constructionism: the case of child sexual abuse. *Journal of Critical Realism*, 16, 3, 268–283.

Pilgrim, D. (2018a) *Child Sexual Abuse: Moral Panic or State of Denial?* London: Routledge.

Pilgrim, D. (2018b) Reclaiming reality and redefining realism: the challenging case of transgenderism. *Journal of Critical Realism*, 17, 3, 308–324.

Pilgrim, D. (2018c) Medical diagnosis: an exemplar of diachronic inference? *Journal of Critical Realism*, 17, 5, 449–465.

Pilgrim, D. (2018d) Are kindly and efficacious mental health services possible? Editorial. *Journal of Mental Health*, 4, 295–297.

Pilgrim, D. and Treacher, A. (1991) *Clinical Psychology Observed*. London: Routledge.

Pilgrim, D., Rogers, A. and Bentall, R.P. (2009) The centrality of personal relationships in the creation and amelioration of mental health problems: the current interdisciplinary case. *Health*, 13, 2, 235–254.

Plummer, K. (1981) The paedophile's progress: a view from below. In B. Taylor (ed.) *Perspectives on Paedophilia* (pp. 12–26). London: Batsford.

Plummer, K. (1991) Understanding childhood sexualities. In T. Sandfort, E. Brongersma and A. Van Naerssen (eds) *Male Intergenerational Intimacy: Historical, Socio-Psychological and Legal Perspectives*. London: Haworth Press.

Plummer, K. (2014) Child abuse and paedophilia: an open letter. http://kenplummer.com [accessed 24 August 2015].

Pojman, L.P. (1998) *Classics of Philosophy*. Oxford: Oxford University Press.

Popper, K. (1959) *The Logic of Scientific Discovery*. London: Hutchinson.

Popper, K. (1962) *Conjectures and Refutations. The Growth of Scientific Knowledge*. New York: Basic Books.

Porpora, D.V. (1980) Operant conditioning and teleology. *Philosophy of Science*, 47, 4, 568–582.

Porpora, D.V. (1993) Cultural rules and material relations. *Sociological Theory*, 11, 2, 212–229.

Porpora, D.V. (2015) *Reconstructing Sociology: The Critical Realist Approach*. New York: Cambridge University Press.

Porpora, D.V. (2017) Dehumanization in theory: anti-humanism, non-humanism and post-humanism. *Journal of Critical Realism*, 16, 4, 353–367.

Power, C. and Aiello, L.C. (1997) Female proto-symbolic strategies. In L.D. Hager (ed.) *Women in Human Evolution* (pp. 153–171). New York/London: Routledge.

Proctor, R.N. (1988) *Racial Hygiene – Medicine under the Nazis*. London: Harvard University Press.

Psillos, S. (2007) Inference. In M. Hartwig (ed.) *Dictionary of Critical Realism*. London: Routledge.

Quayle, E. (2015) Internet risk research and child sexual abuse: a misdirected moral panic? In V.E. Cree, G. Clapton and M. Smith (eds) *Moral Panics in Theory and Practice*. Bristol, UK: Policy Press.

Radford, L., Corral, S., Bradley, C., Fisher, H., Collishaw, S., Bassett, C. and Howat, N. (2011) *Child Abuse and Neglect in the UK Today*. London: NSPCC.

Rand, A. (1964) *The Virtue of Selfishness*. New York: Signet.

Rapp, D.A. (1988) The early discovery of Freud by the British press: general interest and literary magazines. *Journal of the History of the Behavioural Science*, 24, 191–207.

Raynor, E. (1990) *The Independent Mind in British Psychoanalysis*. London: Karnac.

Read, J. and Bentall, R.P. (2012) Negative childhood experiences and mental health: theoretical, clinical and primary prevention implications. *British Journal of Psychiatry*, 200, 2, 88–91.

Read, J., Fosse, R., Moskowitz, A. and Perry, B. (2014) The traumagenic neurodevelopmental model of psychosis revisited. *Neuropsychiatry*, 4, 1, 64–79.

Reich, W. (1946) *The Mass Psychology of Fascism*. New York: Noonday.

Reicher, S. and Haslam, A. (2011) After shock? Towards a social identity explanation of the Milgram 'obedience' studies. *British Journal of Social Psychology*, 50, 1, 163–169.

Relethford, J.H. (2002) Apportionment of global human genetic diversity based on craniometrics and skin color. *American Journal of Physical Anthropology*, 118, 4, 393–398.

Richards, G. (2010) *Putting Psychology in its Place*. London: Routledge.

Richards, H. (2018) On the intransitive objects of the social (or human) sciences. *Journal of Critical Realism*, 17, 1, 1–16.

Riemer, M. and Reich, S.M. (2011) Community Psychology and global climate change: Introduction to the Special Section. *American Journal of Community Psychology*, 47, 3, 349–353.

Righton, P. (1981) The Adult. In B. Taylor (ed.) *Perspectives on Paedophilia*. London: Batsford Academic and Educational.

Roback, A.A. (1961) *History of Psychology and Psychiatry*. New York: Philosophical Library.

Roberts, J.M. (2003) Postmodernism. In M. Hartwig (ed.) *Dictionary of Critical Realism*. London: Routledge.

Robinson, D. (1999) *Nietzsche and Postmodernism*. London: Icon Books.

Rogers, A. and Pilgrim, D. (1991) 'Pulling down churches' – accounting for the British Mental Health Users' Movement. *Sociology of Health and Illness*, 13, 2, 129–148.

Rose, D. (2009) Survivor produced knowledge. In A. Sweeney, P. Beresford, A. Faulkner, M. Nettle and D. Rose (eds) *This is Survivor Research*. Ross-on-Wye, UK: PCCS.

Rose, N. (2013) The human sciences in a biological age. *Theory, Culture & Society*, 30, 1, 3–34.

Rose, S. and Rose, H. (2012) *Genes, Cells and Brains: The Promethean Promises of the New Biology*. London: Verso.

Rosen, G. (1968) *Madness in Society*. Chicago, IL: Chicago University Press.

Rosenau, P.M. (1993) *Post-Modernism and the Social Sciences*. Princeton, NJ: Princeton University Press.

Rosenfield, S. (2012) Triple jeopardy? Mental health at the intersection of gender, race, and class. *Social Science & Medicine*, 74, 1, 1791–1796.

Rossman, G.P. (1985) *Sexual Experience Between Men and Boys*. Middlesex, UK: Temple Smith.

Roth, M. (1973) Psychiatry and its critics. *British Journal of Psychiatry*, 122, 569, 373–378.

Roudinesco, E. (2016) *Freud In His Time and Ours*. Harvard, MA: Harvard University Press.

Ryan Report (2009) Report of the Commission to Inquire into Child Abuse. Dublin: Office of the Minister for Children and Youth Affairs.

Saied-Tessier, A. (2014) *Estimating the Costs of Child Sexual Abuse in the UK*. London: NSPCC.

Salekin, R.T. (2002) Psychopathy and therapeutic pessimism: clinical lore or clinical reality? *Clinical Psychology Review*, 22, 1, 79–112.

Salter, M. (2017) Child sexual abuse. In W. Dekeseredy and M. Dragiewicz (eds) *Routledge Handbook of Critical Criminology*. London: Routledge.

Sandfort, T. (1987) *Boys on their Contacts with Men*. Amsterdam: Global Academic.

Sartre, J.-P. (1998) *Existential Psychoanalysis*. Washington, DC: Regnery.

Sayer, A. (2000) *Realism and Social Science*. London: Sage.

Sayer, A. (2011) *Why Things Matter To People: Social Science, Values and Ethical Life*. Cambridge: Cambridge University Press.

Sayer, A. (2012) Power, causality and normativity: a critical realist critique of Foucault. *Journal of Political Power*, 5, 2, 179–194.

Schilling, E.A., Aseltine, R.H. and Gore, S. (2008) The impact of cumulative childhood adversity on young adult mental health: measures, models, and interpretations. *Social Science & Medicine*, 6, 5, 1140–1151.

Schmidt, F.L. (1996) Statistical significance testing and cumulative knowledge in psychology: Implications for training of researchers. *Psychological Methods*, 1, 115–129.

Schwargel, C. (2014) *The Anthropocene: The Human Era and How It Shapes Our Planet*. London: Synergenetic Press.

Schweder, R.A. (1984) A colloquy of cultural theorists. In R.A. Schweder and R.A. LeVine (eds) *Culture Theory: Essays on Mind, Self and Emotion*. Cambridge: Cambridge University Press.

Screech, M.A. (1985) Good madness in Christendom. In W.F. Bynum, R. Porter and M. Shepherd (eds) *The Anatomy of Madness, Vol. 1* (pp. 25–39). London: Tavistock Publications.

Searle, J. (2007) *Freedom and Neurobiology: Reflections on Free Will, Language, and Political Power*. New York: Columbia University Press.

Sedgwick, P. (1980) *PsychoPolitics*. London: Pluto Press.

Sennett, R. (1977) *The Fall of Public Man*. New York: Knopf.

Sennett, R. and Cobb, J. (1973) *The Hidden Injuries of Class*. New York: Knopf.

Seto, M.C. (2012) Child Pornography Offenders: Characteristics and Risk to Reoffend. Presentation to the US Government Sentencing Commission, www.ussc.gov/sites/default/files/pdf/amendment...and.../Presentation_15_Seto.pdf [accessed 3 January 2019].

Seung, T.K. (2007) *Kant: A Guide for the Perplexed*. London: Continuum.

Shaw, J. and Kendrick, A. (2017) Reflecting on the past: children's services workers' experiences of residential care in Scotland from 1960–1975. *British Journal of Social Work*, 47, 2, 375–391.

Shotter, J. (1984) *Social Accountability and Selfhood*. Oxford: Basil Blackwell.

Shotter, J. (1993a) *Cultural Politics of Everyday Life*. Buckingham, UK: Open University Press.

Shotter, J. (1993b) Becoming someone: identity and belonging. In N. Coupland and J. Nussbaum (eds) *Discourse and Lifespan Development* (pp. 5–27). Newbury Park, CA: Sage.

Shotter, J. and Gergen, K. (eds) (1989) *Texts of Identity*. London: Sage.

Sims-Schouten, W. and Riley, S. (2018) Presenting critical realist discourse analysis as a tool for making sense of service users' accounts of their mental health problems. *Qualitative Health Research*, 29, 7, 1016–1028.

Skinner, B.F. (1957) *Verbal Behavior*. Acton, MA: Copley.

Skinner, B.F. (1971) *Beyond Freedom and Dignity*. New York: Alfred A. Knopf.

Skinner, B.F. (1974) *About Behaviorism*. New York: Knopf.

Sloan, T. (1997) Theories of personality: ideology and beyond. In D. Fox and I. Prilleltensky (eds) *Critical Psychology An Introduction*. London: Sage.

Smedslund, J. (2016) Why psychology cannot be an empirical science. *Integrative Psychological and Behavioral Science*, 50, 2, 185–195.

Smith, C. (2011) *What Is A Person?*Chicago, IL: University of Chicago Press.

Smith, D.L. (2012) *Less Than Human: Why We Demean, Enslave and Exterminate Others*. London: Macmillan.

Smith, E.S., Junger, J., Derntl, B. and Habel, U. (2015) The transsexual brain – a review of findings on the neural basis of transsexualism. *Neuroscience & Biobehavioral Reviews*, 59, 251–266.

Smith, R. (1997) *The Fontana History of the Human Sciences*. London: Fontana.

Snoeyenbos, M.H. and Putney, R.T. (1980) Psychology and science. *American Journal of Psychology*, 93, 579–592.

Solms, M. and Turnbull, O. (2002) *The Brain and the Inner World: An Introduction to the Neuroscience of Subjective Experience*. New York: Other Press.

Sontag, S. (1961) *Against Interpretation*. London: Penguin.

Spearman, C.E. (1904) General intelligence objectively determined and measured. *American Journal of Psychology*, XV, 201–299.

Spielrein, S. (1912) Die destruktion als ursache des werdens. *Jahrbuch für Psychoanalytische und Psychopathologische Forschungen*, 4, 464–503.

Stam, H.J. (2001) Introduction: social constructionism and its critics. *Theory & Psychology*, 11, 3, 291–296.

Stekel, W. (1908) *Nervose Angstzustande und ihre Behandlung*. Berlin/Vienna: Urban & Schwarzenberg.

Stephenson, W. (1953) *The Study of Behavior: Q-Technique and its Methodology*. Chicago, IL: University of Chicago Press.

Stone, M. (1985) Shellshock and the psychologists. In W.F. Bynum, R. Porter and M. Shepherd (eds) *The Anatomy of Madness*, Vol. 2. London: Tavistock Publications.

Sullivan, G. (2018) Collective emotions: a case study of South African pride, euphoria and unity in the context of the 2010 FIFA World Cup. *Frontiers in Psychology*, 9, 1252.

Sulloway, F.J. (1983) *Freud, Biologist of the Mind: Beyond the Psychoanalytic Legend*. New York: Basic Books.

Sunstein, C. (2016) *The Ethics of Influence: Government in the Age of Behavioral Science*. Cambridge:Cambridge University Press.

Suttie, I.D. (1988) *The Origins of Love and Hate*. London: Free Association Books.

Suzuki, S. (1970) *Zen Mind, Beginner's Mind*. New York: Wetherhill.

Szasz, T.S. (1961) *The Myth of Mental Illness*. New York: Harper Row.

Szasz, T.S. (1963) The concept of transference. *International Journal of Psychoanalysis*, 44, 432–444.

Szasz, T.S. (1970) *The Manufacture of Madness: A Comparative Study of the Inquisition and the Mental Health Movement*. New York: Syracuse University Press.

Szasz, T.S. (1976) *Schizophrenia: The Sacred Symbol of Psychiatry*. New York: Syracuse University Press.

Tajfel, H. and Turner, J.C. (1979) An integrative theory of inter-group conflict. In W.G. Austin and S. Worchel (eds) *The Social Psychology of Inter-Group Relations* (pp. 33–47). Monterey, CA: Brooks/Cole.

Tallis, R. (2011) *Aping Mankind: Neuromania, Darwinitis and the Misrepresentation of Humanity*. London: Acumen.

Taylor, B. (1976) Motives for guilt-free pederasty: some literary considerations. *Sociological Review*, 24, 97–114.

Taylor, B. (ed.) (1981) *Perspectives on Paedophilia*. London: Batsford.

Taylor, C. (1964) *The Explanation of Behaviour*. London: Routledge Kegan Paul.

Taylor, L. (2007) The other side of the street: an interview with Stan Cohen. In D. Downes, P. Rock, C. Chinkin and C. Gearty (eds) *Crime. Social Control and Human Rights: From Moral Panics to States of Denial: Essays in Honour of Stanley Cohen*. London: Willan.

Thaler, R. and Sunstein, C. (2008) *Nudge*. London: Penguin.

Thoits, P.A. (1985) Self-labeling processes in mental illness: the role of emotional deviance. *American Journal of Sociology*, 91, 221–249.

Thomas, R. (2007) Risk, legitimacy and asylum adjudication. *Northern Ireland Legal Quarterly*, 58, 1, 3.

Thompson, R. (1968) *The Pelican History of Psychology*. Harmondsworth, UK: Penguin.

Thomson, M. (1998) *The Problem of Mental Deficiency: Eugenics, Democracy, and Social Policy in Britain c. 1870–1959*. Oxford: Oxford University Press.

Thomson, M. (2007) *Psychological Subjects: Identity, Culture and Health in Twentieth-Century Britain*. Oxford: Oxford University Press.

Thornton, E. (1983) *Freud and Cocaine: The Freudian Fallacy*. London: Blond and Briggs.

Toomela, A. and Valsiner, J. (eds) (2010) *Methodological Thinking in Psychology: 60 Years Gone Astray?* Charlotte, NC: Information Age.

Tortorello, F. (2017) What is real about reductive neuroscience? *Journal of Critical Realism*, 16, 3, 235–254.

Toumela, R. (2013) *Social Ontology: Collective Intentionality and Group Agents*. New York: Oxford University Press.

Turner, T. (1996) James Crichton-Browne and the anti-psychoanalysts. In H. Freeman and G.E. Berrios (eds) *150 Years of British Psychiatry: The Aftermath*. London: Athlone.

van Zomeren, M. (2014) Synthesizing individualistic and collectivistic perspectives on environmental and collective action through a relational perspective. *Theory & Psychology*, 24, 6, 775–794.

Varghese, S.A. and Abraham, S.A. (2004) Book length essays as a hybrid genre in science. *Written Communication*, 21, 2, 201–231.

Viki, G.T., Osgood, D. and Phillips, S. (2013) Dehumanization and self-reported proclivity to torture prisoners of war. *Journal of Experimental Social Psychology*, 49, 3, 325–332.

von Bertalanffy, L. (1968) *General System Theory: Foundations, Development, Applications*. New York: George Braziller.

Wagner, W. (1996) Queries about social representation and construction. *Journal for the Theory of Social Behaviour*, 26, 95–120.

Walby, S. (2007) Complexity theory, systems theory and multiple intersecting social inequalities. *Philosophy of the Social Sciences*, 37, 4, 449–470.

Waller, W.W. (1936) Social problems and the mores. *Sociological Review*, 1, 6, 922–933.

Wann, T.W. (1964) *Behaviorism and Phenomenology: Contrasting Bases for Modern Psychology*. Chicago, IL: Chicago University Press.

Ward, J. and Rivers, W. (1904) Editorial. *British Journal of Psychology*, 1, 1, 1.

Watson, J.B. (1913) Psychology as the behaviorist views it. *Psychological Review*, 20, 158–177.

Weber, W. (1968) The nature of charismatic authority and its routinization. In S.N. Eisenstadt (ed.) *Max Weber on Charisma and Institution Building* (pp. 53–54). Chicago, IL: University of Chicago Press.

Webster, R. (2005) *Why Freud Was Wrong: Sin, Science and Psychoanalysis*. Oxford: The Orwell Press.

Weiner, N. (1948) *Cybernetics: Or Control and Communication in the Animal and the Machine*. Paris: Hermann & Cie.

Weiss, P. (1969) *Beyond Reductionism*. New York: Beacon Press.

Weissbrodt, D. and Bergquist, A. (2006) Extraordinary rendition: a human rights analysis. *Harvard Human Rights Journal*, 19, 1, 23.

West, D.J. (2001) Paedophilia: plague or panic? *Journal of Forensic Psychiatry*, 11, 3, 211–231.

Westland, G. (1978) *Current Crises of Psychology*. London: Heinemann.

Wheatley, L. (2019) Foucault's concepts of structure … and agency? A critical realist critique. *Journal of Critical Realism*, 18, 1, 18–30.

Whyte, L.L. (1960) *The Unconscious before Freud: A History of the Evolution of Human Awareness*. New York: Basic Books.

Wilden, A. (1972) *System and Structure: Essays in Communication and Exchange*. London: Tavistock Publications.

Williams, R. (1980) *Culture and Materialism*. London: Verso.

Wilson, E.O. (1975) *Sociobiology*. Harvard, MA: Harvard University Press.

Wilson, M. (1993) DSM-III and the transformation of American psychiatry: a history. *American Journal of Psychiatry*, 150, 3, 399–410.

Wilson, P. (1981) *The Man They Called a Monster: Sexual Experiences Between Men and Boys*. Sydney: Cassell.

Winnicott, D.W. (1965) *Maturational Processes and the Facilitating Environment: Studies in the Theory of Emotional Development*. London: Hogarth Press.

Wittchen, H., Jacobi, F., Rehm, J., Gustavsson, A., Svensson, M., Jonsson, B., Oleson, J., Allgulander, C., Alonso, J., et al. (2011) The size and burden of mental disorders and other disorders of the brain in Europe 2010. *European Neuropsychopharmacology*, 21, 9, 655–679.

Wolfe, C. (2010) *What is Posthumanism?* Minneapolis, MN: University of Minnesota Press.

Wolman, B.B. (1981) *Contemporary Theories and Systems in Psychology*. Amsterdam: Plenum.

Wrangham, R. and Peterson, D. (1997) *Demonic Males: Apes and the Origins of Human Violence*. London: Bloomsbury.

Wurr, C.J. and Partridge, I.M. (1996) The prevalence of a history of childhood sexual abuse in an acute adult inpatient population. *Child Abuse & Neglect*, 20, 9, 867–872.

Wurtele, S.K., Simons, D.A. and Moreno, T.A. (2014) Sexual interest in children among an online sample of men and women. *Annals of Sex Research*, 26, 6, 12–20.

Yehuda, R., Cai, C., Golier, J.A., Sarapas, S., Galea, S., Ising, M. and Rein, T. (2009) Gene expression patterns associated with posttraumatic stress disorder following exposure to the World Trade Center attacks. *Biological Psychiatry*, 66, 7, 708–711.

Young, J. (1973) *The Drugtakers: The Social Meaning of Drug Use*. London: Judson, McGibbon and Kee.

Yuill, R.A. (2004) Male age-discrepant sexualities and relationships. Unpublished PhD thesis. http://theses.glas.ac.uk/theses@glasgow.ac.uk

Zgoba, K.M. (2004) Spin doctors and moral crusaders: the moral panic behind child safety legislation. *Criminal Justice Studies*, 7, 4, 385–404.

INDEX